GOD, TRUMP,
— and the —
2020 ELECTION

STEPHEN E. STRANG

FRONT
LINE

EARLY PRAISE FOR
GOD, TRUMP, AND THE 2020 ELECTION

Stephen Strang is a keen reporter whose prose cuts like a laser into the troubled soul of America and exposes a condition where the elites of our nation have actually turned against it. He lays bare the delusion of the so-called progressives who have steadfastly stood in opposition to our president and refuse to acknowledge any of the good work he has accomplished. *God, Trump, and the 2020 Election* is a must-read for Evangelicals as they go to the polls in the 2020 election.

—PAT ROBERTSON
FOUNDER AND CHAIRMAN, THE CHRISTIAN BROADCASTING NETWORK

Stephen Strang is right: If Evangelicals don't turn out in 2020, Donald Trump will lose and the Left will win—and continue its work of destroying each of the three pillars of the American trinity: liberty, e pluribus unum (out of many, one), and In God We Trust. Why all Christians do not see this is a puzzle. But if enough read this book, it could serve as a wake-up call to the only community standing between our beloved America and her demise.

—DENNIS PRAGER
NATIONALLY SYNDICATED RADIO TALK SHOW HOST
COFOUNDER, PRAGERU

In *God, Trump, and the 2020 Election*, Stephen Strang flawlessly captures the spiritual significance of Donald Trump's presidency in this critical hour. As fewer and fewer Americans value belief in God, Strang's airtight case for reelecting Trump is both timely and urgent. It's a must-read for anyone concerned about the future of our nation.

—GOV. MIKE HUCKABEE
NEW YORK TIMES BEST-SELLING AUTHOR
HOST, *HUCKABEE*, TRINITY BROADCASTING NETWORK

I'm grateful for voices in the media like Stephen Strang who understand the very real spiritual battle behind the 2020 race for the White House. In his insightful new book, *God, Trump, and the 2020 Election*, Stephen looks at our nation, seeing past the political power struggles and shedding light on what's really at stake for our country in the next election. I highly recommend you read this book!

—PAULA WHITE CAIN
SPIRITUAL ADVISER TO PRESIDENT DONALD J. TRUMP
HOST, *PAULA TODAY*; LIFE COACH; AUTHOR

Without hesitation I can say that *God, Trump, and the 2020 Election* may be the most significant book released this year. All Americans—regardless of party affiliation—should read this meticulously researched work, which spells out the implications regarding the outcome of our next election. Stephen Strang is an insightful thinker, a careful researcher, and a consistently accurate commentator. It is absolutely accurate to say that America's identity and future hang in the balance. Nobody explains this better than Stephen Strang.

—ALEX MCFARLAND
PRESIDENT, TRUTH FOR A NEW GENERATION

Stephen Strang is one of the nation's most brilliant political minds. This book blends research on twentieth-century cultural and racial history with an understanding of cutting-edge, twenty-first-century political strategies. Not only that, Strang helps Christians discern how to evaluate which candidate and party policy agendas will invite the blessings of heaven. This a must-read for a pivotal election. And for all its gravitas, it's also a compelling page-turner. Enjoy the read!

—BISHOP HARRY R. JACKSON JR.
SENIOR PASTOR, HOPE CHRISTIAN CHURCH, BELTSVILLE, MARYLAND

This book, *God, Trump, and the 2020 Election*, may well be the most important book Stephen Strang has ever written! Read why Trump must win and why if he does not, it could mean the end of religious freedom in the United States. As America's leading Christian journalist, Stephen quotes Christian leaders on what God is saying through them and the warnings He is giving this generation! Pray that on the day after this coming election we do not wake up in a socialistic, antichrist country. This book will give you the answers to keep this from happening.

—JIM BAKKER
HOST, *THE JIM BAKKER SHOW*

Do you know why Donald Trump must be reelected and what's at stake if he loses? Like me, you may think you know, but in Stephen Strang's new book, *God, Trump, and the 2020 Election*, you'll find the answers to these and other questions that are vital to the health and future of our nation. I intend for it to become a vital part of my daily intercessory prayer life for our country. I believe with all my heart that we will win this election! Our time has come for a mighty and great awakening. However, our God will hold you and me responsible if we sit by and lose it.

—KENNETH COPELAND
HOST, *BELIEVER'S VOICE OF VICTORY*

I encourage you to read Stephen Strang's eye-opening new book about the spiritual forces at work behind Donald Trump's presidency. Incisive and informative, *God, Trump, and the 2020 Election* explains why Christians should vote to reelect Trump based on the facts of what he's done in his first term, what he will do in his second term, and what's at stake for believers if he doesn't win.

—DAVID BARTON
CHRISTIAN POLITICAL ACTIVIST AND AUTHOR

Stephen Strang has been engaged in observing contemporary Christendom for four decades. From his place of prominence his latest book, *God, Trump, and the 2020 Election*, puts in plain English why President Donald J. Trump must win reelection on November 3, 2020. What's at stake is religious liberty. Hint: if Trump loses, Kentucky clerk Kim Davis was just the warm-up act for what's going to happen to your children and mine.

—DAVID LANE
FOUNDER, AMERICAN RENEWAL PROJECT

In *God, Trump, and the 2020 Election*, Stephen Strang skillfully captures the urgency of this moment. In this era of fake news Stephen is a trusted journalist who writes with clarity about the very real struggle in the spiritual realm concerning the presidency of Donald Trump and how important the 2020 election is to the future of our country. I know Donald Trump personally, and he is a godly man who has been leading this nation on a path of blessing. The stakes are high in 2020—perhaps higher than they've ever been. Every Christian should read this book to know how to pray!

—HON. MICHELE BACHMANN
FORMER MEMBER, US HOUSE OF REPRESENTATIVES

God, Trump, and the 2020 Election is a remarkable book. Journalist Stephen Strang sounds an alarm, explaining why Donald Trump's reelection is critical to the future of this nation. Evangelicals supported Trump in 2016 not because he is perfect but because he is a strong leader. He is the most pro-life, pro–religious liberty, pro-Israel president we have ever had. And if the Left regains control, they're going to undo everything this president has done. Stephen understands that although God's hand is on Donald Trump, the church also must arise. We must pray, and we must vote. I encourage you to read this book!

—DR. ROBERT JEFFRESS
SENIOR PASTOR, FIRST BAPTIST CHURCH, DALLAS

Most Charisma House Book Group products are available at special quantity discounts for bulk purchase for sales promotions, premiums, fund-raising, and educational needs. For details, call us at (407) 333-0600 or visit our website at www.charismahouse.com.

GOD, TRUMP, AND THE 2020 ELECTION by Stephen E. Strang
Published by FrontLine
Charisma Media/Charisma House Book Group
600 Rinehart Road, Lake Mary, Florida 32746

Copyright © 2020 by Stephen E. Strang
All rights reserved

Library of Congress Cataloging-in-Publication Data:
An application to register this book for cataloging has been submitted to the Library of Congress.
International Standard Book Number: 978-1-62999-665-3
E-book ISBN: 978-1-62999-733-9

20 21 22 23 24 — 987654321

Printed in the United States of America

To my wonderful wife, Joy, who loved
me even when I was still a Democrat

CONTENTS

FOREWORD

WHEN DONALD TRUMP was elected in 2016, many Americans weren't sure whether he would deliver on his campaign promises. I was one of them. But as much as I was unsure of that, I was sure that Hillary Clinton, if elected, would deliver on hers, thereby eroding and destroying many of the God-given liberties some of us take for granted. I am decidedly glad the American people did not give her an opportunity to do this, and even gladder we gave Donald Trump an opportunity to carry out his promises. But I am even happier to think that he actually has delivered on them. When a politician does that, not only is it refreshing; it is almost shocking.

But the facts are before us. He has appointed justices of an originalist bent and has therefore defended the lives of the unborn and advocated for religious liberty. He has moved to protect our borders and our citizens, and he has fulsomely supported Israel, most dramatically by doing what many presidents promised to do and never did: move our embassy to Jerusalem. And of course he has created jobs and a booming economy. Finally he has labored like Hercules to drain the so-called swamp and has allowed what were once cynically termed "deplorables"—but are actually just freedom-loving Americans—to begin to reclaim our government from the career bureaucrats who had captured it. This is something no less important in our own time than winning independence from the tyrannous British was 244 years ago or preserving the Union from proslavery secessionists was 155 years ago. These are breathtaking achievements.

So approaching the 2020 election, the stakes are just as high as they were in 2016, and in some ways even higher, because when the forces of socialist gloom know their end is nigh, as they certainly now do, they will shriek and fight all the more ferociously. Despite some of the vilest histrionics of those opposed to this president—which should make things clear enough about whom we might best side with if we love our country—many Christians are still grappling with whether to vote for him. This is something they find as unpleasant and difficult to swallow as they likely find his harshest tweets. But many of these people are friends of mine, whom I love. So although I disagree with their stance and find it destructive, I nonetheless hope and pray they might see things differently, and soon. And perhaps this book will help them toward that end.

In this book my friend Stephen E. Strang has masterfully laid out the reasons we should support this president. In *God, Trump, and the 2020 Election* he makes the case that God has raised up Donald Trump to fulfill His purposes for the nation, much as He raised up the biblical king Cyrus to accomplish His purposes during a critical hour in Israel's history. In using Cyrus, God was hardly goading us to applaud Cyrus' paganism, but who can fail to see He was hoping we could nonetheless see and rejoice in the vital role Cyrus played in God's purposes in history?

Stephen challenges us to look beyond the polarizing news stories to see Donald Trump through a spiritual lens. He asks us to consider the possibility that the fierce opposition to Trump is partly a matter of spiritual warfare, something anyone familiar with the events of the last three years must at least have suspected. And he fastens our attention on the fact that Trump's outsized—and even perhaps sometimes bellicose—personality is being used to do something quite wonderful: preserve America's sovereignty and prosperity.

So we are again choosing between two futures for this nation. One is marked by the loss of ordered liberty, by a descent from "the better angels of our nature" and toward a cowardly accommodation with the bullying forces of the bureaucratic elites. The other is marked by the courage of the Founders and their ideological descendants, and it strengthens and inspires us to continue standing to God's glory, in Lincoln's famous words, as "the last best hope of earth."[1]

Though I've said it elsewhere, as we approach the 2020 election, it bears repeating: not voting cannot be an option. Or let's put it another way: not to vote *is* to vote. You may dislike much about a candidate, but God calls us to make the hard choice and pull a lever for one or the other—even if it means voting less *for* a candidate than *against* another. But we have a responsibility to history and to our children and their children, and chose we must.

In this book Stephen makes the case that Donald Trump is the best hope of keeping America from sliding into oblivion. I agree whole-heartedly, and I hope you will join me in praying for our president and our nation, that we might live up to our destiny to be a "shining city on a hill" for the whole world, to the glory of God.

—Eric Metaxas

New York Times Best-Selling Author, *Martin Luther, Bonhoeffer*, and *Miracles*; Host, *The Eric Metaxas Radio Show*

THE BATTLE FOR THE SOUL OF AMERICA

The choice in this election will not just be a choice between
two candidates; it will be a choice between two futures.[1]
—VICE PRESIDENT MIKE PENCE, AT PRESIDENT TRUMP'S
2020 CANDIDACY ANNOUNCEMENT RALLY
ORLANDO, JUNE 18, 2019

THE 2016 PRESIDENTIAL election was many things, but it was certainly not politics as usual. The election of Donald J. Trump as our forty-fifth president was a defining moment in American history. It was a chance for proud patriots to rally with a newfound voice, reclaim our country, and change its trajectory. The earthquake at the voting booths on Election Day 2016 signaled a seismic power shift—not only from one political party to another but from the Washington dealmakers to the American people. It was a message to the special interest groups and left-wing career politicians who had attempted to undermine our country during eight years of the Obama administration that we had had enough.

It was such a significant event that I wrote *God and Donald Trump* a year after Trump's historic election. I made the case that Trump is a unique man with a unique calling who appeared on the American political stage at a critical time in our history. It's as if God raised up this brusque billionaire in the same way He raised up the pagan king Cyrus in the Bible, who allowed the captive Israelites to return to Jerusalem.

Cyrus fulfilled God's purposes in that hour, and now, twenty-five hundred years later, Trump seems to be the man made for this hour. His unique personality and alpha male character traits are now being used to battle our enemies and to defend the country, making him the ideal man to lead the charge in the battle for America's soul.

As a result, Bible-believing Evangelicals who ordinarily condemn the lifestyle Trump lived for many years rallied behind him in unprecedented numbers. They understood that somehow God's hand was upon this man, who may have been the only person in America who could have beaten Hillary Clinton and her corrupt political machine.

In my subsequent book, *Trump Aftershock*, I made the case that despite the attacks and $31.7 million spent on Special Counsel Robert Mueller's deep state witch hunt (which turned up no "dirt"), God has his hand on Donald Trump. After all, how else could he survive the daily attacks and the Mueller investigation and still fulfill so many campaign promises in such a short time?

So how does this relate to you and to America? I'm writing this book nearly a year before the next election because I believe that Donald Trump *must* win and *will* win. Every presidential cycle is a new fight, a new cause, and a new opportunity for the people to decide who should lead the nation. This book explains why Evangelicals should support Trump for a second term based on the facts of what he has done for our base in the first term, what he *will do* in his second term, and what is at stake for Christians if the opposing side wins.

In a word, this book is about God and His purposes as it relates to Donald Trump and his second term. It's about Trump's vision to reverse the loss of American sovereignty and prosperity—a vision I believe he received from God. I believe God wants America to be great because God has raised up this nation, going back to our Founding Fathers, to be a beacon of light and hope for the world. Because of our religious liberty Christianity has flourished, allowing the gospel to be spread across the globe.

As a Christian journalist I will expound on the Christian concept of grace and how it relates to the presidency and upcoming reelection of the first man with no governmental or military background to hold the office. Ultimately I am looking at the election, Trump, and America from what I believe is God's perspective in order to help Christians (and others) see God's hand at work. Yes, I believe Donald Trump *will* be reelected, but I also devote an entire chapter to the serious considerations of those who say he might lose and why.

If you are a Christian, I hope this book gives you a biblical understanding of what God is doing. I also hope it is an articulate, impassioned treatise on why all Christians must support President Trump. My ultimate goal is that by the end of this book you will be convinced, as I am, that the destiny of America is riding on Trump's reelection.

Of course America's future is much more significant than any president's years in office—even Donald Trump's. Yet I hope to demonstrate that a second term for President Trump is vital to America's well-being so he can finish the job he has started and fulfill his unique calling as America's political reformer.

If you are not a Christian, I hope reading this book will give you spiritual insight you won't get anywhere else. The media and politicians see things as Republicans versus Democrats or maybe between conservatives and liberals. They analyze issues and events based on the personalities and agendas of the political protagonists. As the nation becomes more divided, Americans may see it as conflicts between the Far Left and the Right.

However, Christians see things as spiritual in nature. We sense that there is more going on than what we can see with our physical eyes. God is sovereign and has a will that is described in the Bible. Of course man has been debating and analyzing what the Scriptures say about God's will almost since Moses brought down the Law from Mount Sinai around thirty-five hundred years ago. The debate continues today.

I believe there are spiritual forces at work that the Bible calls spiritual warfare. Most Christians realize that the people who oppose our point of view or espouse views that are leading our culture and nation toward more decadence are merely being influenced by forces they probably don't understand. The Bible calls these evil forces "principalities" and "powers" (Eph. 6:12).

I realize that some Christian readers may not agree with me, but for these few pages I ask that you suspend your normal biases and paradigms long enough to consider what I have to say. If we can at least agree that the radical Left is leading our nation into a future disaster from which there will be no turning back, then it's possible to see that Donald Trump is turning the tide.

This book is not all doom and gloom, however. I believe good things are happening as a result of Donald Trump's presidency. I will reveal trends that are not acknowledged by most on the Left but are real nonetheless. The book ends on a positive note because I believe that with Trump's reelection we *can* reverse the loss of America's sovereignty, prosperity, and Christian influence.

Why should this book matter to you? Because you need to understand what we face in the next election and how God's hand is involved in the current presidency. Every voter must understand what Trump will do in his second term to further conservative, biblical principles and establish an outlook for a bright future. Every voter must also understand this will only happen if Christians act now and if we support Trump and vote.

I love America, and I want God's blessing for all Americans. I am passionate about seeing America pivot and return to more traditional values based on the Bible. So come with me on a journey to discover what is happening in our country and what is at stake in the 2020 election and beyond. Find out why I believe Donald Trump must be reelected and what's in jeopardy if he loses.

—STEPHEN E. STRANG
ST. AUGUSTINE, FLORIDA
JULY 13, 2019

PART I

UNDERSTANDING WHAT'S AT STAKE IN 2020

CHAPTER 1

WHY TRUMP MUST WIN

Those who cannot remember the past are condemned to repeat it.[1]
—GEORGE SANTAYANA
SPANISH-BORN PHILOSOPHER (1863–1952)

A MERICA HAS HAD some difficult periods in its history, and I lived through one of the worst. I came of age during the radical anti–Vietnam War era in the late sixties. I remember the riots at the 1968 Democratic convention when radicals tried to take over the party. We saw the same sort of street violence over the Vietnam War that we see today against President Trump in what is almost a repeat of that era.

As a student journalist I covered the riots of radicals at the University of Florida. I reported on the protests after the shooting deaths of four students at Kent State University in May 1970 for the student newspaper. The following year I called in a story to the Associated Press from a pay phone inside the UF administration building after it had been seized by students. I remember the rhetoric and the inflamed passions of the radicals. (The only time I've experienced tear gas was that day, when the police fired it on the students to make them give up the administration building.)

It was an eye-opener for me to see the student newspaper firmly on the side of the radicals, a foreshadowing of today's leftist, "fake news" media. One of the other newspaper staffers even claimed to be a communist. The radical societal changes I saw surfacing when I was a student came as a shock for most traditional Americans; they refused to believe what was happening until it was almost too late. Fortunately, after years of turmoil during the Nixon, Ford, and Carter administrations, some normalcy seemed to return when Ronald Reagan was elected president in 1980.

America has a long history of lively and often extreme political discord going back to the time of John Adams and Thomas Jefferson, whose acrimonious political fight must have seemed extreme after our first president, George Washington, was elected without opposition. But the acrimony then was nothing like what we have seen the last sixty years.

With the Left becoming more and more extreme, it was as if the people said, "Enough is enough." When Donald Trump was elected in 2016, the American people sent a message to Washington that they wanted change. It was a message the political and media elites missed, so they were shocked by Trump's decisive win in the electoral college. Even though Trump lost the popular vote to Hillary Clinton, our Constitution set up a system in the electoral college that protects the small states from being overpowered by the more populous states. Trump won because he took three states the Democrats thought were in their pocket: Michigan, Wisconsin, and Pennsylvania. But he only won by roughly eighty thousand votes spread over all three states—less than 1 percent in each state. "This was not a blowout," said Ralph Reed, a respected conservative political strategist.[2]

Trump's campaign in 2020 is entirely different because while he has been fighting since 2016 to make life better for all Americans, the Left has grown more extreme in its radicalism. It's become more dangerous than it's ever been in the history of our country. Meanwhile Trump has become the unlikely hero of most conservatives, including Evangelicals. They see his courage and his stand for the truth. They see his unprecedented presidential support of religious liberty, life of the unborn, and Israel.

While the country has lurched left over the past few decades, Trump has at least slowed the momentum. Christians have sensed this reprieve, and it has emboldened them to take a stand like they hadn't recently. Conservative news sites—and even Christian ones—are more prominent. Some Christian movies, such as *Unplanned* and *Breakthrough*, have been big hits, whereas before, few Christian-friendly movies even got a slot in a theater. Leaders who may have been intimidated into silence are again taking courage from how Trump speaks the truth and survives the onslaught from the politically correct crowd.

Let's face it, the same people who oppose Trump almost uniformly oppose Bible-believing Christians. If Trump loses, not only do we lose the benefits we have gained from some of his executive orders, but we lose a champion and a real American leader.

Trump Derangement Syndrome

Leftists have taken over the Democratic Party, and their frightening vision for America is fueling their radical agenda. In my previous books I documented how they seemed to go crazy when Trump became president, rioting in the streets after the election and the inauguration. They started fires, broke windows, and battled with police. In some places it was total anarchy, often funded by billionaire radicals such as George Soros. While the electorate made it clear at the polls that they wanted America moving more toward the center, the Left has become emboldened and more radical, espousing an agenda that from a conservative Christian perspective is downright evil.

Historian and philosopher David Barton points out that this polarization shows up in the polls. Fifteen years ago 29 percent of the nation was considered swing voters. Now it's down to 19 percent because so many identify with one side or the other.[3]

To understand the new intensity on the Left, take the gubernatorial race in Georgia in 2018 as an example. Democrat Stacey Abrams lost to Republican Brian Kemp by 55,000 votes. Even so, she received more votes in 2018 than Hillary Clinton did in 2016, partly because she increased black voter turnout in Fulton County (metro Atlanta) by 48.5 percent over 2014. But despite her decisive loss (even after charges of voter fraud and recounts), she still maintains she won and that the election was stolen from her.[4]

Nationally there is also a trend toward higher voter turnout. Before the 2016 election the most votes ever cast for president were in 2008 when Barack Obama won—132 million voters went to the polls. The 2016 election broke that record, with more than 136 million votes cast,[5] and Ralph Reed says voter turnout projections for 2020 may be as high as 155 million to 160 million due to the level of passion for and against the president.[6] Midterm election turnouts are on the rise as well, with 118 million votes cast in 2018 (50.3 percent of eligible voters), up from 83 million in 2014, which was only 36.7 percent of the electorate.[7]

The Left's loathing of Trump has been given a name: Trump Derangement Syndrome. But the Left also loathes conservatives who favor traditional values because we don't go along with their radical agendas of socialistic government control, abortion on demand for any reason leading up to the day of birth, and the belief that sexually anything goes, with anyone, at any time.

It has gone beyond homosexuality becoming acceptable under the law. (Homosexual acts were still outlawed in many states as recently as two decades ago.) Now marriage has been redefined by the 2015 *Obergefell v. Hodges* Supreme Court decision. It even seems we can no longer assume there are only two genders and that everyone is either one or the other, male or female—a concept that is now called "gender binarism." Instead we are told there is a wide range of gender expressions. As David Barton told me, "No longer is gender defined by what's between your legs but by what's between your ears—by whatever you feel you are at that point in time."

In 2019 when the nice-sounding Equality Act was proposed in Congress, almost every Democrat backed it, even though it reached far beyond equality for alternative lifestyles that until recently were considered perverted (and that Christians believe are against God's Word). The law would have forced these new definitions of sexual preference on all Americans, including churches, with penalties and jail sentences for those who opposed it. Thank God it failed to pass.

According to the Heritage Foundation, sexual orientation and gender identity (SOGI) laws such as the Equality Act could harm the following groups of people if that legislation is passed: employers and workers, medical professionals, parents and children, women, and nonprofits and volunteers.[8] In an article published in *Decision* magazine Franklin Graham painted an even more vivid picture of the dangers of the legislation, stating that it "will have catastrophic consequences for…churches and faith-based nonprofits who would lose all protections to hire people who adhere to their Biblical statements of faith. Christians will be persecuted for their sincerely held beliefs as never before. The clear teachings of the Bible on the sins of homosexuality and abortion will no doubt be considered 'hate speech.' It will be a nightmare from which this nation may never recover."[9]

Not surprisingly the Equality Act received the backing of House Speaker Nancy Pelosi as well as former vice president Joe Biden, who said on June 1, 2019, during his campaign for president that the Equality Act would be "the first thing [he asks] to be done."[10] The Democrats failed to pass the bill this time, but what happens if they regain power? That's what is at stake with the 2020 election, like it or not.

Ralph Reed sees the situation as being even more serious. "For the Christian community pretty much everything is on the line. Whether it's religious freedom or support for Israel or America withdrawing from the Iran nuclear deal, the life issue, or the future of the courts—if there is a Democrat elected president in 2020, they're going to reverse everything President Trump has done."

On top of that, he believes Ruth Bader Ginsburg, who will be eighty-seven when the 2020 presidential election takes place, will wait to resign until after the election, hoping a new Democratic president will nominate a liberal, proabortion, anti-religious-freedom justice to the Supreme Court. If that happens, "that justice will sit on that court for thirty to forty years and make it very difficult for us to have the kind of true conservative majority we'd like to have," Reed told me in a recent podcast interview. "They hate Trump. They loathe his agenda. Frankly they disdain us and our biblical values, and they're opposed to our socially conservative–issues agenda."

In Reed's opinion the 2020 presidential election will be a "close, hard-fought, and very competitive contest." He believes President Trump is well positioned for reelection by historic terms. He has no war or foreign policy crisis. He is an incumbent. He has a united party. He will have no significant primary opposition. He also has one of the strongest economies in the post–World War II history of our country, with 3.7 percent unemployment, 2.6 percent GDP growth, and gross domestic income growing at about 4 percent a year.[11] Plus, the stock market is up overall. "These are all good things, so he'll be a very strong and formidable candidate as an incumbent," Reed said.

A year ahead of the election, it's hard to predict what will happen, so we must look at trends. There is an intensity on the Left, especially from newly elected members of Congress. They espouse socialism in America, the world's greatest free market nation, oblivious to the historical fact (evidenced most recently in Venezuela) that socialism never works. In the name of extremist environmentalism Democratic candidates are proposing policies such as the Green New Deal, which goes much further than urging cleaner air and conservation of natural resources—objectives on which most Americans agree.

It's one thing for government to impose environmental rules on industry in terms of what companies can and can't do. Those kinds of moves affect the public through higher prices. The Green New Deal,[12] however, would eliminate carbon fuels and airplanes and, in the end, impoverish the entire country. Is America ready for extreme policies that would outlaw beef or eliminate all air travel? If we can't fly, must we go by ship to Hawaii? And must the ship use solar power since the

Green New Deal would outlaw fossil fuels? It's crazy to imagine, and you'd think such a deal would be roundly rejected by Americans (and it mostly is, although the media and the extreme Left try to make it seem like the latest inevitable trend).

Nancy Pelosi has been doing a balancing act that will continue up to the election. On one side are the darlings of the far Left, Alexandra Ocasio-Cortez and three other very left-wing House members elected in 2018 from deep-blue districts. They could say anything crazy and still get reelected. On the other side is about an equal number of Democrats from districts that Trump carried who barely won their seats. They want to stay away from all that craziness. However, these Democrats don't get much press, so we forget the dilemma they face: how not to make their Trump-loving constituents mad and to still go along with the Democratic agenda, which is becoming more and more radical every day.

"I think the center of gravity in the Democratic Party has shifted to the extreme Left," Reed said. "The energy, the activism, the excitement and intensity are over there now, and I think Pelosi is going to have a hard time containing the swamp fevers of this radicalism and impeachment agenda, and I firmly think the Democratic nominee, whoever they are, is going to have a hard time staying in the center. I think they've kind of lost their bearings a bit. It remains to be seen how that will impact 2020."

THE SILVER LINING

There is a silver lining to all of the negative energy on the Left. Remember how Georgia Democrat Stacey Abrams lost even though she increased the number of voters in Fulton County? That happened because groups such as Ralph Reed's helped get out the vote in even bigger numbers.

The conservative Christian share of the national electorate increased from 33 percent in 2016 to 35 percent in 2018.[13] In Florida the white evangelical share of the electorate increased from 21 percent in 2016 to 29 percent in 2018,[14] and the raw number of white evangelical voters nationwide increased by around 9.5 million between 2014 and 2018.[15] As a result, Republicans Josh Hawley of Missouri, Rick Scott of Florida, and Mike Braun of Indiana won US Senate seats, and Republican Ron DeSantis was elected governor of Florida. "That's how Republicans gained two seats in the US Senate, and in spite of losing both Arizona and Nevada, I think that's why Donald Trump has a real chance to be reelected," Reed said.

In 2018 Reed's organization, Faith and Freedom Coalition, distributed thirty million voter guides to more than one hundred thousand churches and mailed out about 13.4 million pieces of voter education material. The group also sent out thirty-two million digital advertisements on Facebook and other social media platforms and knocked on two million doors, including three hundred thousand doors in Florida alone. The group hopes to double that in 2020. The plan is to knock on the doors of four million evangelical and Christian voters and hand them voter literature that doesn't tell them whom to vote for but lays out the issues.

"I'm not a prophet," Reed continued, "but I think what you saw in 2018 is what we'll likely see in 2020—a very high turnout by historic standards. And I think our people are coming too. Certainly if I have anything to say about it, they will. We're certainly going to do our job."

THE KEY ISSUES AT A GLANCE

So what are the issues that will bring out voters on the Right? I'm not a policy expert, so this is not an exhaustive list of issues. I'm a Christian journalist focusing on the things I know matter most to evangelical voters. To that end here's a quick overview of some key issues:

Abortion: A huge concern is stopping late-term abortion and being certain we have a president who will nominate conservative US Supreme Court justices who will rule favorably on the various heartbeat bills that several states passed in 2019. The bills ban abortion once a fetal heartbeat can be detected, which can be as early as six weeks, and were passed partly to bring the issue before the Supreme Court.

Israel and the Middle East: There's also concern over the Iran nuclear deal and whether the United States continues to give strong support to Israel. For many Christians, including those involved in groups such as Christians United for Israel, this is the top policy issue. Many Christian Zionists even believe our support of Israel is what guarantees God's blessing on America.

Religious freedom: Many Evangelicals believe religious liberty, protected by the First Amendment, is under severe attack—especially by the courts—and that will motivate hundreds of thousands to turn up to the polls to stop these trends. The government power brokers on the left seem to want to replace individual rights with the rights of groups, which would undercut our very Constitution.

Supreme Court justices: The battle over justice appointments is typically viewed through the lens of whether the nominee is an originalist or a postmodernist. Originalists believe the Constitution's meaning is fixed and Supreme Court rulings should be based on what the authors meant when they wrote the documents. Non-originalists and post-modernists believe the Supreme Court should base its decisions on what the text of the Constitution means to modern readers. Because these views can have a significant impact on the justices' interpretations of the Constitution, which affects every aspect of American life, including religious liberties, the Supreme Court nomination process has become a fistfight.

Reed said only time will tell if the Democrats actually "go off a cliff in their extreme leftist agenda." Often at election time they try to seem much more middle-of-the-road and let unelected left-leaning judges accomplish their goals, such as finding "rights" in the Constitution that are not there on issues of same-sex marriage and abortion, for instance.

Immigration: This is an issue so important I devote chapter 4 to a discussion of what the Bible says about borders. Old Testament laws associated with "foreigners" make the case for assimilation, as said "foreigners" living in the Israelite community had to adhere to its covenantal structure. Modern immigration policy, with its emphasis on multiculturalism, is a looming Tower of Babel disaster. Unfortunately some liberal Christians try to frame the immigration debate only as whether Christians should have compassion for the immigrants who are poor (which we should). But Christianity doesn't endorse a suicidal immigration system that gives the country no right to define and defend its borders.

Justice: This is one area where Evangelicals often find commonality with the Left because justice is important in the Bible. Christians see it in moral terms, and I've had black pastors who are passionate about criminal justice tell me that issue is why they stick with the Democratic Party, a topic I discuss in chapter 3. Meanwhile Trump has provided valuable leadership to this important issue of reforming our criminal justice system to give nonviolent offenders a second chance at life. Even though Democrats act as if they have owned this issue for decades, they never accomplished what the Trump administration has accomplished.

Interestingly the concept of prison reform is based on the biblical principles of paying restitution to victims, repenting of past wrongs, working, getting educated, and developing the skills to succeed. As a result, a bipartisan coalition of liberals in the Democratic Party and conservatives and Christians in the Republican Party was built to pass needed prison reform in 2018. But sadly those instances of bipartisan consensus and compromise are few and far between.

Because the Democrats have held the House of Representatives since the midterms, not much is happening legislatively. Therefore the focus of conservative activists such as Ralph Reed is on court appointments in the Senate and working with the administration on executive action such as the Department of Health and Human Services' latest conscience protection. The Faith and Freedom Coalition has a full team of lobbyists in Washington who work on these issues every day. Reed told me he and others are meanwhile building infrastructure and getting ready for 2020. "I want to turn out the biggest Christian vote in US history in 2020," he said.

WHY THE CHRISTIAN VOTE MATTERS

Why is the Christian vote more important than ever? The attacks that have left Christians in a defensive mode are only getting worse. Even respected thinker and author David Horowitz warns that the rising attacks on Christians and their beliefs threaten all Americans—including Jews such as himself. His book *Dark Agenda: The War to Destroy Christian America* should be required reading for anyone wanting to understand objectively what is going on in our mixed-up culture.

First, he lays down how radicalism began in the 1960s as activists started implementing the principles in Saul Alinsky's *Rules for Radicals*. Horowitz explains that was when Democrats began showing their hatred for their political opponents, a departure from traditional American dissent. They began dehumanizing and delegitimizing anyone—including Bible-believing Christians—who disagreed with their left-wing, socialist agenda. Horowitz wrote:

> Stigmatizing one's opponent is a classic radical tactic. It is the
> thirteenth rule of Saul Alinsky's *Rules for Radicals*: "Pick the

target, freeze it, personalize it, and polarize it." Attack your opponents personally and cut them off from any possibility of sympathy. That is why radicals paint their political opponents as homophobes, xenophobes, and Islamophobes. They're not just good-but-misguided people whose religious convictions have led them to a contrasting viewpoint. They are *bad* people possessed by irrational fears of "the others" because they are different.[16]

These dehumanizing terms became cultural norms by the 1990s when political correctness came on the scene—and it applied to everything, not just politics. Today political correctness has gotten so out of control it borders on the ridiculous. For instance, as I write this, Berkeley, California, has just banned the use of gender-specific words such as "manhole" and "manpower" from its municipal code and requires the terms to be replaced with "maintenance hole" and "human effort."[17] And I recently heard on the radio that in San Francisco, the homeless must now be called "urban campers." I couldn't confirm that later, so it's possible someone made it up. But it shows how ridiculous things have become.

When I interviewed him for this book, conservative radio talk show host Dennis Prager shared a sentiment about political correctness similar to Horowitz's. "The Left are Orwell's friends," he said. "They won't say 'illegal immigrant'—you can't even use the title 'illegal alien.' Rather, it's 'undocumented immigrant.' They might as well call bank robberies 'undocumented withdrawals.'"

Donald Trump might not be the first politician to claim to stand up to political correctness, but he definitely took the fight to a whole new level. He wasn't an ideological conservative as much as he was just a street fighter for common sense. Trump's only ideology seems to be patriotism, as Horowitz points out.

During his campaign this was manifest in his concern about not only the state of the country but also the short shrift America had been given in global trade deals, the trillions wasted in foreign wars for which there was no gain, and what Horowitz calls the "porous state of its borders and the precarious condition of its security. [Indeed] his campaign themes made his patriotism clear: *Make America prosperous again, make America safe again, make America strong again, make America great again.*"

He goes on to say that the "haters on the left, in the Democratic

Party and the media generally, have twisted Trump's patriotism and condemned it as jingoistic and bigoted bravado." They've done the same by extension to his supporters, many of whom are evangelical Christians. I've observed that even though Jewish people often don't understand the evangelical subculture, Horowitz is a clear thinker who accurately wrote: "Anyone sympathetic to the unapologetic patriotism of religious people could understand why they were solidly for Trump, despite his flaws."

Horowitz wraps up his book by explaining that Trump seemed to empathize with this community of Christians under attack because he seemed to understand that the same attacks imperiled America's social contract. And Bible-believing Christians in turn continue to support Trump through thick and thin going into the 2020 election because they know that with his election in 2016, what Horowitz calls "the long night of weak Republican leadership and inadequate defense of the Republic was over."[18]

Since Trump's election the crazy extremes of the Left make you wonder if it is shooting itself in the head. And if it is, in a way, that's a good thing. It's like the maxim that paraphrases Napoleon: "Never interfere with an enemy while he's in the process of destroying himself." But if the Left is destroying itself with no vision other than socialism or opposition to Trump, our side must still never become complacent.

"We can't be like a head football coach who gets up in the locker room before the big game and tells the team, 'Hey, don't worry. We're going to win by four touchdowns,'" Reed opined. "No, you should tell them that this game may easily be decided by a field goal with a second left on the clock. Play like that. Play like every single snap could determine the difference between victory and defeat. I don't want anybody going into 2020 thinking we've got it in the bag. I think that was one of the big mistakes Hillary Clinton and the Democrats made in 2016. They were overconfident. They underestimated their opposition, and they paid for it."

The Democrats will definitely bring their A game to the 2020 election, and as I discuss in the next chapter, that's why Christians need to be aware of all the reasons Trump could lose.

CHAPTER 2

WHY TRUMP COULD LOSE

When bad men combine, the good must associate; else they will
fall, one by one, an unpitied sacrifice in a contemptible struggle.[1]
—EDMUND BURKE
ANGLO-IRISH POLITICIAN (1729–1797)

THE FUTURE OF our country is at stake in the 2020 election, and we cannot afford to stand by and do nothing. Albert Einstein once wrote that "the world is in greater peril from those who tolerate or encourage evil than from those who actually commit it."[2] The Democrats will unite and throw everything they have at the next election, and if Christians decide not to rally together and vote according to biblical values, we could see our spiritual enemy win some major battles—in our policies, our leadership, and our rights. If we are to preserve our freedoms, we can't be overconfident. We need to recognize our vulnerabilities, which means we must take a hard look at the reasons President Trump could actually lose.

Not long after Trump's Orlando rally in June 2019 announcing his 2020 candidacy, polls were released saying nearly any Democratic opponent would beat the president.[3] To me that's hard to believe (most polls aren't very accurate sixteen months before an election). After all, under Trump's leadership, the US economy has been booming, the unemployment rate is down, the military is being rebuilt, and our problems with illegal immigration are on the road to being fixed. If Trump is reelected, it's very likely these good trends will only get better.

Although many at the kickoff rally believe Trump will win the upcoming election, others voiced a concern that if Christians don't turn out to vote in record numbers, the Left could win and reverse all the good Trump has accomplished. Yes, Trump's supporters are enthusiastic, but so are the Democrats—and with greater numbers.

Less than two weeks after Trump announced his plans to seek

a second term, *The Hill* reported on a prediction model that accurately forecast four months before the 2018 midterms that Democrats would gain seats in the House. That same model now says President Trump will lose his reelection bid. The Negative Partisanship model, created by Rachel Bitecofer of the Wason Center for Public Policy at Christopher Newport University, predicts Trump will win 197 electoral college votes, while the Democratic candidate will earn 278.[4]

"The complacent electorate of 2016, who were convinced Trump would never be president, has been replaced with the terrified electorate of 2020, who are convinced he's the Terminator and can't be stopped," Bitecofer said. "Under my model, that distinction is not only important, it is everything."[5]

She added: "The Democrats are not complacent like they were in 2016 and I doubt there is any amount of polling or favorable forecasts that will make them so. That fear will play a crucial role in their 2020 victory. We will not see a divided Democratic Party in 2020."[6]

If the Democrats are not complacent, then Trump supporters must not be overconfident. Good approval numbers and a robust economy are no match for an empowered and newly engaged Democratic Party that, along with the Washington establishment, will do anything to stop Donald Trump.

Tom Ertl, whom I got to know in 2016 when he was the national media director of Christians for Donald Trump, wrote an insightful article for NewsWithViews.com, giving the political reality of the "Seven Reasons Why Trump Could Lose in 2020."[7]

Of all the possible roadblocks, Ertl listed overconfidence as the number one obstacle to Trump's reelection. "Overconfidence has been the demise of many a movement, business, individual, and political campaign," he wrote. "It has become a serious problem because there is a real sense within the Trump camp and support base that the 2020 election is in the bag; the very opposite is true."

Ertl believes the ruling establishment and their deep state, which the Trump presidency has exposed, will not rest until Donald Trump is defeated. "America will see an unprecedented amount of Democratic funding and tireless efforts going toward their presidential candidate," he said. "In fact it may not matter who becomes the Democratic nominee because their [electoral numbers], massive fundraising and energies will be at unforeseen levels" for whomever they nominate.

About the same time Ertl published his article, Lara Trump, the president's daughter-in-law, stated on Fox News' *Hannity* show that she believes Trump will be "nearly impossible to beat."[8] On the day the president announced his 2020 candidacy, Trump's campaign manager, Brad Parscale, declared, "I think we win in an electoral landslide."[9] Ertl opined, "This kind of rhetoric has gone from wishful thinking to being absurd to being extremely dangerous."

Even Roger Stone, the author of *The Making of the President 2016* and a longtime Trump confidant, who got caught up in the Mueller investigation, told Alex Jones in mid-2019 he believes the president is in a strong position for reelection. "He has a strong economy, and he has the wind at his back. He is fighting for American interests around the globe. He is fighting to seal our borders," Stone told the controversial broadcaster.[10]

Then he added a note of caution: "But we as conservatives, we as Republicans, we as Trump supporters cannot take victory for granted. We should not assume that this is going to be some kind of landslide, because it's not. Why? Well, because of the mainstream media's torrent of anti-Trump rhetoric by their distortion and their lies and their attacks on this president."

Meanwhile a small group of conservatives was huddling in Washington, DC, to map out a strategy to prevent a Democratic victory. Ray Moore, a prayer leader and Christian educator from South Carolina, was there. In 2016 he played a pivotal role in encouraging then lieutenant governor Henry McMaster to become the first sitting statewide elected official in the nation to support then candidate Trump. Ray's "inside baseball" commentary on that fascinating turn of events was one of the best parts of my book *God and Donald Trump.*

I talked to Ray after the Washington meeting, and he told me that Trump's reelection is not looking certain. He said the consensus at the meeting was that Democrats will do anything and everything to defeat Trump, and they have major billionaire donors lined up to supply them with unlimited funds. Ray predicted we will see voter fraud and ballot harvesting at unprecedented levels such as what took place in Orange County, California, during the 2018 election. Furthermore, the Democrats believe if they can win seven key states, they will easily defeat Trump no matter who is running on the Democratic ticket.

"The key to Trump's victory is for our side to find *new voters*, register them, and get them to the polls," Ray said. "It doesn't matter what the economy is like when the Democrats start vote harvesting. This election will be more difficult than 2016. Right now our side is very complacent; they feel a Trump victory is certain. The opposite could be true. The experts are worried, and we must get out the word on this. All the happy talk of it being easy due to a good economy, his stand for Israel, pro-life judges, and so forth is not good, as it puts our people in a complacent state of mind."

John Graves is president of Vision America, founded by my good friend Pastor Rick Scarborough. He describes himself as data driven, and he was happy to help provide the statistics showing the advantage the Democrats have in the next election. He is a unique leader, a lawyer who also volunteers at Gateway Church near Dallas. His mission is to rally Christians to register to vote and then actually go to the polls.

Graves echoed what others have said: the turnout in the 2020 election will be higher than ever on both sides—possibly approaching 70 percent of eligible voters. Through Vision America—a national association of churches that seeks to mobilize pastors and people of faith to bring spiritual awakening in the culture and government—John is playing an active role in getting Evangelicals to the polls by distributing voter guides showing where the candidates stand on key issues.

"To me, one of the top reasons President Trump could lose would be voter and donor apathy," John told me. "The church must move forward in *humility, diligence, and restraint.* This applies to the 2020 election and all areas. If believers will do those things, this could be a landslide election."

John has an insight he shares when he ministers in churches on the real sin of Sodom and Gomorrah. "Many Christians ignore God's definition of Sodom's sins," he said. "They assume the symptoms of non-biblical sex are the reasons [God destroyed the city] and ignore the roots. Ezekiel 16:49 says, 'Now this was the sin of your sister Sodom: She and her daughters were *arrogant, overfed and unconcerned*; they did not help the poor and needy' [NIV, emphasis added]. Gluttony, pride, and laziness are what lead to the other symptoms we see in our culture."

Through Vision America's outreach to pastors, called Acts 20:28 Pastors, churches large and small are proving that pastors can help reverse our nation's moral decline. Using cutting-edge technology, the organization is able to determine county by county how many pro-life conservatives are registered to vote but unlikely to go to the polls. It then equips pastors and people of faith to educate those disengaged voters and encourage them to vote.

The results of their efforts have been nothing short of amazing. The website for Acts 20:28 Pastors reports that pastors who use their resources see an average voter turnout in their church that is 55 percent higher than the average turnout in their local community.[11] "More and more, pastors and people of faith are seeing that [voting] is a spiritual act and not a political act," John said.

Eight Reasons Trump Could Lose

I applaud Vision America and other ministries that are trying to wake up the church, because the simple fact is that there are political realities that could cause Trump to lose in 2020, including the following that Tom Ertl outlined in the article I mentioned previously.

1. Overconfidence

As Tom noted, overconfidence breeds complacency and laziness because it lulls people into thinking success is automatic. This is a serious threat to Trump's reelection effort. The president's faithful supporters have a sense that his reelection is inevitable and they can just sit back and enjoy the political ride.

This is so similar to what Hillary Clinton's campaign and supporters did in 2016 that I can't help but wonder if Trump's opponents are feeding this kind of presumptive confidence to disengage his base. I hope this book wakes up conservatives to the fact that if the present attitude within the Trump camp continues through 2020, a Democrat will be inaugurated in 2021.

Jay Sekulow, who served as counsel for the president during the Mueller "witch hunt," believes Trump will win by a bigger margin than last time because, as he put it, "the Democratic party has decided to run as the socialist party." But he quickly added: "However, you never take anything for granted, and you've got to run as if you're behind, and that's what he does."

Trump supporters must realize his 2020 reelection effort will be much harder than his surprise victory in 2016. The president is not invincible. The Democrats will not be overconfident this time, and there will be no surprises.

2. Social media censorship

One of the major contributors to Trump's 2016 victory was his ability to use social media to connect with American voters, coupled with alternative media efforts to counter the constant onslaught of anti-Trump rhetoric in the corporate media. But Ertl noted that since 2016 "the radical Silicon Valley establishment has moved on the pro-Trump, conservative and Christian alternative media in a massive de-platforming campaign." The fruits of their success were the Democratic House victories in the 2018 midterms. As Ertl said, "they haven't stopped in their efforts to censor all political opinions that are alien to their neo-Marxist, globalist agenda."

For pro-Trump conservatives the most critical challenge posed by this leftist social media censorship is that it prevents them from communicating with current and potential supporters. The silver lining is that Trump has initiated antitrust legal actions against the social media establishment. Trump's moves to break up Big Tech must be swift and determined. Otherwise, his ability to engage his base and win over new voters will be greatly hindered.

Trump's campaign and supporters "must make an end run around social media censorship and go directly to new voters," Ertl pointed out. Also, Republican lawmakers must join Trump in his efforts to break up Big Tech, and conservatives must create social media platforms that are not under establishment control. Trump will not win if social media censorship continues.

3. Voter fraud

Tom Ertl had this insight about the election: "The one single thing the Democratic Party, at all levels, is best at is voter fraud, and they are very proud of their refinement of creating illegal votes. Joseph Stalin's comment 'The people who cast the votes decide nothing; the people who count the votes decide everything' has been the inspiration of big-city Democrat operatives for decades. In fact voter fraud is so prevalent in large Democratic urban areas that the art of stealing votes is part of every Democratic candidate's election strategy and considered normal behavior.

"The 2020 Democratic voter fraud effort will be concentrated in key swing state cities of Philadelphia, Pittsburgh, Detroit, Milwaukee, Minneapolis, Miami, Orlando, Las Vegas, and Cleveland. I am sure the planning has already begun," he wrote.

The Trump campaign is aware that the states that propelled Trump to a 2016 electoral victory were won by the thinnest of margins. Had Democratic operatives added a few more votes in their large cities, Trump would not have won. Consider these 2016 election statistics:

- In Pennsylvania, Trump won the twenty electoral votes by only 44,292 votes, or 0.7 percent of the votes cast.

- In Michigan, only 10,704 votes gave Trump a 0.2 percent margin to get the state's crucial sixteen electoral votes.

- In Wisconsin, which Hillary Clinton did not consider in play, Trump won by only 22,748 votes, or 0.8 percent.

- In my home state of Florida, where both houses in the Legislature, the governorship, and a majority of those we send to Congress are Republican, Trump won by a razor-thin 1.2 percent, or 112,911 votes, to give him twenty-nine electoral votes. (On election night as I watched the returns from the New York Hilton with other Trump supporters in what turned out to be a victory party, when the count from Florida came in, I knew Donald Trump would win.)

If the vote tallies of those four states had been reversed, Hillary Clinton would have had an electoral victory of 307–231. Compare that with the 306-to-232 margin Trump won by. If even 38,875 votes in Pennsylvania, Wisconsin, and Michigan had been reversed, Clinton would have earned a 278–260 electoral college victory. Trump's win in 2016 was razor-thin.

For the Trump campaign to overcome Democratic voter fraud, the campaign must work with state and federal officials—both federal agencies overseeing the election process and Republican-controlled state houses and legislatures—to investigate and prosecute election fraud. This cannot wait until December 2020; that will be too late. The question Ertl posed in his insightful op-ed is, "Do the Republicans have the fight and the will to stop Democratic voter fraud? So far they haven't."

For what it's worth, I think my eighty-eight-year-old mother was the victim of voter fraud in 2016. A lifelong Republican, she now lives in an assisted-living facility not far from me. She no longer drives, so I took her to her precinct in a predominantly Democratic part of Sanford, Florida. When we showed up with her voter card and ID, we were told she had already voted and were turned away.

Since my mother is forgetful, I knew there was a possibility she sent in an absentee ballot, forgot about it, and hadn't told me. But at this stage in life, I don't think she's sophisticated enough to fill out the ballot and find a stamp to mail it on her own. But I couldn't prove my suspicions, and the election workers could provide no proof other than a record in their computer, so we left. Since then I've taken her to early voting locations, where we both vote, and as her power of attorney I can help her fill out her ballot, something I think she can no longer do on her own. But voting early comes with its own risk of fraud, leading to the next way Trump could lose.

4. Ballot harvesting

Because absentee voting has increased nationwide over the last decade, ballot harvesting has become a growing concern. This political term refers to the process of paper votes such as absentee ballots being collected and delivered to polling locations by third parties. As you can imagine, this process is rife with opportunities for fraud and deception.

The extent of Democratic mischief in this area is not fully known, but many point to ballot harvesting as the reason Democrats gained four congressional seats during the 2018 midterms in a Republican stronghold like Orange County, California. Statewide, Democrats claimed all but seven of California's fifty-three House seats. It is likely no coincidence a massive number of Democratic ballots appeared there on Election Day. It was estimated that more than 250,000 ballots were dropped off in Orange County alone.[12]

If no one is prosecuted or jailed for illegal ballot harvesting, the Democrats will continue to engage in these activities. Again, federal agencies that oversee elections and the state houses of government must help bring an end to these practices. It is laughable that while the mainstream media obsess over fake news reports of Russian election meddling, they practically ignore the real election meddling the Democrats have carried out in every modern federal election.

I like the way Ertl put it in his op-ed: "While Republicans hold rallies in huge stadiums for Trump, Democrats strategically work to flood America with illegal immigrants [who will become] Democrat voters. We have great enthusiasm, but they have a strategy to win. Our side has great rallies; their side wins elections."

5. Economic collapse

One of Trump's greatest accomplishments in his first two and a half years in office has been turning on the US economic engine. The growing economy is clearly an area of strength for Trump as he faces reelection. His "America first" economic policies that are helping to revive flagging industries, increase wages, and bring a stock market boom will go a long way in attracting working-class voters from the Midwest, who have a history of supporting Democrats because they claim to be prolabor.

It should also be noted that the nation's economic condition is especially significant for incumbent candidates. Only two presidential incumbents in the last fifty years have failed to cinch a second term (Jimmy Carter in 1980 and George H. W. Bush in 1992). Since history shows that incumbents do well even when their first elections and terms were contentious, many believe these two exceptions were caused by the tough economic times the country was facing during their campaigns. (We could add Gerald Ford, except he was never elected and only became president when Richard Nixon resigned. Although not considered an incumbent, Ford did not win his bid for reelection in 1976 due in large part to the tough economy.)

Trump's current campaign dependency on his economic successes and the rise in the stock market is a perfect setup for the central bankers and international financiers to stage an economic collapse just before the election in 2020. A similar economic downturn in September and October of 2008 propelled Barack Obama to victory in his first presidential run.

"Considering the immense debt of the US Treasury and the tenuous condition of the American dollar, presently held as the world reserve currency, it may not take much for our global financial masters to contrive an orchestrated economic collapse and to turn Trump into a one-term president," Ertl observed. "Bad economic news always hurts the party in the White House. The hope here is that if this is attempted by the global financiers, Trump would move against the private Federal Reserve and nationalize it."

6. More war in the Middle East

President Trump is known for his often threatening rhetoric against Iran, and this puts him in a troubling political situation made worse by the way Western media and the Washington establishment seem to be constantly pushing the United States toward a war with Iran.

If Trump initiates a war with Iran, his chances of being reelected will be destroyed. A war with Iran cannot be won. Iran is not like Serbia, Libya, or Iraq—nations that don't have strong militaries. Not only is Iran a formidable military power; it has over eighty million citizens, many of whom could be recruited as soldiers. A war against Iran would be long and expensive, and it would create an international public opinion nightmare for the president.

On top of that, Trump campaigned against the senseless and expensive Middle Eastern wars that marked the presidencies of both Bushes, so he must avoid one—even if he must continue to punish Iran for bad behavior. Remember, all they respect is strength, not weakness, as the Obama administration demonstrated when it actually gave Iran billions of dollars and the most poorly negotiated deal in US history.

7. Evangelical Never Trumpers

I believe the term Never Trumper represents a very dangerous strain both in the Republican Party and among self-described Evangelicals who still hold to the feeling that they should vote for anyone but Trump (even if the Democratic challenger is the most extreme leftist in the Democratic Party). They should have an epiphany as Dr. Richard Land, the respected president of Southern Evangelical Seminary in Charlotte, North Carolina, did.

Land disliked Donald Trump so much in 2016 that he favored any of the other seventeen candidates for the Republican nomination. But "when it [came] to a binary choice between Hillary Clinton and President Trump, it took me about one nanosecond to determine that at the very worst, the president was the lesser evil versus Hillary Clinton," he said. "And frankly, he's done far better than I thought he would."

Land believes some Evangelicals were so offended by some of the comments Trump has made and his past behavior that they just decided to vote for neither Hillary Clinton nor Donald Trump. "I call that the 'Pontius Pilate syndrome,' where you ask for a basin of water, and you wash your hands and say, 'I'm not going to get involved in anything as contaminated as politics,'" Land told host Fred Jackson on American Family Radio. "Well, my theology tells me that when I'm confronted with a choice between a bad choice and a worse choice, if I don't help support the bad choice, then I become morally culpable for helping the worse choice prevail. So I think it's a combination of a lack of understanding of how the real world works and sort of a desire to be above the fray."[13]

When Trump won 81 percent of the white evangelical vote in 2016, he faced the constant demonization and public opposition of the evangelical Never Trump leaders. When *Christianity Today* did polls on whom evangelical leaders were backing in 2016, only one or two said they backed Trump.[14] Robert Jeffress, the pastor of Dallas First Baptist Church and an early Trump supporter, told me, "They missed it, and I think a lot of those [Never Trump] Christian leaders were miffed that they had so little influence over rank-and-file Evangelicals who didn't listen to them and voted for Trump anyway."

In previous elections there were Evangelicals who voted for Democrats. Usually those Christians are much more liberal, not just concerning politics but also in social and theological issues. I discussed this with Doug Wead, a longtime friend who was instrumental in helping Evangelicals get access to the White House during the Reagan and George H. W. Bush administrations. He told me that Barack Obama actually got a much higher evangelical vote than Hillary Clinton did. To explain the reason, he pointed to a *Washington Post* op-ed by Michael Wear, director of religious outreach for Obama's 2012 campaign, called "Why Did Obama Win More White Evangelical Votes Than Clinton? He Asked for Them."[15]

There are a certain number of Evangelicals who favor gun control and think protecting the environment is important, so they are predisposed to vote for Democrats if the Democratic Party will give them a chance. Wead explained that many of these Evangelicals didn't vote for Hillary Clinton because they felt unwanted. For example, the week of the election a group of celebrities went into a soundstage and recorded a song, which ended with the lyrics "Jesus f***ing Christ, please vote." If you look it up on YouTube, you'll see there were a half-million hits on this video of celebrities using Jesus' name as profanity to get out the vote for Hillary Clinton. Wead believes many Democratic-leaning Evangelicals were probably alienated by this, which is why Clinton garnered fewer evangelical votes than Obama. (She got only 16 percent in 2016, compared with 26 percent for Obama in 2008 and 21 percent in 2012.)

Still, these liberal Evangelicals are a factor that can't be ignored. Franklin Graham recently criticized these members of the "Christian Left" in *Decision* magazine.

"Using new terms like *Progressive Christianity* and the *Christian left* may sound appealing to some," Graham wrote, "but God's laws and standards do not change...(Malachi 3:6). Progressive Christianity is simply another name for theological liberalism and its accompanying permissive lifestyle that ignores God's call to holiness and obedience. There is really nothing progressive about it, other than an increasing slide into sin and disobedience."[16]

Pastor Jeffress agrees. He loves quoting Ronald Reagan as saying, "*Status quo*...is a Latin phrase for 'the mess we're in.'"[17] And that may be the crux of the divide between the 80 percent of what I call "red Evangelicals" and the 20 percent who tend to be "blue Evangelicals." One has to wonder if the status quo will be good enough as the country moves further left. Or is a disrupter what we really need to bring a much-needed course correction?

As in 2016 forecasters have presumed that Evangelicals who voted for Trump will remain the president's most reliable voting bloc. His economic policies that put America first, Supreme Court nominees, and very public pro-life stance have endeared him to much of Protestant Christianity. However, the 2016 Never Trumpers, Ertl noted, along with "advocates of the modern social justice movement that has adopted cultural Marxism, are leading a large number of Evangelical millennials into the Far-Left Democratic camp."

Many of the Evangelicals who were skeptical of Trump but ultimately voted for him in 2016 no longer doubt his ability to lead. By all standards it seems Trump could win upwards of 80 percent or even 90 percent of the evangelical vote in 2020.

Die-hard Never Trumpers could become an obstacle to reaching these levels if they make a concerted effort to suppress evangelical voters for Trump. If the president's evangelical support falls to the low 70 percentiles, he will have a hard time winning in some of the swing states.

8. Division fatigue syndrome

While there is Trump Derangement Syndrome, there is also "division fatigue syndrome" on the part of some conservatives, partly because of the steady drumbeat of negative press coverage but also because of the president's combative tweets, which critics blame for causing division in this country. I don't believe Trump caused the divisions. But his willingness to be a disrupter of the status quo is bringing the divisions to the surface. Many have observed that Trump doesn't start fights, but he won't back away from one. It was his willingness to stand up to bullies on the Left that made millions of Americans vote him into office. But if he wants to win a second term, he can't continue to alienate so many groups—including those who support his policies.

Someone told me she turns off the TV because she's so tired of hearing about Trump's latest tweet that made someone else upset. It may surprise you coming from someone like me, who is so supportive of the president, but I've come to the conclusion that a segment of the electorate may think a sleepy Joe Biden is preferable to a constantly combative Trump. I voted for Mitt Romney in 2012 even though he alienated Evangelicals. But several million Christians stayed home rather than voting for a candidate whose policies were better than Obama's but whom they didn't like. I hope the same doesn't happen in 2020 with Donald Trump.

THE "NEW AMERICAN MAJORITY"

Trevor Loudon, a New Zealander who now lives in Florida, has studied the Left and communism for years. He believes the Left, and specifically Jon Liss and his organization called the Freedom Road Socialist Organization (FRSO), is trying to do a repeat of Jesse Jackson's Rainbow Coalition from the 1980s. Liss has been operating under the radar for decades, building political influence as he leads the FRSO, which Loudon says "grew out of the Maoist New Communist Movement of the 1970s and has maintained ties to the People's Republic of China." The FRSO works in partnership with the Communist Party USA and the Democratic Socialists of America in an alliance called the Left Inside/Outside Project, and Loudon reports that this unholy alliance has "infiltrated the Democratic Party in every state in the union."[18]

When Jesse Jackson started the Rainbow Coalition in the eighties, its goal was to mobilize millions of Democratic-leaning people of color to become voters, thus defeating Ronald Reagan and giving the Democratic Party's Far Left permanent control over this country. Back in 1980 minority voters made up 12 percent of the electorate in America, and most of those minority voters were black.[19] Today minority voters are around 28 percent of the electorate and include Hispanics and other groups.[20]

According to Loudon, San Francisco lawyer Steve Phillips has played a key role in the Democrats' new strategy. The Rainbow Coalition inspired Phillips' approach, and his fortuitous marriage into the Sandler family fortune has given him the influence and resources to make it a reality. Phillips, a self-confessed student of Marx and Lenin and graduate of Stanford University, was Jesse Jackson's California student coordinator in 1988. With Sandler money and his Rainbow Coalition background, Phillips has become a major player in the Democratic Party and a leader of the Democracy Alliance, an unsavory coalition of around one hundred leftist millionaires and billionaires, including George Soros, Tom Steyer, and Norman Lear of People for the American Way.

With Steve Phillips' guidance and his connections to networks of grassroots communist activists mainly in the South and Southwest, the Democracy Alliance has seen Democrats in California gain a four million voter edge over Republicans in voter registrations. Virginia, once a reliable Republican state, has turned almost blue because of this program, and several more Southern states are on the same trajectory.

Loudon told me that with Democracy Alliance money these leftists have consolidated twenty voter registration organizations from fifteen states into the State Power Caucus for the purpose of registering ten times as many voters in 2020. That's right, forty million new anti-Trump voters. If they reach only 20 percent of that goal, they will flip North Carolina, Arizona, Georgia, Florida, and possibly even Texas from Republican to Democratic control. That will give them a "new American majority," a concept Phillips touted in his 2016 *New York Times* best-selling book, *Brown Is the New White*.

Endorsed by Senators Kamala Harris and Cory Booker as well as John Podesta, former chief of staff to Bill Clinton and counselor to Barack Obama, *Brown Is the New White* is the guidebook for the Democratic/communist revolution now unfolding ever so slightly under the radar. In a way, by writing *Brown Is the New White*, Steve Phillips has become the new Saul Alinsky. The way Phillips calculates, 23 percent of the electorate are "progressive people of color." Add that to the 28 percent of the electorate who are reliable white Democratic voters, and you have 51 percent—what Phillips calls the "New American Majority."[21]

"The only thing stopping permanent Democrat power is that some of the 23 percent of 'progressives' of color don't vote regularly," Loudon told me. "So instead of spending billions of dollars to shift

1 or 2 percent of centrist voters into the Democrat column, the new strategy is to sign up tens of millions of new black and Hispanic voters in the South and Southwest in mass voter registration drives. Then you inspire them to go to the polls by running leftist 'candidates of color.'"

Recent examples are Stacey Abrams and Andrew Gillum, both black, who almost won the Georgia and Florida governorships in 2018. Loudon labels them as hard-core leftists, and both were longtime Steve Phillips/Democracy Alliance protégés.

Phillips and his money were also behind Democrat Doug Jones, who defeated Republican Roy Moore in a 2017 Alabama special election to fill the US Senate seat Jeff Sessions vacated when he became US attorney general. At a rally targeting black voters, the leader of the Vote or Die campaign said, "Too many working class and poor people will die if Roy Moore wins," because health care, housing, and other social programs would be rolled back.[22] During the subsequent midterm elections, the group distributed pamphlets all over Alabama depicting President Trump as a white supremacist and an ally of the Klan.

"Florida, Georgia, and Alabama were merely trial runs for the real deal in 2020," Loudon said. The State Power Caucus is now applying what it has learned in these states on a national scale to oust Donald Trump. But according to Loudon, defeating Trump is merely a means to an end. Loudon said Liss' real goal "is to build a new mass socialist party that will eventually be able to challenge for state power."

Time will tell who among the many 2020 Democratic presidential hopefuls gets the nomination. But it's significant that four of those who declared early were leftist candidates of color: Tulsi Gabbard, Kamala Harris, Julián Castro, and Cory Booker. Loudon says all of them are connected to Steve Phillips in some way, and it's almost certain that at least one of them will be on the Democratic presidential ticket, if not this election cycle, then later.

Loudon agrees with Donald Trump Jr., who recently told Fox News the 2020 election "is about communism versus freedom."[23]

Laments Loudon: "The Democrats and their communist allies plan to use minority voters to create a majority that can never be overturned. If they win in 2020, they will then legalize 22 million overwhelmingly pro-Democrat illegal immigrant voters (as Hillary Clinton promised to do within one hundred days of taking office), and conservative Christians and Republicans will become a permanent (and very much persecuted) minority in their own country—forever."

AMERICA'S FUTURE IS ON THE LINE

In Trump's current term in office Americans have witnessed the exposure of three powerful enemies of the United States: the corporate media, the deep state, and the Democratic Party.

It is hard to believe how radical the Democrats have become. They are now a party whose passion and vision are to destroy anything that is virtuous. They despise the Christian faith, glory in killing babies, and promote any form of human debauchery. They enthusiastically support the invasion of the southern border and give aid and comfort to the invaders. The Democratic Party has become a political institution of evil and is hell-bent on pulling down what remains of America's Christian heritage and culture. We cannot allow such people to run our government.

The 2020 election will be critical and historic. What Trump offers the country is a chance to hold back these Democratic forces of evil, the ability to change the Supreme Court and the federal judiciary for a generation, and the additional time needed to further expose and battle the Washington establishment and deep state.

The global establishment will hit Trump with everything in its vast financial and political arsenal. Trump, who has empowered and inspired an increased worldwide awareness of the importance of national sovereignty, will be singled out for its vengeance.

This is the very reason Trump's reelection is so important. He is a historic political reformer who has totally changed the geopolitical narrative to the real issue of our time: nationalism versus globalism. The global establishment has seen, in two years, its one-hundred-year plan for a total consolidation of its financial, political, and institutional power into a world government implode before its very eyes.

The global elite, social media, corporate press, and Democratic Party will join forces to defeat Trump in 2020. The American people will witness the most political, corrupt, well-financed election battle in presidential history.

Engagement in the fight for a Trump reelection and a conservative House and Senate is a worthy pursuit—just the thought of a radical Democrat or socialist president should be enough to compel any sane

American to action. It will take a heroic effort by the Trump campaign leadership and his individual supporters to bring millions of new Trump voters to the polls to have any hope of victory.

I hope this chapter was a reality check to the tenuous situation conservatives face. Trump supporters must out-plan and out-work our formidable opposition if Trump is to be reelected.

If Donald Trump is going to win, we must also reach out to those in the black community who often vote Democratic despite their shared values with many evangelical Republicans, and I'll discuss this in the next chapter.

CHAPTER 3

BLACK AMERICANS, DEMOCRATS, AND TRUMP

I am a Republican, a radical Republican, a Black Republican, a Republican dyed in the wool....It is the party of law and order, of liberty and of progress, of honor and honesty, as against dis-loyalty, moral stagnation, dishonest voting, and repudiation.[1]
—FREDERICK DOUGLASS (1818–1895)
FORMER SLAVE TURNED ABOLITIONIST,
ORATOR, AND STATESMAN

MY FAMILY MOVED from Iowa to segregated Florida in 1962. John F. Kennedy was president, and Martin Luther King Jr. wouldn't share his "I Have a Dream" speech for another year yet. As a child I was shocked to see that my new doctor's office had separate waiting rooms for black and white patients. Drinking fountains were marked "white only," and I attended segregated schools until integration started being enforced when I was in tenth grade.

I quickly learned most white people in Florida were Democrats, a holdover from the days of Reconstruction. In 1964 when Martin Luther King Jr. marched in St. Augustine, Florida, over integrating not only the lunch counters but also the public beaches and swimming pools, I remember reading that Florida's Democratic governor, Farris Bryant, had to call in the National Guard to protect black demonstrators from violent segregationists. I can remember reading the news of how ugly things got. But those demonstrations and the resulting bru-tality may have helped pass the 1964 Civil Rights Act a few weeks later. People in St. Augustine still talk about it.

After Reconstruction following the Civil War most black Americans were Republicans. White Southerners hated Republicans so much that the vast majority of elected officials in all former Confederate states, including Florida, where I live, were Democrats. These Democrats abridged the rights of black Americans by passing statutes that have come to be known as Jim Crow laws. Most segregation laws in the South were passed by Democratic-controlled legislatures and signed by Democratic governors.

Many people today don't realize what became known as the Democratic Party was founded in the early days of our republic and led by slave owners such as Thomas Jefferson and Andrew Jackson, among others. The Republican Party, by contrast, was founded in 1854 when the Whig Party failed to stop the expansion of slavery into the West.

Democratic Southern states began seceding from the Union after Republican Abraham Lincoln was elected president in 1860. More than six hundred thousand Americans on both sides lost their lives in the bloody Civil War that followed. Lincoln freed all the slaves in the South with the Emancipation Proclamation, while Democrats in the North supported making peace with the Confederacy, which would have continued slavery and prevented the United States from becoming the great nation it has become. Had the Confederate States of America continued as a separate nation, the United States would today be more like Canada and not the powerhouse that in the last century was able to save the world for democracy in two world wars.

With this historical record many Republicans struggle to understand why an overwhelming majority of the black community, even those who are socially conservative, register and vote as Democrats. Most also say they dislike Donald Trump, even now, when as president he has done more for the black community than most presidents in history, lowering black unemployment rates, passing prison reform, and appointing men such as Dr. Ben Carson as secretary of Housing and Urban Development and Dr. Jerome Adams as surgeon general.

WHY BLACK VOTERS FLED THE GOP

The switch from Republican to Democrat began during the Great Depression when Franklin D. Roosevelt implemented the New Deal, which provided government programs that benefited many in the black community. As a result, by 1960 two-thirds of black Americans were Democrats.[2]

That year a phone call would move black voters even further toward the Democrats. In October 1960 Martin Luther King Jr. was arrested while participating in a sit-in in Atlanta. After several days in prison he was released without bail like the other protestors, but he was immediately arrested again for a probation violation related to traffic charges and sentenced to hard labor at a maximum security prison.

With the presidential election just weeks away, both the Republican candidate, Richard Nixon, and his Democratic opponent, John F. Kennedy, wrestled with how to respond. Neither wanted to alienate crucial Southern white voters. Nixon decided to say nothing, but Kennedy called King's wife, Coretta Scott King, expressing his concern for her husband and offering to help if he could. Another call from Kennedy's camp to Georgia officials led to King's release the next day.[3]

Before this, many in the black community were skeptical of Kennedy. He had been tepid on civil rights, and as Election Day neared, Kennedy had been meeting privately with white Southerners to assure them he wouldn't be an aggressive proponent of civil rights.

"King's release had an immediate and profound impact on the black community, unleashing a wave of support for Kennedy," wrote Steve Levingston, author of *Kennedy and King: The President, the Pastor, and the Battle Over Civil Rights.* "In a single day, the senator beat back years of skepticism about his commitment to racial justice."[4]

Kennedy won 70 percent of the black vote and beat Nixon by a narrow margin in the popular vote. But even as president Kennedy was reluctant to push too hard for civil rights legislation lest he lose the support of Southern white Democrats.[5]

After Kennedy was assassinated in 1963, Lyndon Johnson worked to pass the Civil Rights Act in 1964. The irony is that Johnson, a Southerner, had the reputation of being a racist who allegedly cynically said behind the scenes that by passing the Civil Rights Act, "I'll have those n***ers voting Democratic for two hundred years," a viral quote that has been circulating since the 1990s. The implication is that he was pushing the civil rights bill as a political ploy for the Democratic Party, not because he genuinely wanted equality for black Americans. Ronald Kessler published this infamous quote in his book *Inside the White House: The Hidden Lives of the Modern Presidents.* While some question its authenticity, no one can deny it would have been in keeping with Johnson's character to have said it.[6]

According to the "fact-checking" website Snopes.com, Johnson, the thirty-sixth president, "reportedly referred to the Civil Rights Act of 1957 as the 'n***er bill' in more than one private phone conversation with Senate colleagues. And he reportedly said upon appointing African-American judge Thurgood Marshall to the Supreme Court,

'Son, when I appoint a n***er to the court, I want everyone to know he's a n***er.'"[7]

Historian Doris Kearns Goodwin said Johnson also remarked:

> These Negroes, they're getting pretty uppity these days and that's a problem for us since they've got something now, they never had before, the political pull to back up their uppity-ness. Now we've got to do something about this, we've got to give them a little something, just enough to quiet them down, not enough to make a difference. For if we don't move at all, then their allies will line up against us and there'll be no way of stopping them, we'll lose the filibuster and there'll be no way of putting a brake on all sorts of wild legislation. It'll be Reconstruction all over again.[8]

There's speculation that these comments were made to appease seg-regationist Democrats in the South so they would support Johnson. But it's also the way many Southerners talked in that day—especially if those Southerners were members of the Ku Klux Klan. Sound like an outlandish accusation? Not according to a government memo the *Washington Post* discovered in the JFK files, which were released to the public in 2017. If the memo's claim is true and Johnson was a one-time member of the KKK, it certainly casts a shadow on his involvement in the Civil Rights Act—not to mention his establishment of domestic programs called the Great Society intended to eliminate poverty and racial injustice.[9]

As a young teen I remember people talking about the Ku Klux Klan in Florida, but I never ran into any members myself. However, they were strong enough around Lakeland, Florida, where I went to high school, that in the 1970s they actually held a march down the main street of Lakeland.

Some believe the mass exodus of any remaining black Republicans happened a few days after Johnson signed the proposed Civil Rights Act into law in 1964. At the Republican National Convention, Barry Goldwater, a strong conservative who notably opposed the Civil Rights Act, was nominated as the GOP's presidential candidate. Because Johnson, a Democrat, had signed the bill into law, and Goldwater, the new Republican candidate, opposed it, many believe this is the moment the GOP lost the rest of its black members.[10]

Bishop Harry R. Jackson Jr., pastor of Hope Christian Church, a

Pentecostal congregation in Beltsville, Maryland, and a passionate advocate for racial unity, helped me understand another major twist in our political history that changed the Republican Party's image and brand. It has to do with the exodus of Strom Thurmond from the Democratic Party in 1948 to become the Dixiecrat Party presidential candidate. Years later he and some of his associates became Republicans.

Here's what happened: As the Democratic Party became more modern and liberal, it recognized the need to treat black Americans more equitably. A right-wing Democratic splinter group developed called Dixiecrats (also called the States' Rights Democratic Party), and it became strong enough to run Thurmond for president. They were against federal regulations, which they thought interfered with states' rights, and they were opposed to the civil rights agenda of the Democratic Party. They carried over one million votes in the South in 1948.

Strom Thurmond and other prominent Dixiecrats ultimately became conservative Republicans, and their defection to the Republican Party came at the same time President Johnson began to lead the Democratic Party toward an aggressive civil rights agenda. This left many black Americans confused about the Democratic agenda.

Meanwhile the Christian school movement began during the time that prayer and Bible reading were removed from public schools. Interestingly the nation was beginning the long process of desegregating public schools and universities at the same time. As a result, many black Christians have been suspicious about the racial motives of the Christian school movement. Since Republicans have advocated school choice, Christian schools, and homeschooling, a false narrative arose that Republicans were attempting to dodge the desegregation of schools back in the 1960s.

Today Democrats can count on around 90 percent of the black vote. Hillary Clinton got 89 percent, and in 2012 Barack Obama got 93 percent.[11] Even black Christians and social conservatives who oppose same-sex marriage and abortion often vote a straight Democratic ticket. I've had black preacher friends say they overlook the bad policies of the Democrats (such as abortion and gay marriage) in the same way white Christians overlook the many faults of the Republican Party just because the Republicans back certain Christian causes. To these individuals it's important that Democrats seem to support social justice issues, often having to do with civil rights or prison reform. That all sounds nice. I can back those issues too. But the term *social justice* has been co-opted by the Left as a euphemism for socialism.

The black church is so important in the black community that in some ways being a conservative black Christian is more socially acceptable than being a conservative white Christian. It is commonly accepted that the Democratic Party is less religious than the GOP, and it is also true that Democrats are less religious than their Republican counterparts. But what the pollsters found was that while *white* Democrats are less likely to be religious than Republicans, *nonwhite* Democrats—generally black or Hispanic voters—are more similar to Republicans than to liberal Democrats on a whole host of issues, including faith.[12]

The most recent Pew study of these issues reports that "belief in God as described in the Bible is most pronounced among US Christians. Overall eight-in-ten self-identified Christians say they believe in the God of the Bible, while one-in-five do not believe in the biblical description of God but do believe in a higher power of some kind. Very few self-identified Christians (just 1%) say they do not believe in any higher power at all."[13]

A 2014 Pew study of religious participation concluded that nonwhite Democrats are as religiously committed as Republicans when it comes to praying and attending church. And when you narrow the survey results to black Democrats, they are even more religiously committed than Republicans. Nearly half (47 percent) of black Democrats say they attend church at least weekly, and about three-quarters pray daily (74 percent) and say religion is very important in their lives (76 percent). There are some ways that Republicans and nonwhite Democrats do not resemble each other, such as their views on abortion: 58 percent of nonwhite Democrats and 57 percent of black Democrats said abortion should be legal in all or most cases, whereas just 38 percent of Republicans held this view.[14]

CONSIDER THE FACTS

Black Christians share so many core values with Republicans that I find it hard to understand why they still vote Democratic. I know Republicans are often viewed as racially insensitive, but consider these facts, which most Americans don't know or have forgotten:

- The Republican Party was founded as the abolitionist party in 1854.

- Five of its original nine platform planks dealt with ending slavery, giving full civil rights to emancipated slaves, and giving black Americans the right to vote.

- Abraham Lincoln was the first Republican president.

- The Democrats chose to divide the nation in war rather than liberate their slaves.

- Democratic representative Preston Brooks caned Republican senator Charles Sumner almost to death for continuing to speak against slavery on the floor of the Senate.

- Democrats founded the Ku Klux Klan.

- Democrats overwhelmingly opposed the Thirteenth, Fourteenth, and Fifteenth Amendments, which gave citizenship rights to former slaves, while Republicans overwhelmingly supported them. (And these were Northern, not Southern, Democrats.)

- Democrats instituted most Jim Crow laws, which were intended, among other things, to keep black Republicans from voting because at that time, all liberated slaves belonged to the party of Lincoln. The Democrats knew it, and that is why they came up with Jim Crow laws, to circumvent the rights the Thirteenth, Fourteenth, and Fifteenth Amendments gave the freed slaves. It was not about white versus black—it was the Democrats disenfranchising newly liberated black Americans.

- The first twenty-three black men elected to Congress were all Republicans.

- The first black senator was Hiram Revels, who some have said should have his name on the Russell Senate Office Building. They wouldn't even have to change the initials. It would still be RSOB. Senator Russell was a Democrat and a racist, so why is he honored with a building named after him?

- The Democrats ignored the civil rights laws the Republicans established during and after the Civil War and moved to legalize segregation through decisions such as *Plessy v.*

Ferguson, which used the "separate but equal" doctrine to uphold racial segregation. That ruling was overturned during the tenure of Republican President Dwight Eisenhower when *all* the Southern states had Democratic governors, some of whom were keeping black children from attending public school.

- The Republicans fought to integrate the public schools while governors such as Democrat J. L. Lindsay Almond of Virginia actually shut down public schools to keep from integrating them. Many Southern states, such as Alabama and Georgia, also passed laws attempting to circumvent the *Brown v. Board of Education* ruling.

- Democratic senator Robert Byrd of West Virginia was the top officer, the Exalted Cyclops, in a local KKK unit and a mentor to Hillary Clinton and Barack Obama. He was called the "conscience of the Senate" by the former Democratic senator from Florida Bill Nelson and many others, even though he frequently used the N-word and was an unrepentant member of the KKK.

- Al Gore's father, the Democratic Senator from Tennessee from 1953 until he was defeated in 1971, joined Senator Byrd in the filibuster to oppose the Civil Rights Act of 1964, which as it turned out was already the Fourteenth Amendment of the Constitution but had been ignored by Democrats for decades.

"I am still shocked that any black person in the country could identify with the party of the KKK, Jim Crow, slavery, oppression, discrimination, and segregation," said Nina May, an antiabortion activist, founder of the Renaissance Foundation, award-winning independent filmmaker of several documentaries and educational videos, and producer of TV shows. She is also the wife of respected Christian attorney Colby May.

"I was raised as a Democrat in the South, where every Republican was referred to as an 'N-lover,'" she told me. "It was watching the way the Democratic governors and Democratic elected officials were treating blacks that made Southern whites like me shun that party and instead embrace the party of Lincoln. We were ashamed of the

Democrats and rejected their devilish ways. They still use the same oppressive, bullying, segregationist tactics they've always employed."

A resident of Virginia, Nina also has harsh words about the current Democratic governor of Virginia, Ralph Northam, who was quoted in 2019 as saying a baby who survives a botched abortion would be kept comfortable until the mother and doctor decided to end its life.[15] Democrats may call that a woman's choice, but I call it infanticide. President Trump referred to it in his 2019 State of the Union address as executing the baby,[16] which in my opinion was an accurate choice of words.

By the way, it was well known that while in medical school Northam appeared in a photo that showed one man in blackface and the other wearing the KKK's trademark white hood and robe.[17] This would have been unforgivable if a Republican had done it. Yet it's interesting that the controversy has died down and Northam is still in office.

"True to form, the Democrats suggest it's OK to kill a baby after it is delivered; they have not changed their position on children's rights to either have a good education or even live," Nina May said. "Slavery has morphed into abortion as their new cause to champion. Black America needs to be reintroduced to the party that was founded to liberate their ancestors, and if anyone should pay reparations...it is the Democratic Party."

Regardless, most of the black community continues to vote along Democratic Party lines—although something strange happened in the 2016 election. While only 8 percent of black Americans voted for Trump, many stayed home rather than voting for Clinton. The *New York Times* found that 4.4 million Obama voters stayed home on Election Day, and more than a third of those no-shows—1.6 million—were black.[18]

Trump's 2020 campaign manager, Brad Parscale, said Trump can quadruple the 2016 black voter turnout in 2020, according to an article in 2019 in RealClearPolitics by Philip Wegmann titled "Trump Bets on More Black Support in 2020. (He Might Need It.)." Wegmann quoted a Daily Beast article in which longtime GOP strategist Ed Rollins said, "Democrats can't win unless they get Obama levels of black voter turnout. Unless they can get back those levels, it makes it awful hard for them to win the White House."[19]

A month after the election, Trump said he "did great with the African American community. So good. Remember the famous line, because I talk about crime, I talk about lack of education, I talk about no jobs. And I'd say, what the h*** do you have to lose? Right? It's true. And they're smart, and they picked up on it like you wouldn't believe."[20]

Despite Trump's efforts to reach out to the black community and create economic opportunities for all Americans, he is still frequently branded a racist. Conservative black commentator Candace Owens holds black leaders who are being spotlighted by leftist media responsible for this false narrative. She recently defended Trump against racism accusations from black leftists, saying, "Black support for Donald Trump has doubled since this time last year. You guys can try to pretend that he is pushing in a racist era in this country when in fact we know the Democrats are the racists. [They] have always been the racists, the parties never switched, and you should know this....You know that the people under the hood of the KKK were Democrats, and the parties never switched. And it's a shame you should defend...our community being attacked because we support Donald Trump because we understand that we have better economic opportunities under him than we ever had with Obama....I'm really done with this. I'm done with this racist narrative."[21]

Owens has also come to Trump's defense amid the Twitter war between the president and four freshmen congresswomen known as The Squad, who falsely accused the president of racism. When it comes to Twitter, I'm certainly not going to say that Trump never puts his foot in his mouth, but my hope is that more black Christians and conservatives will begin to see through the leftist smoke screen and realize the truth.

People like rapper Kanye West give me hope. Recently he began hosting what he calls Sunday Services and released an album titled *Jesus Is King*, which points to the new direction he says he wants to take his life and music. West, who met with Trump at the White House in 2018, said his faith in Christ set him free from the Democratic Party, which he said had brainwashed the black community.[22] At a Sunday Service in October 2019 he told the crowd that it was the Republican Party that freed the slaves and said it is "mental slavery" to make political decisions based on race. "You black, so you can't like Trump?" West said. "I ain't never made a decision only based on my color. That's a form of slavery, mental slavery."[23]

Whatever has motivated the new path West is on, I applaud him for courageously stepping out to shatter the thinking that you're betraying the black community if you have your own independent thoughts about politics. If more black voices will follow the example of Owens and West and resist the lies of the Left, I believe we can heal the divide and unite over the values on which we all agree.

HEALING THE RACIAL DIVIDE

In the black community Trump had to persuade pastors almost one by one that he wasn't the racist the Left made him out to be. Back in 2015 Mark Burns, a black pastor from South Carolina, was invited to a meeting with some evangelical leaders at Trump Tower. When I interviewed him for a podcast, Burns told me, "I really didn't know a lot about Donald Trump other than he was the guy who said, 'You're fired!' He had just made the announcement that he [was] running for president, so my wife and I attended this meeting."

Burns recalls the excitement he felt to meet Christian leaders such as Dr. David Jeremiah and Jentezen Franklin at that gathering. When all the leaders sat down, he found himself directly opposite Trump, and the first thing Burns noticed was that Trump was carrying his mother's Bible.

"I didn't think I was going to make a real impact, but I felt a boldness come over me," he said. "I [asked God], 'Do I belong at this table?' I heard the Holy Spirit say, clear as day, 'You belong here. You belong here.' And then He gave me the words to ask a question that others wanted to ask but didn't: 'Mr. Trump, many of us African American leaders took some heat just coming to this meeting. So clearly there's a disconnect between you—the Republican Party—and the black community. What's your plan to bridge that gap?'"

The question didn't faze Trump. On the contrary, the future president got excited and said, "Thank you for asking that question. This is why I wanted to bring everyone together. I would like to learn more about how we can make this better for the African American community."

Trump's response told Burns and every other black leader in that room that the business mogul would be a president for all races, contrary to what popular opinion would dictate. Burns said he heard God tell him, "Show the world that [Trump] is not a racist."

The Christian leaders prayed over Trump that day. A cell phone video taken by his wife, Tomarra Burns, and posted on her Facebook page went viral with 1.9 million views. It showed Dr. David Jeremiah praying and asking God to send a strong black American who would walk with Trump and help him bridge that racial gap.[24] Not too long afterward Burns was asked to speak in Trump's place at Bob Jones University. Other Republican candidates were going to speak, but Trump wasn't able to make it. Bob Jones University was only ten minutes from where Burns lived, so he agreed. When it was his turn to speak, "I just began to pour my heart out with what I thought the Holy Spirit was telling me to say. And the place went crazy—great response."

Burns says many—especially on the political left—scheme against Trump's presidency even though he's done so much for minorities and for the nation as a whole. And although many have questioned and attacked Burns for his strong commitment to Trump's vision for the United States, he refuses to back down from what he believes God has revealed to him.

Since that meeting in 2015 Burns—cofounder of the NOW television network—has unashamedly spoken in defense of the president, calling out false allegations and unfair attacks from the Left. I can't help but admire his strength to stand firm.

It's nothing new to call Trump a racist. Democrats have been using the epitaph to label any Republican they don't like. A recent article in RealClearPolitics said, "This condemnation…has become something of a litmus test in the Democratic primary, with candidates lining up one after the other to decry the current occupant of the Oval Office."

The article interviewed Paris Dennard, "who is on the president's Commission on White House Fellowships [and] says he can't take that criticism from Democrats seriously so long as Ralph Northam remains governor of Virginia. If liberals really cared about racism, he argued, they would have run Northam out of office."

> What's more, [Dennard] continued, the African American electorate views Trump through "one of two lenses." Publicly, the black community is more likely to criticize the current administration lest they lose friends, face backlash, and risk having "their 'black card' be taken away." Privately, he asserted, those same voters will take a look at the policies of the president: "There [are many] black Americans who look at this president in terms of what he is doing and how their lives are. I think they come away believing that Trump is doing what he said he was going to do for the black community." Perhaps a

second term for Trump hinges on this silent black majority, assuming it exists.[25]

REPUBLICANS HAVE DROPPED THE BALL

While the Republican Party may be the party of Lincoln, Burns points out it does very little outreach to the black community, as if there's no hope of winning their votes. And black leaders who rise in the GOP aren't always supported. I saw this up close and personal a decade ago, and it left me disillusioned too when a group of establishment Republicans stabbed a black preacher friend of mine in the back when he ran as a Republican for a US Senate seat from his home state.

I met my friend in the 1990s when he was a rising star in the Republican Party. He was also pastoring a growing church that now has twenty-two thousand members, sits on a beautiful campus, and is widely respected. He is an accomplished leader and would have made an excellent Republican senator, but the entire incident was so negative my friend is no longer a Republican and asked that I tell this story without using his name.

While doing research for this chapter, I pulled out an old issue of *Charisma*, where we first wrote about my friend's reason for getting involved in politics: "I hope to make the world a better place through my work as a pastor and as a public servant," he said. "I want to minister the gospel of Jesus Christ and win the lost. But I also want to work within the political process to ensure that Judeo-Christian values are installed in the public policy and public life of this nation." He also listed his goals as to "create jobs, reform...government and 'find ways to help those at the bottom end of the ladder, primarily through education'"—priorities that are neither Republican nor Democrat.

Originally a Democrat, he became a Republican when he read the platforms of both parties. He told *Charisma*, "With my value system, to my chagrin, I found that I agreed more with those Republicans than I did the Democrats." The article also described him as an "ideological maverick who doesn't seem to mind bursting the stereotypical bubble of black political belief and loyalty" and a man who was willing to "[swim] against the tide."

Then a series of events happened that show how nasty party politics can be when he lost his bid to unseat the US senator from his state—an incumbent Democrat who was about as liberal as they get.

At that time, the Republicans had the majority in the Senate, but they had the chance to elect another Republican by running a black man—my friend—who would peel away enough black votes to win the race. Often a political party will strategize to support a single candidate in the primaries who it feels can go the distance. This saves the candidate the expense and wear and tear of winning a primary election so they can focus their time, financial resources, and energy on winning the general election. This was the strategy when he declared his candidacy.

However, the National Republican Senatorial Committee apparently didn't agree with the plan. Senator Elizabeth Dole of North Carolina, who headed the committee at the time, apparently didn't believe a "black preacher" could win. So she recruited a white man who won the primary but lost badly to the Democrat. In fact in that election Republicans lost six seats in the Senate and Democrats took control. So much for Elizabeth Dole's ability to lead! She was replaced as chairwoman after the disastrous midterms and got her comeuppance when she lost her own bid for reelection to the Senate two years later.

How do I know so much about this race? Because I supported my friend even though I live in Florida and couldn't vote for him. I maxed out my own contributions and raised tens of thousands more in donations because of my respect for him as a leader. I felt it would be good to have a strong Christian like him in the Senate. But he lost because, in my opinion, the Republican establishment did him in. How sad. If he had been in the Senate, he would likely have cast the deciding vote on key issues such as Obamacare. He would have been a good role model for others in the black community who wanted to make their way to the Republican Party. Instead he is no longer a Republican, and I don't blame him.

It's no wonder black Americans don't feel warm and fuzzy toward the Republican Party. It's a loss for the nation as a whole too because there are many in the black community, such as my friend, who would be able to speak from a prophetic perspective if they were in office. This came up when Harry Jackson interviewed me before his Rise Up prayer event for America, where we spoke about the importance of having a prophetic perspective of our nation.

In addition to being a pastor, Jackson serves as presiding bishop of the International Communion of Evangelical Churches and hosts *Hope Connection*, a thirty-minute television show that airs on several national networks. Not only is Jackson a strong voice for biblical values in the social sphere, but he's also passionate about racial reconciliation—to the point that he cofounded the Reconciled Church initiative. And he's not afraid to speak the truth about hard topics such as abortion and same-sex marriage.

During the interview he talked about our need to look at the nation's issues from a prophetic perspective. He believes God is speaking to America and wants to promote an agenda. It's not a black or white agenda, nor is it a Republican or Democratic agenda. Instead it's "God's own understanding of righteousness and justice." The question is, Will His people listen?

Charles Flowers—senior pastor of Faith Outreach Center International in San Antonio—participated in the interview. He pointed out that a herd mentality afflicts many in America. For instance, he said many in the black community think that if you are socially conservative and therefore support conservative candidates, you are betraying your ethnic identity. "You know the series…'Am I still black if…?' that kind of defines whether or not you meet what the normative thought is around black people?" Flowers said. "So am I still black if I watch Fox?…Am I still black if I don't immortalize slavery and the atrocities associated with it?"[26]

That herd mentality, Jackson said, easily leads the American people to make bad choices. "The answer is the Word of God applied to our lives and having almighty God come and bless America. But I believe the renewing of our mind according to the Word of God will release a prophetic perspective that will cause us to be blessed and not cursed."

Jackson believes we can't blindly follow either political party. Instead we need to be biblically informed and heed what God is trying to do in America. I couldn't agree more.

Yet the perception exists in the black community and media that if you're black, you must be a Democrat. Not only that, they vilify every black person who is Republican or supports President Trump. A good example is Omarosa Manigault Newman. When she was on Trump's White House staff, the Left and media maligned her, saying she was selling out African Americans—as if the black community should uniformly oppose Trump just because most are Democrats. Yet when she turned on Trump by writing a negative book in 2018 and bashing the president in media interviews, she became the darling of the same media, even if the attention was only short-lived.

Of course Omarosa (whom I met at the Trump election party in 2016) is in a class by herself. Most black Americans who back the president do not turn their backs on him because they see what he's accomplishing and what he's doing for the black community. That's the point I'm making here. The president wants to reach the black community, and I hope they will begin to see that, as have Diamond and Silk, the hilarious sisters whose wit and wisdom have made them famous on the internet and cable news. Or Candace Owens and many others.

Pastor Burns believes more blacks will support Trump in 2020, increasing from 8 percent in 2016 to 15 percent. He also believes Trump will get 30 percent of the Hispanic vote. They may seem ambitious, but he says these are "doable numbers."

Pastor Burns may be in the minority in the black community, but he believes in Trump. "We're going to win 2020," he said. "God told me this."

When it comes to the black community, I am not advocating for the Republican Party. In fact there is a lot not to like about the Republican establishment, as the way Elizabeth Dole and the Republican establishment treated my black preacher friend shows. As I've written before, I registered as a Democrat at age nineteen and for more than twenty years voted in Democratic primaries—although I usually voted Republican in the general election as the Democrats moved further to the left and further away from what I believe are godly principles. I tell people today I'm a "reluctant Republican." Usually I vote for the candidate, not the party.

But while Republicans are far from perfect, on the important issues the people they run for office and their official party platform are much closer to what I believe. So I hope many black Americans will make the same odyssey I have and that they will see from the facts I've outlined in this chapter and the ugly history of the Democrats that they have no option but to support the Republican candidate.

Today the Democrats' extreme leftist policies do not benefit all Americans, especially those of color, whom Democrats take for granted and use to advance their own political aims. Nowhere is this clearer than at the southern border, where Democrats seem more concerned about inflaming passions than finding solutions to the immigration crisis. With an eye toward changing voter demographics in key states, Democrats have made the border the new election battleground, dismissing the real threats of unbridled immigration because they seem to believe every new immigrant is a new vote for the Democrats.

What does this mean for America, and how should evangelical Christians view this crisis?

CHAPTER 4

GOD LOVES BORDERS

A nation that cannot control its borders is not a nation.[1]
—RONALD REAGAN
FORTIETH PRESIDENT OF THE UNITED STATES

P RESIDENT DONALD TRUMP'S controversial border wall has been dominating the news ever since he famously rode down the escalator at Trump Tower in June 2015 to announce he would run for president. The media seemed unable to believe he would make the wall a focal point of his 2016 campaign, yet many now believe it could be a critical factor in his bid for reelection.

Critics may complain about our president's bold agenda to build a wall, but many of them don't realize this concept isn't new, and the president inherited a mess. The debate surrounding illegal immigration—and even talk of building a fence—goes back as far as Ronald Reagan's presidency. Construction of a fourteen-mile stretch of fence along the San Diego-Tijuana border began during George H. W. Bush's administration and continued into Bill Clinton's first term. In 2006, during George W. Bush's administration, the Secure Fence Act authorized hundreds more miles of fencing.[2]

Yet while the issue has become almost a stalemate in Washington, the subject of borders is not merely a topic of political debate. It can also be viewed with spiritual eyes. We have to look no further than the Bible to learn that walls are biblical and God loves borders.

In a recent sermon series called "Border Control," Pastor Matthew Hagee, son of John Hagee of Cornerstone Church in San Antonio, described the Bible as a book of borders. He said God put borders around everything He created and that the current problems at the nation's physical border are merely an outward symptom of a supernatural border problem. As a country we've crossed the line on biblical mandates regarding gender, abortion, sexuality, and marriage. We haven't stayed within the boundaries God has given us in His Word. Because of that our view of borders has changed. Borders used to be thought of as blessings, Hagee says, but now they are burdens.[3]

Pastor Jim Garlow put forth a similar theory regarding today's "anything goes" society. He said people don't like borders in their lives, and that sentiment extends to not wanting borders around countries.

God imposed biblical borders, but people hate them. They don't want rules. They want to be able to kill babies if the pregnancy is unwanted; they want to be able to end it even though they are ending a human life. Sexually they want to do anything with anyone at any time. They don't realize that God created boundaries as a means of protection.

If one nation gets out of line, borders make it more difficult for them to spread their poison, their toxicity, their evil ways to the next country. Garlow contends that God established borders for a reason—even geographical borders are permitted by God and even blessed by God; He establishes nations.

President Trump has decided that he's going to focus on blessing the people in this nation, and that's what all governing officials should do in their own country. As part of this focus, Trump sees through the manipulation of nations such as China, which originally established tariffs to help its economy because it was a developing country. Although China's economic picture has changed drastically since then—in 2018 the Chinese boasted a GDP worth 13.6 trillion US dollars[4]—it still establishes enormous fees for any product that comes into its country. (It's also worth noting that China's economic growth has more recently slumped to its lowest level since 1992 due in part to tariffs and trade friction with the United States.[5])

Francis Myles, author of *Why God Hates Open Borders* and pastor of Lovefest Church International in Tempe, Arizona, also preached a powerful sermon about how God establishes borders. His message is taken from Acts 17:26, where Paul tells the Greeks on Mars Hill that God created every nation on earth from one blood and established "their boundaries." Boundaries are God's idea, Myles said, and anyone who wants open borders is in rebellion against Him.[6]

These are not the only leaders who view the battle over the wall through a spiritual lens. Dr. Alveda King—niece of Martin Luther King Jr.—wrote an article about Trump's wall for Newsmax that caught my attention and prompted me to interview her.[7] Not only does she believe borders are God's idea; she also sees a spiritual reason behind many liberals' biased animosity toward Trump. She makes a comparison to the biblical story of Ezra and Nehemiah, who helped restore Jerusalem after the Babylonian captivity. At that time, Ezra served as a teacher of the law to the people of Israel, and as governor Nehemiah helped rebuild Jerusalem's wall.

"And they had Sanballat and Tobias and the naysayers saying, 'Come down off the wall! Don't build the wall! Come down and talk to us and let's discuss,'" Alveda said. "Nehemiah, by the Spirit of God, knew that he couldn't come down off that wall, or it wouldn't happen. And that's what we're seeing here."

Today's naysayers want to delay Trump's border wall with unproductive discussions. But those anti-wall protesters don't realize just how badly we need a wall. After all, much illegal immigration directly supports drug cartels. "The drug cartels are advertising," she said. "[They say], 'Give us the money, and we'll get you across.' But no! They're really doing that to profiteer with the drug market. We even have some evidence that some of the little children are not even the children of the families they're with. They are renting the children to look as though they're families, to help the cartels get the people across the border."

In fact these drug cartels go so far as to trick people into crossing the border illegally. Many travelers think what they're doing is legal because the cartels tell them they will take care of their paperwork as long as they pay them a certain sum of money. But those lies are costly.

Alveda also pointed out that the wall is not merely Trump's agenda. On the contrary, she said members of law enforcement, the medical community, and others are pleading with Trump to put a strong regulatory system in place. The United States is and should always strive to be a compassionate nation, she said, but because of the problems stemming from illegal immigration, we need order. We need a wall.

"Without the order that is required to help and assist and serve the immigrants, they are suffering," she said. "We welcome immigrants to America—absolutely. But there is a process, and the president is working on that process."

King pointed out that a video clip is circling the internet right now of President Obama saying we need to put politics aside and stop the flood of immigrants coming into our country.[8] She wonders why it was fine for Obama to make this call to action, but not Trump. I can't help but wonder the same thing.

A GOP-funded website called BorderFacts.com raised the same

question. A section labeled "What They Said" includes a slideshow of comments on immigration from former presidents Bill Clinton and Barack Obama, former secretary of state Hillary Clinton, and Senate minority leader Chuck Schumer.

The website quoted Obama from a 2013 State of the Union address, when he said, "Real reform means strong border security," and noted that his administration had put "more boots on the Southern border than at any time in our history" and reduced "illegal crossings to their lowest levels in 40 years."[9]

Two years later, during her second presidential campaign, Hillary Clinton said, "I voted numerous times when I was a senator to spend money to build a barrier to try to prevent illegal immigrants from coming in. And I do think you have to control your borders."[10]

Bill Clinton expressed similar sentiments in a 2005 State of the Union address when he said, "It is wrong and ultimately self-defeating for a nation of immigrants to permit the kind of abuse of our immigration laws we have seen in recent years, and we must do more to stop it."[11]

Also included among the comments was a quote from a 2009 speech Schumer gave at an immigration law and policy event, where he said, "When we use phrases like 'undocumented workers,' we convey a message to the American people that their government is not serious about combating illegal immigration, which the American people overwhelmingly oppose. If you don't think it's illegal, you are not going to say it. I think it is illegal and wrong, and we have to change it."[12]

Not only have all of them flip-flopped on the issue; they and other long-term Democrats are the ones who have done nothing for decades and allowed the problem to escalate to its current level.

I agree with a recent tweet from Charlie Kirk, founder and president of Turning Point USA.

> Chuck Schumer has been in office for 38 years
> Nancy Pelosi has been in office for 32 years
> Maxine Waters has been in office for 28 years
> Joe Biden was in office for 44 years.
> Yet they blame all of America's problems on Donald Trump,
> who hasn't even been in office 3 years?[13]

Wilfredo "Choco" De Jesús, former senior pastor of New Life Covenant Church in Chicago, one of the largest US congregations in the Assemblies of God, has been a consultant to President Obama and has also met with President Trump. Recently he was elected treasurer of the General Council of the Assemblies of God, one of the highest positions in that denomination. As a Puerto Rican American from Chicago's Humboldt Park, he sees the controversy from a unique perspective. He told me he is amazed by the hypocrisy of the Democrats on the topic of immigration. In 2009 they controlled both the House and Senate and could have passed comprehensive immigration reform.

"Barack Obama said in his first year of office he would address this issue of comprehensive immigration reform, and he lied to the people," Choco told me. "President Trump inherited a mess. Now he's there to clean it. So you need somebody who's strong-willed and says, 'I'm going to clean this mess.'"

He believes President Trump has tried to work with the Democrats to find a solution, but the Democrats won't cooperate because they want to make the president look bad. "There's hypocrisy on both sides," he said, so "I just say let's fix it—build the wall. But let these people have a pathway toward citizenship in five or seven years. I'm not for amnesty, but at least create a pathway and work with the president."

Choco believes a country that spends upwards of one hundred million dollars on one military jet should be able to afford to build a wall to protect our country. "I say to my Democratic friends, give them the money for the wall—just as long as the wall has doors. There's nothing wrong with trying to secure the border. You just can't have chaos. I've been to the border. I've seen it, and it's unfortunate, but we have a system that's been broken [for] more than twenty years, since Ronald Reagan."

In addition to government inaction, some also believe the Democratic Party has a hidden agenda to change voting demographics through immigration. Brigitte Gabriel, founder of ACT for America and a *New York Times* best-selling author, made this point in her latest book, *Rise: In Defense of Judeo-Christian Values and Freedom.* Gabriel said refugees are given jobs in strategic election states such as Iowa, Michigan, Georgia, and Texas. "Notice these are all states that voted for Donald Trump," she wrote. "This creates a significant interest among Democratic politicians who want to import more welfare-dependent voters in areas of the country that will prove advantageous for them."[14]

A COMPLICATED ISSUE

The issue of immigration is complex, to say the least. Mexico as a nation-state does not send immigrants to the US; the dysfunctional nature of its society does. Mexico's biggest problem is corruption, which is advanced and sustained by the drug lords. There are honest men and women in government and law enforcement, courageous people who are trying every day to do the right thing. But it is a struggle.

I learned this from my longtime friend Marc Nuttle of Oklahoma City. He is a lawyer, an author, a consultant, and a businessman who has advised US presidents, leaders of foreign countries, state officials, and corporations. He is one of the smartest people I know. He said the United States should enforce its laws across the border and begin to prosecute the warlords of Mexico. "It may not be easy," Nuttle said, "but it can be done. We did it in Panama when we arrested and imprisoned Manuel Noriega."[15]

The current border crisis seems to have struck a nerve, as evidenced by the fever pitch of the debate on news talk shows. What is this raw nerve? Nuttle said it is the awareness of most average Americans that our nation has some serious problems, and Donald Trump seems to be the only one who will say so or propose solutions. These inherent problems include immigration and an unsecured border, as well as a visionless foreign policy, an unsustainable budget, a broken infrastructure, and a populace that no longer sees itself united in purpose.

"But this is not what makes the nerve raw. [It's what] makes the nerve sensitive," Nuttle wrote in his weekly policy briefing, called *The Nuttle Report*. "What makes it raw is a dysfunctional do-nothing Congress, a condescending intelligentsia that thinks its wisdom is better than anyone else's, and a disrespectful, arrogant press."

As Donald Trump is identifying these problems, Marc said it's as if the public is breathing a huge, collective sigh of relief and saying, "Finally someone is speaking to the reality of the situation!" Congress is so dysfunctional that it cannot offer any answers on how to secure our borders, which is what frustrates the public and produces a raw nerve. Nuttle said it may be difficult to secure the border, but it can be done, because Israel built a wall.

Yes, the US-Mexico border is much longer than Israel's—roughly four and a half times as long in fact. But why not let the American people decide what sacrifices they are willing to make to secure the border. "It's not that the issue is difficult," Nuttle said. "It's that no one will honor the people's honest intentions to discuss options."

The corporate media ignores the documented fact that criminals are crossing the border. The illegal immigrant who fatally shot Kathryn Steinle, an innocent woman, in San Francisco has seven felony convictions and had been deported five times.[16] The press made very little mention of this repeat offender. But to Nuttle what's most upsetting is that Congress, the media, and the intelligentsia don't seem to want to secure the border, and they appear to have no compassion for how having an unsecured border impacts Americans mentally and physically.

Nuttle wrote:

> It is important to remember that, as the United States of America, we respect and are open to immigrants. We are a nation of immigrants. Our future economic stability depends upon immigration, but our laws must be respected if we are to maintain order.
>
> One solution is to embrace the culture and stability of the Hispanic family in America. Family-owned businesses per capita are a very high percent of the Hispanic community. They are well-run, innovative, and profitable businesses. They are a growing employer for the general population. We should recognize them for the stabilizing force that they are, and bring them to the forefront of the debate on immigration.
>
> The Hispanic community suffers because of the current negative dialog surrounding immigration. We should champion them as the future for the assimilation of a changing workforce. They along with other family-owned and small businesses are the front door to training, placement, and creation of new jobs.
>
> The [president and Congress] should promote the American business model. Fifty percent of the non-farm adult workforce in the United States work for a small business of 25 employees or less. These small business owners provide services and efficiencies for large business to compete in the world marketplace. This large and small business equation in our country is unique in the world trading system. No law or regulation

should be passed or imposed without first measuring the impact on this unique American business model.[17]

Today identity politics and racial divides threaten the unity of these United States. Politicians spout rhetoric advocating one division of society over another for the dominance of one societal argument over another. No statesman except Donald Trump is speaking to the vision of a unified America. He's providing the leadership people deserve based on love and respect.

"Treating each other fairly is the goal," said Nuttle, and he quoted Oswald Chambers, who put it this way: "What we call the process, God calls the end."[18] Is that Pollyanna-ish? Nuttle asked rhetorically. "Only if we don't believe in binding principles. No one has a right to control the system just for their benefit. The pursuit of happiness, as each person defines happiness, requires unrestricted pursuit. This is what our Founding Fathers hoped for the generations."

Recently Steve Deace, a talk show host on *The Blaze*, noted that Fox News' Tucker Carlson accurately pointed out "the painfully obvious fact that Rep. Ilhan Omar (D-Minn.) loathes the very country that rescued her from oppression and then elected her to Congress. If we don't learn from that stupidity vis-à-vis our nation's immigration policy...the natural consequences will be both existential and deserved."[19]

Carlson went on to say:

No country can survive being ruled by people who hate it....
[Omar] scolded us and called us names; she showered us with contempt. It's infuriating. But more than that, it's also ominous. The United States admits more immigrants than any country on earth, more than a million every year. The Democratic Party demand we increase that number and admit far more. OK, Americans like immigrants, but immigrants have got to like us back.[20]

As I was writing this book, two respected leaders traveled to the border to see the situation for themselves. Upon returning, they tried their best to get out the word on what they saw, which differs from the leftist view often presented in the media.

One was Sam Rodriguez, the president of the National Hispanic Christian Leadership Conference, who appeared on Fox News with

Shannon Bream to refute allegations made by freshman New York congresswoman Alexandra Ocasio-Cortez, an avowed socialist. AOC, as she's called in the media, had made statements in 2019 that our border facilities were like Nazi concentration camps and that some detainees had been told to drink from toilets.

"I must be living in a parallel universe somewhere," Rodriguez told Bream, adding that he's a devoted Trekkie. "There must be some sort of breach in the space-time continuum."

After hearing the news reports that children were living in deplorable conditions at the detention center outside El Paso, Texas, Rodriguez contacted the White House to gain access to the facility. He was permitted to walk through unrestricted and ask questions freely. "I did not find soiled diapers. I did not find crying children. I did not find deplorable conditions," he said. "Quite the opposite. I found amazing people on both sides trying to make a very difficult circumstance better. So I don't know where everyone else is visiting."

He asked the border patrol agents—most of whom were Latino—if what he was seeing had been staged. "[They answered], 'Pastor Sam, absolutely not. You are looking at the very thing that existed here for a number of weeks.'"

He said he also learned that the attorneys who reported seeing soiled diapers and other appalling conditions never actually toured the center. "They never visited what I visited. They took that information, anecdotally, from interviews with children—with children, mind you—from the age of two to the age of seventeen."

Rodriguez, who is neither a Democrat nor a Republican, told Bream both political parties have failed miserably to fix the broken immigration system: "We got here because Congress . . . is playing politics with millions of individuals, with the sovereignty of our nation, and with the protection of our border."[21]

Around the same time, Dr. James Dobson, a venerated evangelical leader, visited the border at McAllen, Texas, at the invitation of the White House. He then sent out a widely circulated letter to his constituents, partly to fulfill a promise to the border patrol agents he met to set the record straight on what is really happening.

"I came away with an array of intense emotions," he wrote. "First, I was profoundly grieved over the misery of thousands of people. Second, I felt a deep appreciation for those who are doing their best to help in an impossible circumstance. Third, and frankly, I was angry at the political fat cats who have deliberately allowed this chaos to occur for political or financial gain. They, and their friends in the fake media, have told the American people that there is no crisis at the border! Shame on them all."

Dobson said his heart aches for those caught up in the debacle at the border. But he added:

> Lest I be misunderstood, let me make clear that I am among the majority of Americans who want the border to be closed to those who attempt to enter illegally. There has to be a better solution than this. I have wondered, with you, why the authorities don't just deny these refugees access to this nation. Can't we just send them back to their places of origin? The answer I received was "No," for reasons I will explain.
>
> Only 10 percent of the detainees are Mexicans. This year alone, people have come to our southern border from 127 countries, including Bangladesh, Pakistan, Turkey, India, China, Albania, El Salvador, Guatemala, Honduras and other nations around the world. They speak their native tongues, which means they can't be understood by each other or the staff. What are we to do with them? The Mexican government will not take them back, and there is no place to send them. Our current laws do not permit us to repatriate them to their country of origin. This is a disaster with no solution or projected conclusion.

Then Dobson makes this profound point about what will happen if we do nothing: "Their numbers will soon overwhelm the culture as we have known it, and it could bankrupt the nation. America has been a wonderfully generous and caring country since its founding. That is our Christian nature. But in this instance, we have met a worldwide wave of poverty that will take us down if we don't deal with it. And it won't take long for the inevitable consequences to happen."[22]

LEARNING FROM THE CRISIS IN VENEZUELA

As leaders such as Dobson and Rodriguez speak out, the truth about the situation is becoming better understood—as well as the risk of allowing this flood of immigration to continue.

To see what unfettered immigration does to a once prosperous country, we must look no further than Venezuela, which is experiencing economic turmoil. Inflation in 2019 was at 10 million percent, resulting in food shortages and people starving across the nation.[23]

Recently I met Michael Sabga, an evangelical Christian and successful businessman who was born in Venezuela but now lives in St. Augustine, Florida. He remembers the days when Venezuela had one of the most coveted economies in all of Latin America. "It was a prosperous, beautiful, great country to live in with a great education system, great economy, buildings, highways, and one of the most advanced medical facilities in the world," he said. "The country had real freedoms like in the US." So what happened?

The borders between Colombia and Venezuela were very porous— and still are, he said, because there's never been an actual fence or wall. In the 1980s and 1990s the situation was terrible in neighboring Colombia because heinous drug cartels such as Pablo Escobar's Medellín Cartel and the Cartel de Cali were terrorizing the nation. As the nation became a war zone, the quickest and easiest thing for Colombians to do was flee to neighboring Venezuela. The country was so rich and there was so much work available that it essentially became a haven for poor Colombians seeking a better life.

"For two decades the migration of these people was so intense that it got to a point where the Venezuelan system couldn't deal with them anymore," Sabga told me. "They couldn't support them. They couldn't offer them education. And what you ended up with was what we call belts of poverty around the cities."

Neither the government nor the religious institutions could keep up with the needs of the immigrants, and soon the poor communities were being isolated from the rest of society. That's when Hugo Chávez began speaking the language of the common people and offering the poor a future that looked very bright—a future that included a lot of giveaways.

"He was definitely a communist," Sabga said of Chávez. "He was definitely a follower of Fidel [Castro], of the Marxist ideologies, which meant that soon he was changing the constitution and infiltrating the electoral system so they're always winning. And there were many instances in which Hugo Chávez brought in these voting machines, electronic machines, where he got to control the results."

It didn't happen overnight, but soon the oil industry, the basis of the Venezuelan economy, was being run incompetently by Chávez's cronies in the Venezuelan government. When the US oil industry pulled out of Venezuela because conditions were so bad, the oil industry collapsed. Soon there was no money to pay for the electrical grid, the water system, or the health care system.

"That money is basically gone," he said. "And they're not going to replace that money. They're basically letting the country fall into an abyss."

Sabga sees some frightening parallels between the United States and Venezuela. And he hopes we will learn valuable lessons from watching what happened to the once prosperous South American nation.

"The most important thing right now is we have to stop this immigration flow in the southern border of the US—and at some point the northern border because we're going to have a problem with Canada as well," he said. "The number one reason that Venezuela fell into the chaos they're in today is very simple: open borders and no control of immigration. This is what started the whole thing, and this is what is happening in the United States. We have to find a way to stop that flow."

I sincerely hope the United States pays attention to Venezuela's hardship and realizes that if we do not deal with the immigration crisis we're facing, we could suffer greatly later on.

Meanwhile there is hope coming from the Hispanic evangelical community for a solution to the immigration problem. While Washington seems deadlocked, the National Hispanic Christian Leadership Conference (NHCLC), founded by Sam Rodriguez, has connections so strong on both sides of the political aisle that David Brody of the Christian Broadcasting Network (CBN) called the group the "evangelical whisperer." The group has managed to form close friendships with both the Trump White House and Democratic House Speaker Nancy Pelosi, who called the NHCLC when she read that millions of illegal immigrants would be deported.

"She figured her voice on this sensitive topic wouldn't move the needle with this White House," Brody wrote, "so she turned to, at least on the surface, what may seem an unlikely choice: the conservative evangelical community, specifically her friends (that's right, friends) at the [NHCLC]."

Brody's report continued:

A source with knowledge of the immigration discussions between House leadership and the Hispanic evangelical community tells CBN News that the Pelosi phone call was to top leaders at the NHCLC with a desperate plea to have them convince the White House to pull back on the impending raids, which at the time was reported to involve millions of deportations. The NHCLC did indeed pick up the phone and dial 1600 Pennsylvania Avenue. A source close to the White House acknowledges that the NHCLC discussed the impending raids with administration officials, and they were assured that the activity by Immigration and Customs Enforcement would be limited in scope, targeting a few thousand illegal immigrants who had defied court orders to deport, not millions.[24]

When Pelosi held a press conference that week, she said she had "called some people of faith" and felt their calls to President Trump "made a difference."[25]

I asked Tony Suarez, the NHCLC's executive vice president, about the organization's relationship with Pelosi. He explained: "The position of the NHCLC has always been to be at the table. It doesn't matter who else is at the table. We want to be the hands and feet of Jesus to anyone in need and to be like a Nehemiah and be able to speak truth to power and to speak on behalf of the people of God.

"That's why we felt it was important to be a part of the Faith Advisory Council when we were invited by then candidate Trump," he continued, noting that he and Sam Rodriguez served on the council as private citizens and not as representatives of NHCLC. "It's why we felt it was important to be at the table when Speaker Pelosi invited us time and again. That does not mean we condone or endorse everything that each of these elected officials does, but it does mean we are there to be a voice for the voiceless and to be a voice on behalf of the church. And that's what we've tried to do."

I'm privileged to be on the board of the NHCLC, so I know firsthand it is a very conservative organization that respects the rule of law but also believes the Bible commands Christians to be compassionate. "Those views have led the NHCLC into uncharted territory where they have the ear of both conservative immigration officials inside the White House and progressive Democratic leadership in the House of Representatives," Brody reported.

One issue the NHCLC supports is protecting "Dreamers"—young undocumented immigrants who were brought to the US as children—from deportation. In fact Brody reported, "It was this issue that brought the NHCLC and Nancy Pelosi together about a year ago. Since then, the relationship has only gotten better, and a trust has developed despite the closeness that Rodriguez and the NHCLC have with the White House."

Brody said Pelosi hopes the NHCLC will be a compassionate bridge to the Trump White House. "She trusts them," he said, "and the feeling is mutual."[26]

As for a comprehensive solution to the border crisis, that's trickier. The NHCLC has made clear to Democratic leaders in the House that Congress must come up with the ultimate solution. Suarez told me, "To get any piece of legislation done, be it immigration, be it something with religious liberty or criminal-justice reform, we know that it has to be done in the halls of Congress. That's how our government works."

He explained that Americans sometimes lose focus, thinking the president makes these things happen. "But the White House does not dictate law to our country; it's done in the halls of Congress," he said. Like many of us, he's frustrated with Congress' inaction. "Some of the personalities that are currently involved—Pelosi, [Chuck] Schumer, [Dick] Durbin, and others—have been in leadership for over two decades. So they've been a part of these conversations for well over twenty years.

"We have a humanitarian issue at the border, and the people responsible—the only branch of government that is truly responsible for fixing it—still can't come to an agreement," Suarez said. "It doesn't matter if the House is under Republican leadership or Democratic leadership. This is something the House has failed us on time and time again."

I share his frustration that for thirty years our elected officials have campaigned on immigration but failed to deliver on their promises. I agree with Suarez when he says, "We've reached the point where we, the people, have to hold elected officials accountable. If you're going to *campaign* on the issue, then you have to *act* on the issue."

Before the NHCLC (and the relationships Rodriguez forged with Presidents Bush, Obama, and Trump), Hispanic Evangelicals had little voice in Washington. In fact previous administrations and most inside the Beltway viewed all Evangelicals with suspicion, as we will see in the next chapter.

CHAPTER 5

WASHINGTON AND EVANGELICALS BEFORE TRUMP

Mark my word, if and when these preachers get control of the [Republican] party, and they're sure trying to do so, it's going to be a terrible...problem. Frankly, these people frighten me. Politics and governing demand compromise. But these Christians believe they are acting in the name of God, so they can't and won't compromise. I know, I've tried to deal with them.[1]
—BARRY GOLDWATER (1909–1998)
FIVE-TERM SENATOR FROM ARIZONA AND 1964
REPUBLICAN PRESIDENTIAL NOMINEE

E VANGELICALS HAVE BECOME loyal to Donald Trump because we see him as a champion of our values. Instead of pandering for votes from religious conservatives and then treating Evangelicals as if they don't exist, which some leaders have said Ronald Reagan did, Trump listens and acts.

Today there are many Evangelicals in the Trump administration, from Secretary of State Mike Pompeo to Vice President Mike Pence. Mike Evans frequents the White House, and he told me that you can't walk ten feet in the West Wing without running into an Evangelical.

But it hasn't always been so. Until Jimmy Carter exploded on the national scene in the mid-1970s Evangelicals were not seen as a voting bloc, and the term *born-again* was not widely used outside conservative churches.

Of course before the 1960s there was at least a religious veneer on the nation's political scene. Back then there were moral issues of war and peace and disputes (often violent) between labor and management. But today's hot-button issues were nowhere on the scene. Prayer was considered legitimate in schools when I was a child, abortion was so secretive it was unheard of, and homosexuality was definitely in the closet.

After World War II, Christians were scandalized by behavior that to many today doesn't seem so bad. For example, Harry Truman liked to drink bourbon and play poker with his friends. To him religion was primarily ethical behavior derived from a Protestant tradition, and he didn't speak much about it. However, he quoted Scripture, perhaps because he had read the Bible through twice by the time he was twelve, and when it came to recognizing the Jewish state, it was evident that his worldview had been shaped by his knowledge of Scripture.

It's widely accepted that Presidents Roosevelt, Eisenhower, Kennedy, and Johnson had marital infidelities, not to mention Bill Clinton. But until Clinton, marital unfaithfulness was something no politician talked about and the media ignored.

When Truman was still president, a thirty-three-year-old Billy Graham was interviewed in *Christian Life* magazine about how the 1952 election was the most important since the Civil War. The reason: the drift toward socialism. I have a copy in my office because the interview was done by my late mentor Robert Walker. Now, six decades later, what was said seems quaint.

For example, the article talked about the religious faith of both candidates—Dwight Eisenhower and Adlai Stevenson—and noted, among other things, that both drank and smoked. It said Eisenhower, the Republican who won, was raised in the Brethren in Christ denomination but hadn't belonged to a church while he was in the army. It also said he quoted the Bible in speeches and that some of his closest advisers were sincere Christians.

The article said Stevenson, the Democrat, was divorced and a member of the Unitarian Church. But in answer to how religion would influence him as president, he wrote something we would be surprised to read from a Democrat today: "I believe that Christian faith has been the most significant single element in our history and our tradition. From the beginning it has been the most powerful influence in our national life," adding that he tried to live by what the prophet Micah wrote: "to do justly, to love mercy, and to walk humbly with God."[2]

Billy Graham was among the first in modern times to use the term *evangelical*, which conservative Christians began using to refer to themselves to avoid being lumped in with liberal "social gospel" Christians on one side or "fighting" Fundamentalists on the other. He was also one of the first high-profile Christian leaders to be welcomed in his role as Christian leader to the White House. Beginning with Truman he visited every president at the White House through George W. Bush until he was too old and feeble to travel. Barack Obama and Donald Trump went to visit him in his North Carolina home.

"One of Us"—or Not

Jimmy Carter, a Southern Baptist Sunday school teacher before he was governor of Georgia, popularized the phrase *born-again*. He famously told a *Playboy* interviewer during the run-up to the 1976 election, "I've looked on a lot of women with lust. I've committed adultery in my heart many times."[3]

Then *Newsweek* named 1976 "The Year of the Evangelical,"[4] and the same year, a book titled *The Miracle of Jimmy Carter* by veteran journalists Howard Norton and Bob Slosser persuaded many conservative Christians to vote for Carter. I remembered thinking this Baptist Sunday school teacher was "one of us,"[5] and I supported him even though at the last minute I decided his policies were too liberal and voted for Ford.

While we knew Dwight Eisenhower was a Presbyterian (when in the White House), John F. Kennedy was Roman Catholic, Lyndon Baines Johnson was Disciples of Christ, and Richard Nixon was a Quaker, no one talked or speculated if they had been born-again. When Gerald Ford became president, he invited Billy Zeoli, a fellow Michigander, to be the White House chaplain. I knew Zeoli, and we had dinner in Grand Rapids a few years after Ford left office. He had a colorful personality and loved to tell stories about how he led Gerald Ford to the Lord at a prayer breakfast in Washington when Ford was still a US representative from Michigan.[6] That means Ford, not Carter, was actually the first *born-again* president.

When Carter became a disappointment as president and grew more and more liberal, Evangelicals were among the first to rally behind California governor Ronald Reagan, a Hollywood actor who "had a past." (Sound familiar?) And much like the current occupant of the White House, Reagan received a prophetic word in 1970 from the late George Otis that he would be president.[7] (I will discuss prophetic words about Donald Trump in chapter 11.)

Bob Slosser, at one time the assistant national editor for the *New York Times*, had been swept into the burgeoning Charismatic movement during that time, and he wrote years later about how the prophecy took place. Reagan was governor of California and under a lot of pressure in his reelection bid, yet he took time to meet at his home in Sacramento with a group of friends who had flown up from Southern California. The group included Pat Boone and his wife, Shirley; Harald Bredesen; and George Otis. Herb Ellingwood, a staffer who later worked in Reagan's White House, was also present.

Someone in the group asked if they could pray for the governor and his wife. The Reagans agreed, and the seven held hands in a circle. Slosser wrote that suddenly "the Holy Spirit came upon" Otis, who began prophesying specifically to Ronald Reagan as if God were speaking, referring to Reagan as "My son." The prophecy went on to tell Reagan that his "labor" was "pleasing."

Slosser describes what happened next: "The only sound was George's voice. Everyone's eyes were closed. 'If you walk uprightly before Me, you will reside at 1600 Pennsylvania Avenue.' The words ended.... Reagan took a deep breath and turned and looked into Otis's face. All he said was a very audible, 'Well!'"[8] However, years later, a few days after Reagan was elected president, he told Pat Boone he remembered that prophecy and had thought of it many times over the years.

Pat Boone and Ronald Reagan would also play a role in opening doors to the White House for a young motivational speaker, now historian and television pundit, named Doug Wead, who ended up being an instrumental liaison between Evangelicals and the White House.

Because I've been friends with Doug since I was a teenager, I asked him to recount this period of his life for this book. His experiences give us a front-row seat to the way several US presidents viewed Evangelicals. It's a perspective you won't hear in the media or find in any other books on the subject.

AN EVANGELICAL CONNECTION
TO THE WHITE HOUSE

In 1979, a few years after the US pulled out of Vietnam and it fell to the communists, there was a humanitarian crisis in Cambodia, next to Vietnam. Wead heard about it, flew to Cambodia, took lots of pictures, and saw how terrible it was. The day he returned to the US, he was invited to a dinner at the home of Ronald Reagan in Pacific Palisades, California.

"I was filled with stories about Cambodia, and that made an

impression on them," Wead said. "It was not because I was so colorful in my stories but because the day before, I'd been in Cambodia,
so I was just overflowing with astonishment at what I'd seen. So the
Reagans remembered that night because it was pretty dramatic."

That week was also historic. The night before, the famous Roger Mudd
CBS Reports interview with Ted Kennedy about Chappaquiddick had
aired. And the next Tuesday, Reagan flew to New York and announced
his candidacy for president.

Little did Doug Wead know that one thing would lead to another,
and a decade later he would play a major role in the White House,
opening doors for other Evangelicals. But the experience would also
allow him to see up close and personal that the Washington establishment (what we now call the deep state) did not want anything to
do with these goody-two-shoes conservative Christians—despite what
they might say publicly.

When Reagan ran for president, Wead was already known as an
author. As far back as 1972 he had written books on the Charismatic
movement. He wrote the biography of legendary Assemblies of God
missionary Mark Buntain called *The Compassionate Touch*. He also
wrote *The Great Multi-Million Dollar Miracle* about Trinity Bible
College (TBC), where his late father, Roy Wead, was president. I
remember that book because my late father, A. Edward Strang, was on
the faculty at TBC during that era.

I got to know Doug because his uncle Karl Strader was my pastor.
At the time, Doug was a rising evangelist in the Assemblies of God
only five years older than me, and I always looked up to him. As a
young man he preached at some of the biggest Charismatic churches
and was known to be a go-getter.

He was also known as a maverick within the Assemblies of God,
meaning he was gutsy and didn't seem to care who he offended if he
thought he was in the right. In that era he anonymously published a
short-lived magazine called *Restoration*, in which he ran articles about
what he thought the Assemblies of God denomination should do—
things they would never publish in their own publications. He hired a
young journalist to edit it as a freelancer in 1977—me. (I did the work
under a pseudonym because I had just started *Charisma* magazine,
and I was on staff at an Assemblies of God church in Orlando. I didn't
want to get in trouble if the Assemblies of God was to take issue with
anything in Doug's magazine.)

By 1974 Doug had begun speaking for corporations at motivational rallies. This work took him all over the world speaking or writing. When Doug got back from Cambodia, he knew he had to help those people, and it had to be done fast. "Who can raise money quickly?" he asked himself. He knew the answer: his buddies who had huge followings on television.

So he persuaded Pat Boone to host a dinner at his home in Southern California. Rex Humbard, Oral Roberts, and Jim Bakker flew in. Robert Schuller drove over from Garden Grove. Wead, who lived in Springfield, Missouri, at the time, invited the Roman Catholic bishop from Springfield, Bernard Law, to attend so the event would be ecumenical. (Later Law was named a cardinal in Boston and became infamous after a *Boston Globe* investigation revealed he had been covering up child sex abuse perpetrated by priests in his archdiocese. He resigned in disgrace.)

One of the guests gave a little speech that night about how the televangelists should do something to be altruistic to help the Cambodian people because the televangelists had a reputation of mainly using their broadcasts to raise money to stay on the air. Looking back, it seemed almost prophetic, considering the televangelist scandals that would happen a few years later.

Apparently Robert Schuller didn't like what he heard, because he told one of the attendees that Pat Boone was sure naive to sponsor such an event. He, Oral Roberts, Rex Humbard, and other televangelists were always gravely concerned with raising enough money to keep their ministries on the air and wouldn't likely ask people to give to other causes on their airtime. Almost immediately afterward Pat and Shirley Boone made appearances on CBN and PTL, appealing to their audiences, and were able to raise close to a million dollars, resulting in the formation of the foundation Save the Refugees, which later became Mercy Corps.

Bob Maddox from the Carter White House also had been invited that night, and that opened the door for a big fundraiser at the White House for Cambodia—the first of many. Wead packed the event with his corporate contacts and then invited evangelical leaders he knew— Jim Bakker, Pat Robertson, and others.

A year later, when Reagan was in the White House, he remembered Doug Wead and his Cambodian fundraiser, and he allowed Wead to hold several more of the events at the White House. One of them was attended by George and Barbara Bush.

Long before Paula White Cain or Trump's Faith Advisory Board or a state dinner hosted by the sitting president, here was a former Assemblies of God evangelist-turned-motivational speaker inviting evangelical leaders to fundraisers in the East Room at the White House, and it wasn't even considered an evangelical event! (I knew Doug back then and remember hearing about the fundraisers, but I never attended. However, Doug did open doors for me to meet with the Bushes later.)

In Washington, Wead quickly learned that most of the Washington Republican establishment didn't like Evangelicals and didn't trust them. This was especially true of the blue-blooded Bushes, who attended one of Doug's fundraisers at the White House when Reagan was president. They liked Doug but had no idea he was an Evangelical. That, Doug told me, was a blessing in disguise.

"Because we had our first dinner in the Carter White House, it was considered a bipartisan event and was not religious at all," he said. "And so the Bushes didn't know of my evangelical background till I was with them for several years. And then when they knew, they felt, 'Oh, here's somebody we know, somebody we can trust. Let's listen to what he has to say.'"

Wead's writing gifts also opened doors. First, he penned *Reagan: In Pursuit of the Presidency—1980* before Reagan's upset victory over Carter. Since then he has written books about the children of presidents and even the parents of presidents. (When Trump defeated Hillary Clinton, Doug wrote a book I enjoyed reading called *Game of Thorns*, which captured the behind-the-scenes intrigue of the 2016 election in both the Trump and the Clinton campaigns. I was surprised, however, that despite the huge role Evangelicals played in that election the book said very little about Evangelicals.)

In Washington it was not popular to be an Evangelical, and Wead knew it. So he got to know the Bushes and later worked his way into their White House by being secular, not religious. "I met the Bushes as a non-Evangelical, which was very important. I came into their orbit through Peter Teeley, who was the former press secretary for Jacob Javits, a liberal senator from New York who was Jewish, so they didn't associate me with Evangelicals," he told me, adding that there was such antipathy and bias toward evangelical Christians "that if I had come into their orbit as an evangelical Christian, I'd never gotten where I got."

It was good the Bushes trusted Doug, because he helped win over the *born-again* vote for George H. W. Bush in 1988, the year CBN founder Pat Robertson ran for president. Bush rewarded Doug with a role as special assistant to the president when he was inaugurated in 1989. It was a senior-level role that included being a liaison to veterans, law enforcement organizations, and celebrities, as well as various religious groups.

It wasn't the first time a Republican president had appointed a religious liaison. President Ronald Reagan appointed a delightful white-haired grandmother named Carolyn Sundseth, formerly with YWAM. I knew her and published her book, *Barefoot to the White House*, in which she shared her improbable political odyssey. But Sundseth was at a lower level. Wead was a "commissioned officer." Nevertheless, many in evangelical circles thought of him as the new Carolyn Sundseth, who was enormously popular among Evangelicals who knew her.

Wead became friends with the family, even befriending George W. Bush, who had recently become a born-again Christian himself. Doug said that during this time, Junior (George W. Bush) was also trying to beat alcoholism. In Alcoholics Anonymous they told him he needed to find new friends. So when he moved to Washington to help his dad's campaign, he was looking for new friends and trying to find God to help him kick his drinking addiction. That's how he and Doug became friends.

In 1986 the Christian Booksellers Association (CBA) convention was in Washington, DC, and Doug arranged for a large group of CBA industry leaders to meet with then vice president Bush at the official vice presidential residence, the Naval Observatory in Washington. It was an interesting and eclectic group. In addition to the Christian publishers, others such as Jerry Falwell Sr., Tammy Faye Bakker, and Jimmy Swaggart had flown in. Looking back, it was ironic these people were in the same room at that time, considering the televangelist scandals that would happen less than a year later.

At this gathering not only did Bush mingle and pose for pictures, but he talked a little about his vision for the nation and hinted that he would be running for president. The publishers in the room mostly passively listened to his spiel. The preachers pushed to find out whether he was born-again. Bush, what I call a High Church Episcopalian, believed in Christian principles as taught by his church. But he was uncomfortable describing himself as "born-again." Yet that's all this crowd wanted to hear. I always wondered why Wead hadn't coached him ahead of time on what to say to conservative Christians.

Then, in 1988, Bush discovered so many evangelical Christians were backing Pat Robertson that he won the Iowa Cavalcade and later came in second in the caucus—something Wead had been warning the Bush campaign could happen. Bush came in third. Even though Evangelicals, also known as the Moral Majority at the time, had coalesced around Ronald Reagan, the Bushes hadn't seriously considered Evangelicals a group worth wooing.

The Moral Majority, founded by Jerry Falwell Sr. in 1979, came together as a response to serious shifts in the country's cultural and political landscape at the time. The organization provided a way for various conservative groups to band together as a united political force against social and cultural changes that were undermining the country's moral foundations. After helping Ronald Reagan win the presidential election in 1980, the group officially disbanded in 1989. But it paved the way for what came to be known as the religious Right. Today's politically minded Evangelicals can credit our influence in Washington, in large part, to Falwell's trailblazing "pro-family and pro-American" coalition of conservative social values.

Upon realizing the Moral Majority's ability to successfully rally conservatives behind a presidential candidate, suddenly the Bush campaign wanted to know everything about this large, but largely unknown (to them), group that had proved so powerful for Robertson. Wead compiled more than one thousand pages of memoranda giving background on several hundred evangelical leaders. "I wrote them generically. But then vice president Bush would send these memos back to me with little notations on them such as, 'What about this?' 'What about that?' He really got into the minutiae of everything," Doug said.

Bush was apparently intrigued by the Charismatics. He found out one of his key supporters in Texas was a Spirit-filled, tongues-talking Christian. So one day he asked her if she would speak in tongues for him so he could hear what it was like. As Wead tells the story, "She said, 'Well, I can't, I can't just do that,' and he said, 'You can't?' She said, 'No, the Spirit has to move me.'"

After Bush didn't seem to know what to say at the event I attended in 1986, each time he'd meet with Evangelicals, he would do his homework and afterward would ask Wead, "Why did they ask this? What did I say? How did they hear it?" as if the different groups were speaking different languages. Bush may not have been perfect at it, but he was good enough that Evangelicals began to accept him as a born-again Christian.

About the same time, the vice president was being introspective, asking himself, "Why am I running for president?" Wead said this was important in his spiritual odyssey. "As you go through that whole process of running for president, you have to ask yourself why. Why are you doing this? You spend the whole year at it, really. It makes you really think about your purpose in life, and if you are a person of faith, it makes you think about God."

When Wead got to the Bush White House, he saw how little influence Evangelicals had in the capital. Out of the 749 federal judges at the time, only four claimed to be born-again Christians. "That's astounding. That's almost 40 percent of the population claims to be born-again. And there's only four federal judges, if you can believe that," Wead recalled.

Once Wead discussed this with Antonin Scalia, himself a devout Catholic, who told him that at some point there ought to be an Evangelical on the Supreme Court because of the sheer numbers of the group. At the time, there were three Jewish justices and six Catholics on the Supreme Court.

During the 1980s Oral Roberts and some other organizations were under scrutiny by the government and even claimed they were being harassed by the IRS. (This was long before the Obama administration was accused of doing the same thing to conservative Christians and Tea Party groups.)

"So I was able to use my position to say to the president, 'Look, we want evangelical support, but they say it goes two ways. Why is your government harassing them and trying to put them out of business and disqualifying them?'"

When Bush asked what he meant, Wead would give examples of the IRS pressuring ministries such as Oral Roberts' with endless audits and lots of questions.

These Washington biases were never discussed openly. No one questioned why Evangelicals—said to be about 40 percent of the US population at that time—were barely represented.

During this time there were unconventional groups such as "house churches" in Charismatic and evangelical circles that the IRS was refusing to recognize as churches. After all, they didn't have a building, and their services weren't necessarily on Sunday morning. When they met, it didn't resemble the liturgy of more established churches.

"So that's where all of these laws came into place that the church had to have sacraments, all these things that the IRS says a church has to have that the Bible doesn't say a church has to have. But the IRS does. It's all based on the fact that their understanding of Christianity was limited. And it was basically Catholic," Wead said.

Finally Wead found one person in the IRS who seemed reasonable to work with. It turns out he was one of seven regional directors of nonprofits, and he was the one all the major ministries said was the most reasonable. He was a Catholic but Charismatic. So Wead invited him to the White House and took him to the White House Mess, a private dining room for senior staff, directly under the Oval Office.

Wead asked him about bias in the IRS. When he denied bias, Wead said, "Then why are you the only one who understands the evangelical perspective? A lot of the ministries are complaining that the IRS is biased and trying to put them out of business." Wead asked him to help find others so he could report to the ministries that were complaining of being attacked. The man objected, saying there could be no religious test for office.

Wead countered, "'If there is no religious test for office, how come 40 percent of the country are born-again Christians, and none of them are in the top three hundred positions in the IRS? Tell me that's not unconstitutional.' He said, 'OK, I get your point.'"

After a couple of months the IRS official came back and told Wead he couldn't find any other Evangelicals or Charismatics. Today we think of the bureaucracy as being mostly liberal and maybe hostile to conservatives. But Wead says that sort of bias toward conservative Christians has been going on for years in the Washington Beltway, even though the millions of churchgoing Evangelicals came to be seen as a voting bloc.

Still today Wead knows national politicians who look at Trump and figure he picked up the evangelical vote because he was in the right place at the right time. Intellectually they may be conscious of the fact that Evangelicals are an important constituency. But no matter how often they see reports about the group's size, they don't fully comprehend it, or even believe the numbers, until they actually encounter

Evangelicals. "You can live and die in that Northeast Corridor without ever meeting one," Doug told me.

While Gerald Ford understood Evangelicals, he may have lost the election because he was willing to play down his own born-again experience. Ford let the Evangelicals vote for Carter and opted instead to pursue Catholic voters, who were a bit scandalized by Carter and his born-again testimony. As a result, Ford won Illinois with more Catholic votes but lost Missouri, Kentucky, and border states such as Tennessee because of the evangelical votes that went to Carter. That really got a lot of the political class' attention.

Wead is full of stories hearkening back to his beginning as a Pentecostal evangelist. And if there's a miracle aspect, so much the better. He likes to tell one about Ronald Reagan getting healed of ulcers. Reagan told him that his ulcers got so bad when he was governor of California that he reached the point where he went into the private bathroom in his governor's suite and was in such pain that he said, "God, You're going to have to kill me or heal me. I can't go on with this anymore." With that he dumped his medicine down the toilet and claimed he never had any pain from ulcers ever again.[9]

Reagan wrote about this experience in a letter to his dying father-in-law dated August 7, 1982. His account is a little different: Reagan said his ulcers got so bad during his first year as governor of California that he was in constant pain, ranging from discomfort to sharp attacks, and he kept an antacid in his desk at work, in his briefcase, and at home. He spent months like this. Then one morning he got up as usual and went into the bathroom, but as he reached for the antacid, he just knew he didn't need it. He later encountered several people who said they had been praying for him, and he attributed his healing to the power of prayer.

Reagan wrote that he put his medicine back on the shelf, not that he flushed it down the toilet, but either way, he was miraculously healed, and he wasn't afraid to tell others about it. And who's to say Reagan didn't leave out some of the more colorful details in his letter, which he wrote to encourage his father-in-law to follow Christ.

Wead is confident in his account. "I heard him with my own ears tell me that. And he didn't know that I was raised as a Pentecostal. There were several people standing around him when he told this story. But it's possible someone told him because we tried to plant things like that with Bushes. So I know it can happen." Wead paused before adding, "I believe in healing, but I'm not sure I'd have faith to flush my medicine down the toilet."

Despite Reagan's personal faith, his and subsequent Republican administrations kept Evangelicals at arm's length. Wead said there was so much bias in that era against Evangelicals he knew that if someone applied for a job in the administration and the person attended Gordon-Conwell Theological Seminary, they would drop the resume in the wastebasket. And the applicants from Biola or Wheaton or one of the Pentecostal colleges didn't even get that far.

This contempt went all the way to the top. George H. W. Bush pretended to listen to evangelical leaders but then did what he wanted. After Bush was elected president and was deciding whom to appoint to various positions, Doug Wead invited about twenty-five evangelical leaders to make suggestions on whom he should select. The group included Paul Crouch of Trinity Broadcasting Network (TBN), Beverly LaHaye of Concerned Women for America, and Dr. James Dobson, founder of Focus on the Family, who sat straight across from the president-elect.

When he was asked to speak, Dobson remembers saying: "Mr. President, 43 percent of your vote came from Evangelicals and people who identify as pro-life. Now we understand you are considering appointing Louis W. Sullivan to be Secretary of Health and Human Services. He is pro-abortion. Would you, Mr. President, throw it in the face of all these people who voted for you because they think you are pro-life?"

Bush leaned back in his chair, put his hands behind his head, smiled, and said, "Well, I can tell you that you're not going to have to worry about that." Then he changed the subject. Two weeks later he appointed Sullivan, who served all four years of Bush's term. (Fortunately, though Sullivan made pro-choice comments before his appointment and was endorsed by Planned Parenthood, he flip-flopped on the issue and supported Bush's pro-life policies while in office.)

I know the story is true because I was in the room. I was honored to be invited and sat quietly at the end of the table next to Jerry Falwell Sr., who also said very little that day. Others gave advice about various policy positions important to Evangelicals. Dobson is absolutely right. Bush ignored our advice and did what he wanted.

"I really loved him," Dobson said of Bush. "I wrote one of my newsletters about him. I believe he really did love the country. But I'm not sure that he was deeply committed to a conservative social position. His wife, Barbara, didn't like it, and who you are married to influences you," he said, adding that Laura Bush a decade later was much less conservative than her husband when he was president.

However, George W. Bush was more sophisticated in his knowledge of born-again Christianity than most of the other Washington politicians, primarily because (according to Doug) he had vetted all of Wead's memos for his father. However, Junior, as Wead calls him, didn't want anyone to know he relied on other people's research.

"Now, Trump is not that way about anything," Wead told me when I asked him to compare the two presidents. "He's just transparent. So it's pretty hard to see Trump as manipulative and sophisticated when he is not manipulative and sophisticated about anything, let alone his faith."

Paula White Cain, the president's longtime friend and spiritual adviser, shared a story that illustrates Wead's point. During Trump's early days in office some evangelical leaders were meeting with him to discuss Supreme Court appointments. Paula said somebody in the meeting threatened Trump and said, "Our organization will sue you if you lie to us and don't follow through on what kind of judges you put on the bench." The president is known for hitting back, but she said he just smiled very calmly and said, "You aren't going to have to sue me," meaning, "I'm going to give you the judges you want because I want them too."

Wead wasn't in that meeting, but the president's response doesn't surprise him. "Trump is real, and I think the Evangelicals know he's real," Wead said. "And this began before Paula with Norman Vincent Peale. Trump loved his sermons. He loved what today we call the prosperity gospel. Peale was a forerunner of that. The power of positive thinking was a cultural revolution in its time."

During the Bush era the anti-evangelical bias was so great that Wead devised ways to send signals that born-again voters would get but wouldn't let the press identify the Bushes as evangelical. He would give them phrases to work into speeches such as "wonder-working power" or other familiar song lyrics. His copious memos would tell them which NBA stars were Christian so they could be seen in public with them. Evangelicals knew the connection, but the press didn't. "So you get the advantages without the animus," Wead said.

THE END OF AN ERA

I knew Doug when he worked for George H. W. Bush, and I knew he was close to both father and son Bush. Years later, when I met and interviewed George W. Bush, Doug was nowhere around. I never knew why; then I found out about "the tapes." The *New York Times* reported in 2005 that Wead had recorded hours of phone conversations over a period of years that revealed what the younger Bush really thought about his political opponents, campaign strategy, and even a few of his youthful indiscretions.

Being a historian, Wead said he wanted to have his comments on the record for posterity. He says he knew Bush Junior would be a major figure, even before he became president. He said if he could have recorded Gandhi or Martin Luther King Jr. or Churchill, he would have. He told the *Times* he only recorded in states where it is legal to record without the other party's consent. And he never made money on the tapes. In fact they were revealed when he was proving a fact in one of his books to a *Times* reporter—a fact that was not footnoted but proved Wead's point.

After Wead let a reporter listen to several of the tapes (which the *Times* speculated was to promote one of his new books), the *Times* made the tapes' existence a huge story because they offered an unvarnished look at the sitting president in unguarded conversations with a friend:

> Variously earnest, confident or prickly in those conversations, Mr. Bush weighs the political risks and benefits of his religious faith, discusses campaign strategy and comments on rivals. John McCain "will wear thin," he predicted. John Ashcroft, he confided, would be a "very good Supreme Court pick" or a "fabulous" vice president. And in exchanges about his handling of questions from the news media about his past, Mr. Bush appears to have acknowledged trying marijuana.[10]

The tapes also revealed what Bush Junior said about certain Evangelicals, especially Dr. James Dobson, who later condemned Wead for making the recordings. "I know Doug Wead," Dobson said. "I am shocked by his breach of trust and his relationship with then governor Bush, who had welcomed him into his confidence."[11]

It was big news for a few days; then the controversy died down. Bush had already been reelected, so it didn't hurt him politically. And while the tapes were a little titillating, what they revealed, in my opinion and those of others, wasn't that bad.

But Americans United for Separation of Church and State, which misses no opportunity to bash Evangelicals, seemed to enjoy reporting that Bush appeared to waffle at one time on his opposition to abortion. The group highlighted a conversation from September 1998 when Bush told Wead about an upcoming meeting with Dr. James Dobson:

> "He said he would like to meet me, you know, he had heard some nice things, you know, well, 'I don't know if he is a true believer' kind of attitude," Bush said.
>
> Bush said he planned to assure Dobson of his opposition to abortion and dispel rumors that he did not consider the issue important.
>
> "I just don't believe I said that. Why would I say that?" Bush asked Wead.[12]

The *Times* also reported that Bush apparently decided against Gen. Colin Powell and former Pennsylvania governor Tom Ridge as candidates for vice president in 2000 because they were pro-choice and Bush feared selecting either of them would upset Dobson and alienate conservative Christians. "'They are not going to like it anyway, boy,' Mr. Bush said. 'Dobson made it clear.'"

Wead told me he felt bad for any offense to Christian leaders—most of whom he had spent his early years promoting to presidents—and offered the tapes to Bush. Since then he has continued to write about history and appears weekly on Fox Business Network.

Twice he joined presidential political campaigns, serving as a senior adviser to Ron Paul in 2012 and later to his son, Sen. Rand Paul, in 2016. I ran into Doug in the spin room watching Sean Hannity interview various candidates after one of the political debates held in Orlando. Doug did his best to convince me Ron Paul was the guy to support. I wasn't convinced.

It was the last time I saw my old friend. Little did I know when we met in the late sixties where life would take us and that for a period of time Doug would be the evangelical doorkeeper to power in Washington.

Before he retreated from public life, Ronald Reagan gave one last speech at Wead's charity dinner, where he said about his old friend,

"Doug Wead, your excellent service in government, at the White House, and in the private sector leading the effort for famine relief in Africa and Asia is a reminder that wherever we work, we can work to serve others."[13]

Like my friend Doug Wead, Donald Trump isn't perfect and is sometimes misunderstood and maligned in the press. But evangelical Christians know that God can use people despite their imperfections, a topic we will explore in the next chapter.

PART II

UNDERSTANDING

DONALD TRUMP

CHAPTER 6

GOD USES IMPERFECT LEADERS

*The best of men are only men at their very best. Patriarchs,
prophets, and apostles—martyrs, church fathers, reformers,
puritans—all, all are sinners, who need a Savior. They may be
holy, useful, honorable in their place—but sinners after all.[1]*
—J. C. RYLE (1816–1900)
ENGLISH WRITER AND EVANGELICAL PASTOR

DENNIS PRAGER, A popular talk show host, can't understand why conservative Jews and evangelical Christians are criticized as hypocritical for supporting a man as imperfect as Donald Trump. So Dennis made this one of the "Ultimate Issues Hour" discussions on his radio show and invited me as his guest. He talked about how he, a committed Jew, has defended Evangelicals many times, saying the ones who claim Trump supporters are giving religion a "black eye" are "staggeringly immature."[2]

The reason, according to Prager, is virtually anyone, including those on the Left, will support a sinful person if that individual supports the policies they like. Prager offered a hypothetical example: if a Democrat who is known to be dishonest supports abortion rights, the Left would vote for that person if the opponent was pro-life even if that person was a highly moral person.

"Theirs is a phony argument. The Left lies with the ease that you breathe. We're voting for a president, not a pastor. People sin, my friend," Prager said to his listeners. "Grow up."

This echoed the way Jerry Falwell Jr., the president of Liberty University, put it: "We are not electing a pastor in chief; we're electing a commander in chief."[3] Like Prager, he made that comment to explain how he could support a man who is well known as far from perfect.

I didn't vote for someone who promised to live a Christian lifestyle; I voted for someone who promised to defend *my* right to live that way. Why, then, when we support Trump do we feel the need to give a disclaimer that we don't necessarily agree with all his tweets but we admire his policies and what he has accomplished? Maybe because we don't see the bigger principles at work.

Ralph Reed, a respected political activist who was the first executive director of the Christian Coalition in the 1990s, was in Jerusalem when the US Embassy was moved there from Tel Aviv in 2018. While attending the events celebrating the opening of the embassy, he heard Danny Ayalon, former Israeli ambassador to the US, make the point that Jews believe only flawed men make great leaders. The rabbis teach in fact that you should never put someone in leadership who doesn't have a flaw in life.

"If someone is self-righteous and convinced of their own goodness, they won't feel the need to redeem their past by bearing good fruit and doing great deeds. But if they have experienced real failure or a major setback in their lives, they are more likely to approach leadership or service redemptively," Reed told me.

He said this explains why Trump is such a great leader who is so committed to keeping his promises. Despite his past mistakes and failures—or perhaps because of them—he wants to do the right thing. Whatever one thinks of him, it is undeniable that when it comes to defending life, defending the rights of Christians, and defending Israel, he is seeking to act in a way that is right and advances good.

I was so intrigued I contacted Ayalon in Israel to learn more. He explained that throughout the millennia the sages have written in the Mishnah and Gemara that the public should select a leader over them "who is blemished." And why is that?

"I think for two main reasons," Ayalon said. "One is that he will be humble and will understand he's flawed and will not think that he's 'god' like the emperors of China or Japan or the French kings such as Louis XIV, who considered himself the center of the universe, and others in recent history. And the second reason is that he can be more accountable to the public."

Every Christian knows from Sunday school that God has always used flawed leaders. You can look at most of the characters of the Old Testament, from Abraham to Moses to the many kings of Israel, and see they were not perfect, but God used them anyway. The apostle Peter is a powerful New Testament example of this as well. We see him try and fail to walk on water, hastily cut off a soldier's ear in the Garden of Gethsemane, and deny knowing Jesus three times on the night He needed him the most—all before he became a miracle-working preacher of the gospel, an author of Scripture, and a pillar of the early church.

There are many examples of this throughout American history as well. You need look no further than Abraham Lincoln, whose long list of "failures" includes losing his job; going bankrupt in business; having a nervous breakdown; being defeated in many political pursuits, including two unsuccessful runs for the US Senate; and failing to receive the nomination for vice president. President Harry Truman is another example, going bankrupt as a haberdasher before he ran for local office in Jackson County, Missouri.

A GREAT LEADER

It's ironic and hypocritical that many on the Left are so desperate to criticize Trump even though he is doing a great job of making America great again. Suddenly they criticize his lifestyle, although before he ran for president as a Republican, they saw nothing wrong with his past and he seemed to be the darling of the liberal media. Has he done and said things that don't reflect the teachings of the Bible? Yes. He's imperfect, but according to the rabbis, that makes him a great leader.

Ayalon recognizes the criticism of Trump for what it is—politically motivated and coming mostly from those who are Left socially and the extreme Left politically.

"I'm not a judge," Ayalon said of Trump. "But I'm saying that a leader, just like in the old biblical times, should be judged by the benefit [he or she] gives the people in terms of supplying security and well-being or welfare and economic benefits. In my opinion Trump is doing an amazing job—starting with putting the United States first as the world leader militarily, technologically, economically, culturally, you name it. That's because it's not just a matter of having the capabilities to be great but actually being great."

Ayalon's insight as a Jew helps Christians remember that God has always used flawed leaders. We must avoid the trap of trying to defend the tired, old accusations against Trump's bad behavior and instead think biblically.

"If I look at Hebrews 11 and all the faith heroes God listed, I could run a successful political campaign that would disqualify each from public service in America," historian David Barton told me. "For example, I could show you that despite God's own choice, David should not be your national leader. After all, he can't control his kids—his son Absalom tried to kill his father and did kill his brother. His son Amnon raped his sister, and [David] never said no to his son Adonijah. He's a terrible father! And he's so arrogant that he ignored God and numbered the troops. He also committed adultery with Bathsheba and murdered her husband, Uriah. We should never choose him to be a national leader! But God did choose him, and he was one of the greatest leaders in Israel's history."

In the same way, Christians overlook the good Trump has done and focus on all the mistakes he's made and all the perceived weaknesses he still struggles with.

"As Christians we have created artificial standards for our leaders that God doesn't have for His leaders in the Bible," Barton said. "I have flaws, Trump has flaws, and we can point them out in a self-righteous manner. Or we can look at Hebrews 11 and see all these great leaders had serious flaws but God definitely still used them."

Barton says conservative Christians should "look at what the president has done for the economy, but especially standing for religious liberty, appointing righteous judges, protecting unborn life, and supporting Israel—so many of the things the Bible specifically talks about. No president in our lifetime has gotten done as many biblically correct things as he has."

Because of this Barton says Christians must be willing to support Trump and not allow the Left to undermine his conservative agenda any longer. He points out that we don't have to win every American to our way of thinking—we just need to win more than we have now.

Author Lance Wallnau has made the same point. "Figures like Churchill, Lincoln, and George S. Patton don't step out of cathedrals onto the stage of history, yet we canonize them later as instruments God raised up to meet a singular crisis, he said.[4] None of these men were conventional Christians, and they had many detractors in the clergy, yet each played a pivotal role in history. They stood strong against the enemies of freedom and helped safeguard our way of life and Christian heritage.

History has shown that Winston Churchill was the right man at the right time to be used by God, yet he was also not a very popular person. In fact Churchill was described with terms that are often used in association with Donald Trump. He was called an "'aristocratic adventurer' who lacked good judgment and political skills." He was considered "rootless...unstable...unsound...an undeniable cad." He was "an embarrassment" to important people in the Conservative Party. And he was viewed as impetuous—"'a real danger' who...tended not to count the cost of his endeavors."[5]

The British didn't like him until they needed someone very strong to defeat the Nazis. He didn't have many fans within the Christian community, either. The conservative Christians of the day in Britain didn't like the fact he smoked cigars and loved drinking brandy. Churchill was a deeply flawed man, but God still raised him up to save Western civilization.

Winston Churchill seemed to know this, according to one of his biographers, his own great-grandson the late Jonathan Sandys. In *God and Churchill: How the Great Leader's Sense of Divine Destiny Changed His Troubled World and Offers Hope for Ours*, Sandys makes the case that his famous great-grandfather felt a call from God his entire life that he was to save Western civilization. A case can be made, of course, that he did just that when he stopped Hitler from taking over Great Britain. In the face of Hitler's military might, Churchill had to resolve to move ahead anyhow and to never quit. Churchill was a strong leader, and his example shows that God uses whomever He wants.

John Graves of Vision America makes the same point: "Thank God for a leader like Churchill. He was not the most polished or polite of leaders but was used to save many lives in a time of war. We are at war now for the soul of our nation."

That's what I see in Donald Trump and why people support him despite all the criticisms thrown at him. In that respect Trump resembles the indefatigable British prime minister, who often went against convention, decorum, and his own party to badger the people of Great Britain into defending their country against Hitler's Third Reich. Churchill was viciously attacked by the media in his day.

Today Donald Trump invites the same kinds of bitterness and resentment by raising alarms about the unraveling of American society at a time when our political elites, buttressed by the media, are denying that anything is wrong. Like Churchill, Trump is the target of opposition forces seeking to silence him for his bluntness and to stop him from speaking from the heart about problems the political establishment has been sweeping under the carpet for generations.

True leaders such as Churchill show strength of character in the face of adversity. Granted, Britain was in a life-and-death struggle with Nazi Germany, which threatened to destroy all of civilization. Forgive me if you consider this hyperbolic, but the situation today in America is almost as serious, considering the world we might have entered had Hillary Clinton won the election instead of Trump. It's a world where we could have lost our constitutional protections to our religious freedoms. In this case our struggle wasn't with guns, tanks, and planes—it was a political battle over the presidency and the direction of our nation now and for generations.

THE CHANGE AGENT AMERICA NEEDS

I believe we are blessed to have a leader like Donald Trump, who has such a strong sense of purpose at this critical moment in history. He takes orders from no one but seeks input from all, even his enemies. Money can't buy him; he has plenty of that. Politics eludes him, and he seldom follows the party line. His signature is not for sale. He has promised not to put special interests before national interests, vowing to the American people in his 2020 candidacy announcement speech: "My only special interest is *you!*"[6]

Trump is like Gen. George Patton in many ways, in that he believes in his destiny and his duty and he wants to do the most direct and sensible thing. Patton was one of the best American generals, yet he had a foul mouth and a serious problem with anger. In that very dark hour of World War II he won a significant battle that reveals the mercy of God.

In December 1944, in the days leading up to the Battle of the Bulge, Germany's last offensive campaign of World War II, the weather was horrible. There was a terrible fog, to the point that the soldiers couldn't move much, and air support was impossible. So Patton ordered Third Army chaplain Colonel James H. O'Neill to write a prayer for good weather. Then he ordered the prayer to be distributed to all the soldiers in the Third Army. He also ordered a training letter on the importance of prayer be distributed to almost three thousand organizational commanders and just under five hundred chaplains.

Patton and his men called out to God. The soldiers prayed God would lift the fog, and He answered them. A few days into the Battle of the Bulge "the enshrouding rain and fog—typical for the season and counted upon by the Germans as a continuing shield from Allied air power—suddenly began to break. The Germans were dismayed;

American forecasters were taken by surprise. 'Flying weather' brought swarms of Allied planes. Hundreds of enemy tanks were destroyed in their tracks, while a systematic bombardment of German troops in the forward positions was begun."[7]

This true story—which was a major turning point in WWII—gives me a lot of respect for Patton, who may not have been religious but believed in the power of prayer. "I am a strong believer in Prayer," Patton once said. "There are three ways that men get what they want; by planning, by working, and by praying. Any great military operation takes careful planning, or thinking. Then you must have well-trained troops to carry it out: that's working. But between the plan and the operation there is always an unknown. That unknown spells defeat or victory, success or failure. It is the reaction of the actors to the ordeal when it actually comes. Some people call that getting the breaks; I call it God. God has His part, or margin in everything. That's where prayer comes in."[8]

Patton may not be remembered as a religious man, but he was described by Chaplain O'Neill, who penned that famous prayer, as having "genuine trust in God, intense love of country, and high faith in the American soldier." Similar words might be used to characterize President Trump. In fact political pundit Marc A. Thiessen said Donald Trump "is not the most religious president we have ever had, but he may be the most pro-religion president."[9]

I think Thiessen is exactly right. But Trump's victories for religious freedom are not the story the leftist media wants to tell. While "fake news" outlets love to highlight Trump's flaws and past moral failures, Trump is fulfilling his promise to protect Americans' religious liberty, to the point of imposing sanctions on Turkey over wrongfully imprisoned pastor Andrew Brunson. Thanks to Trump's persistence, Turkey did free Brunson, who is finally home safe with his family.

Veteran broadcaster Arthelene Rippy of Christian Television Network in Clearwater, Florida, remembers both Franklin Delano Roosevelt and Harry S. Truman. "If you look at all the presidents since then, they all had their strengths and weaknesses," she said. "But no one compares to the strengths of this president [Trump]. As our culture grows darker, he's the change agent we need."

I agree with her. We've had some great presidents and some bad presidents, but at a very critical time in history I believe God raised up this outsider to shake the United States out of its comfortable slide toward globalism.

David Barton feels the same way about Trump. He admits Trump was not his first choice during the Republican primaries in 2016 but quickly adds, "I will say, hands down, I don't think a single one of the Evangelicals, whether Huckabee, Carson, Rubio, or Cruz (and they're all my friends), could have gotten done what Trump has."

Not only that, Barton thinks none of them would have tried all the things Trump has. As Christians doing Christian things, they would have gotten their brains beat in. But Trump has been getting things done that are important to Christians, yet "nobody's going to accuse him of trying to create a theocracy, which they would with the others," Barton said. He sees this as a positive because it makes Trump uniquely bulletproof from such accusations in these areas.

"Not only that, Trump is stubborn and tough enough that he doesn't care what people say. Nobody's been willing to fight as hard for these values and these principles, and he's been so good at principles—as good as Reagan was. I think Trump has stood firmer for principles, and in a more hostile climate than any other leader we've had in our lifetime."

The Bible teaches God is sovereign and uses whom He wants, with or without the approval of the most pious or legalistic among us. Yet some people, even if they barely know anything about theology, will criticize Trump. I mentioned this to Prager when I told him how a CNN anchor asked me if Trump was supposed to ask for forgiveness, referring to the "gotcha question" at the Iowa Family Leadership Summit when he said he'd never asked for forgiveness. Of course Trump isn't theologically sophisticated and didn't know how he was supposed to answer. And his comment has been just one more thing his opponents use to criticize him. Paula White Cain counters this criticism of Trump by saying that in her role as a close family friend and spiritual adviser she has witnessed firsthand where "he has said he was sorry for a situation or asked forgiveness for a situation, and he acknowledges where there needs to be repentance or forgiveness or action."

It's like a prominent preacher friend of mine said in a sermon once: "All of us and sin, and all of us have done things that we regret, and some people just have gotten caught."

I've been taught there is a progressive work of grace called sanctification. Committed Christians believe in the ongoing work of the Holy

Spirit in all of our lives. So I believe it is pretty hypocritical for anyone to cast a stone at Trump because of his past.

Paula also notes that during the time she has known Donald Trump, she has seen "a progressive change in his life. I have seen the work of the Holy Spirit." She adds that she knows the Lord has to work on her to have more patience or not lose her temper, and she sees that in Trump. "This is a man who absolutely does have a walk with God and who definitely has values and convictions and lives by those," she said.

It's the same thing I told Prager on his show: there are imperfections in all of us. I said every person who has accepted Christ knows what it is to be forgiven, including me. I'm glad my worst moments in life aren't published on the front pages of the nation's newspapers, and I think most Christians have done at least a few things they wouldn't want publicized. I liked the way George W. Bush put it when asked about his youthful indiscretions: "When I was young and irresponsible, I was young and irresponsible."[10]

Ralph Reed told me that Trump doesn't always know the right evangelical terms to use, and he doesn't usually speak in Bible verses. But he does the right thing when it comes to supporting priorities in the Christian community. "Trump has done everything he could to defend Christians, contrasted to Jimmy Carter, who was a Sunday school teacher most of his life and who did nothing to help Christians," Reed said.

SOMETHING WINSOME

While there may be a lot to criticize about the president (isn't that true of all politicians?) and while some don't like the brusque personality of this billionaire from Queens, there is also something winsome about Donald Trump. You can see it in his huge rallies, where he is funny and relates to the crowd by espousing the issues important to them. When I interviewed him in 2016, I found him to be respectful and even a bit humble—not at all like his public persona. In promoting my books about Trump, I've had to defend him in my interviews, and I make this point from my own experience.

Jerry Falwell Jr. was one of the first evangelical leaders to support Donald Trump for president—and he received flak for it from both liberals and conservatives. But he has had an opportunity to see up close what is really going on in the Trump White House.

"I'm proud I supported Donald Trump," he said. "And since he's entered the White House, I've stayed in close touch with him, talking to him about once a month. It has become a close friendship. I'm so pleased with how he's kept his promises. He's appointed justices to the lower courts and the Supreme Court who I believe will uphold the Constitution. On matters related to religious liberty, the president has been a godsend. And his deregulation strategies have brought about prosperity for businesses and the American worker. He's done all the things he said he was going to do—even with all the attempts to thwart his administration by fake Republicans in the Senate and all the folks on the left who will stop at nothing to overthrow a duly elected president."

In addition, Falwell sees Trump as "somebody with resolve and backbone," unlike the typical politician, who puts their finger up to see which way the wind is blowing and are so scared of their shadow and criticism from the press they waffle on every issue.

"Trump just marches ahead. He doesn't care how much criticism comes his way. And the people don't care either. The people don't care what the press say anymore because they've lost all credibility. That's what Americans have longed to see in their president—somebody who will stand up for the country, stand up for what's right and not back down in the face of adversity."[11]

How to Tell Your Friends to Vote for Trump

If you're a Christian, you know what it is to have faults and be forgiven. You may even see God's hand on Donald Trump. But what about the vast majority of Americans who do not share your worldview—who listen to those in the media and culture who don't like his tweets, are turned off by his bravado when dealing with foreign powers, and dislike some of his policies?

Chances are you work with these people or live next door to them. You may even have extended family members who dislike Trump so much it makes family gatherings difficult. How do you persuade them to reelect the president?

In 2016 many questions existed about Trump. Many conservatives didn't know if he was really a conservative or how he would govern. Now we see his many accomplishments and that he delivers on what he promised. But leading up to the 2016 election, although many conservative Christians didn't like the policies (and corruption) of Hillary Clinton, they just couldn't bring themselves to vote for

Trump. A woman who felt this way reached out to Pastor Jim Garlow on Facebook and asked him what to do.

For many years Jim was pastor of Skyline Church near San Diego, California. He was one of the main pastors who helped pass California's Proposition 8 in 2008, which amended the state constitution to say that marriage should henceforth be defined as the lawful union of one man and one woman. More recently Garlow cofounded the Jefferson Gathering, a weekly worship service for members of Congress in the US Capitol in Washington, DC.

After thinking it over, he fired off a fourteen hundred–word reply explaining his perspectives on the election. That message was picked up and shared almost twelve thousand times on Facebook in a matter of days.[12] Realizing he had struck a chord, Garlow, whom I've known for more than twenty-five years, contacted me and asked if I might be interested in seeing what he had written.

His rationale was so good and so succinct that I asked him if he'd allow us to publish the article on our organization's website, and he agreed. We posted it as an op-ed on August 11, 2016, two weeks after the Democratic National Convention in Philadelphia.

The article began by saying that "the Democrat and Republican party platforms are as different as night and day." In his opinion they were "as far apart as evil vs. good....I don't care for the 'right vs. left' nomenclature. I am far more concerned with 'right vs. wrong.'"

Then he used an analogy only a pastor could bring to a political discussion, saying, "As a pastor, I would rather deal with a church attendee who is blatant and brash in his sinning than one who is devious, lying, cunning, and deceptive. Both are problematic, but one is easier to deal with than the other. If I were a pastor bringing correction to a parishioner, I would prefer dealing with a 'Trump type' any day over a 'Hillary type.' The chances of making progress with the 'Trump type' are many times greater."[13]

The article made sense to people. It contained concrete reasons to vote for Trump even if there were things you didn't like about him. It was shared again and again, becoming by far the biggest article in the history of Charisma News. By Election Day it had been shared more than four million times!

So what do we do now? Many of the issues are the same regardless of who the Democrats nominate for the 2020 race. At the same time, Donald Trump needs to continue his policies and the upward trajectory this nation is taking. It's not just "make America great again." Now it's "keep America great." Here are talking points based on Garlow's article that you can use with family and friends who need to be sold on supporting Donald Trump in 2020:

- "Not voting is not a viable option, contrary to what the 'purists' claim." A lot of disagreement exists, he acknowledged, but refusing to vote for either candidate merely increases the Democrats' chances of winning the presidency. So pretending to be more honorable or more righteous is not wise. It is not noble. It is wrong.

- Garlow pointed out that America has been blessed with three great freedoms: political, economic, and religious. Few countries in the world have ever had that honor. Donald Trump appears angry and aggressive in his public statements because he perceives that all three of those freedoms are at risk, and he has promised that his administration will continue to defend this great heritage.

- Even if the privilege of appointing additional conservative Supreme Court justices were the only reason to vote for Trump, that ought to be enough. Trump's marriages, his casinos, and his rants on Twitter don't come close to justifying the decision to sit out the 2020 election. "Every rational person knows the Supreme Court appointments are paramount," Garlow said.

  Ohio Pastor Frank Amedia, who stumped for Trump during the 2016 campaign and prophesied that he would become president, agrees with Garlow's point but adds a warning that "there's a false sense of conservativism in the Supreme Court right now. Unfortunately most of the justices are still voting liberal, so we need one or two more true conservatives."

- On the positive side, Garlow said, is the fact that Trump continues to surround himself with good people, including Christian Vice President Mike Pence. As a billionaire builder and businessman, Trump knows how to pick great managers, and he knows how to delegate. Garlow expressed his belief that Trump's choices for cabinet positions will continue to be men and women of principle, many of whom will

be Christians and all of whom will be fair-minded conservatives. Do these good people impact him? There's a very good
chance they do.

- If you stop to consider Trump's beliefs on each of the major
  issues he addressed throughout his first campaign and presidency, it would be very hard to find fault with any of them.
  Garlow suggests Trump gets it right on at least 75 percent
  of the issues. Compare that to the Democratic front-runners,
  who most conservative Christians would agree are wrong on
  100 percent of the issues.

- There is one more issue that many people fail to consider
  closely enough, and, according to Garlow, it could be the
  biggest issue of all: the Left's relentless push for globalism—
  which is more than a geographical issue. It's not simply about
  eliminating borders. It is a spiritual issue that is demonic at
  its core. It means the dismantling of American sovereignty,
  opening our borders to the world, and abandoning our great
  heritage of freedom and independence based on the Christian
  worldview of the Founding Fathers. Globalism would transform this country into something we no longer recognize,
  and the Democrats thrive on that possibility.

  Garlow suggested that Trump's outspoken resistance to
  the globalist agenda may be the main reason the Left hates
  him. "Think 'principalities and powers,'" he warned. This is
  "extremely serious."

  Amedia, who also sees things through a spiritual lens,
  shares Garlow's concern. He believes globalization is "the
  breeding ground for the Antichrist spirit." Here's how he
  explained this perspective to me:

  "[We're seeing] opposition to the globalization that was
  gaining fervor and finding its path in the previous administration," Amedia said. "Why? Because I think we're
  beginning to see the budding of Babylon. The spirit of
  Babylon, the economic system of Babylon is beginning
  to spring up. That means this is the true system of the
  Antichrist. So our eyes should be looking very, very clearly
  at what's happening right now."

  Under Trump, Amedia believes globalization has been
  halted to the point that it's being dismantled. "We see that

in the [European Union]—any members of the EU that tried to oppose Trump have found themselves in chaos," Amedia said. But Amedia doesn't think Trump is conscious of the spiritual implications of globalism. Instead he sees Trump as merely a vessel God is using to accomplish His purposes.

- Donald Trump has demonstrated support of the Christian pro-life position, while the Democrats continue to push an agenda where there are no limits to a woman's right to kill her unborn child—which now extends all the way up to the minutes before she gives birth. Planned Parenthood traffics in body parts from the babies its clinics have killed,[14] which is as evil as anything the Nazis ever conceived.

- Amedia agrees with Garlow as to the importance of the issue of abortion. He sees improvement, pointing out that nineteen states have laws that could be used to restrict the legal status of abortion. Of these, eight states will automatically ban abortion if *Roe v. Wade* is overturned. Nine states have retained their abortion bans that preceded the legalization of abortion. In reality only thirteen states have laws that protect access to abortion.[15]

   "As believers, protecting the life of the unborn is dear to us; it's dear to removing curses from this nation. And I don't think anybody can argue that it's not dear to the heart of God. That has to be kept in the forefront," he said, adding that God is using Trump to accomplish some incredible things to protect the unborn.

   I agree. In fact that's part of the reason I moved away from the Democratic Party. I couldn't in good conscience vote for people who support ungodly causes such as abortion.

- Donald Trump is building a strong military to defend this nation, which is the main purpose of government. He has not hesitated to call Islamic terrorism what it really is. He has pulled the US out of Obama's terrible Iran nuclear deal and not backed down to the saber-rattling tactics of Iran in response.

- Trump understands that America stands at "11:59 p.m. on the 'cultural clock,'" as Garlow put it.

We are racing toward the end, morally, economically, militarily, and spiritually. America has begun to regain its position as the world's leading superpower, but a Democratic inauguration in 2021 will roll back all those gains and hasten our final destruction. Trump has begun to slow down the nation's descent, and with God's help I believe he can reverse it. But we have to give him the chance to finish what he's started.

In 2016 many Christians wanted to vote for Trump, but they had to be given permission because they felt he had failed most of our usual litmus tests. Garlow gave them the permission they needed in 2016. Four years later many no longer question voting for him because they can clearly see his track record. In the next chapter I hope to convince any who are still unsure. All they must do is look at his accomplishments and how he keeps his promises.

CHAPTER 7

PROMISES MADE, PROMISES KEPT

A promise must never be broken.[1]
—ALEXANDER HAMILTON (1755–1804)
FOUNDING FATHER AND AMERICAN STATESMAN
IN A LETTER TO HIS SON, 1791

PRESIDENT TRUMP CHOSE to announce his bid for reelection at the Amway Arena in my hometown of Orlando on June 18, 2019. I've been to many events at the arena, and none were more enthusiastic—not even when the Orlando Magic pulled off an improbable win! More than one hundred thousand people had applied for the twenty thousand seats. People began lining up forty hours ahead of time, and six hours before Trump spoke, people joining the growing line were told it was more than a mile long.

Street vendors and political volunteers worked the crowd for several city blocks as thousands passed the time in the oppressive Florida heat and humidity. Not even a strong afternoon storm could dampen the atmosphere of anticipation. News crews from around the world were there to capture the mood as the massive crowd of hopefuls waited for hours to get inside. One Trump supporter told a reporter why he felt braving such conditions for hours was worth it: "We're excited to see the president, but we also hope the Democrats see how many of us are here and get a clue that they are doing everything wrong!"

If you watched it on TV, you know the audience in the filled-to-capacity arena was beyond enthusiastic long before the president came out to deliver a seventy-six-minute trademark speech, telling all the things he's accomplished in his first term. I captured the spirit of some of his remarks in the opening paragraphs of the introduction to this book. As far as the crowd that night was concerned, our country needs four more years of Trump keeping his promises to the American people.

I was there in person to see the arrival of celebrities including Mike Lindell, CEO of MyPillow; and Lou Holtz, a legendary football coach, as well as several well-known political figures such as Florida senators Marco Rubio and Rick Scott and Florida governor Ron DeSantis. But what surprised me the most were the many Christian leaders who made the effort to fly in and support Trump. I saw Jentezen Franklin, Jerry Falwell Jr., Pastor Robert Jeffress, Bishop Harry Jackson, Dr. Alveda King, Pastor Tom Mullins, Pastor Darrell Scott, and more. I talked with these Christian leaders as we waited for the rally to begin, and the consensus seemed to be that they thought Trump would win.

A columnist in the left-leaning *Guardian* who covered the event agreed that Trump is "cruising toward reelection," adding, "Trump may be historically unpopular, but he is popular enough to be (comfortably) reelected. His supporters have agency and urgency, the two things the Democrats are still lacking. They have [only] 500 days left to create this, together, rather than apart."[2]

No matter what else you can criticize the president for, he keeps his word. At his huge rallies he likes to say, "Promises made, promises kept." (When I interviewed her for this book, Paula White Cain said she used that expression in an interview, and then others picked up the phrase. Now it has become one of his administration's slogans.)

The list of what he has accomplished is stunning, even if it's ignored by the mainstream media. He hit the ground running in January 2017. Early into his term he began achieving results domestically and internationally for the American people. Since taking office, he has strengthened American leadership, security, prosperity, and accountability.

While critics are quick to blast Trump's perceived mistakes and flaws, the president has one character trait that many other politicians lack: he keeps his promises. Just look at our now-booming economy, muscular diplomacy, and new embassy in Jerusalem. Even his support of religious liberty is in response to a promise he made to a roomful of pastors during his campaign.

I believe President Trump has made a huge difference in his first term. But despite all the progress there are other issues he must focus on. One is the nation's overwhelming debt, which Trump has not been able to bring down yet. Part of the reason for that is the tremendous deficit he inherited from past presidents, while the other part is that he simply hasn't focused on it thus far.

This is also a concern to Gordon Robertson, and we talked about it when he interviewed me on CBN's *700 Club Interactive*. I agree with Robertson, who hopes that in the next term Trump will make it a point to deal with our nation's crippling debt. I believe he can do it; after all, he thinks like a businessman, not a politician.

During that interview I made the point to Robertson that the president is making such an impact that he is a disrupter of our government's deep state.[3] And as a disrupter it makes sense that his personality can often be abrasive. Overall he has moved our nation in the right direction, and I look forward to seeing what his next move will be.

Meanwhile the American economy is stronger, American workers are experiencing more opportunities, confidence is soaring, and business is booming. President Trump has reasserted American leadership on the world stage, secured vital investments in our military, and stood up against threats to our national security, all while putting the American people first and making government more accountable.

Jerry Falwell Jr. says President Trump has exceeded the expectations of his supporters. Yet the Left, instead of acknowledging the genuine successes of the Trump administration, is growing in its animus toward the president. Refusing to acknowledge the roaring economy and a renewed sense of optimism and national pride, some on the Left (and some on the Right) are succumbing to an irrational loathing of the president that has been called Trump Derangement Syndrome. And so the rift between the Left and the Right has grown deep, and our national politics are more polarized than ever.

To counter this lack of fair coverage by the mainstream media, or maybe to make political points with his base, President Trump trumpets his accomplishments in his many speeches. One place where the nation was closely watching was in his 2019 State of the Union address, where, along with enumerating his accomplishments, he supported biblical values.

Some have said it was the most pro-life State of the Union Address our generation has ever heard. Pastor Paula White Cain called the address "absolutely astounding." Pausing for a moment, she continued, "And I would go even further to say that he was anointed [as he spoke]," adding that she knew millions of people were praying and fasting that the president would "be the mouthpiece God would breathe through."

TRUMP PROMISED TO SUPPORT PRO-LIFE ISSUES

One of the highlights of Trump's speech was his strong emphasis on pro-life values.

"There could be no greater contrast to the beautiful image of a mother holding her infant child than the chilling displays our nation saw in recent days," Trump said. "Lawmakers in New York cheered with delight upon the passage of legislation that would allow a baby to be ripped from the mother's womb moments from birth. These are living, feeling, beautiful babies who will never get the chance to share their love and their dreams with the world. And then we had the case of the governor of Virginia, where he stated he would execute a baby after birth."

The president didn't stop there. He then boldly called members of Congress to action, encouraging them to outlaw this insane and barbaric law.

"To defend the dignity of every person, I am asking the Congress to pass legislation to prohibit the late-term abortion of children who can feel pain in the mother's womb," he said. "Let us work together to build a culture that cherishes innocent life. And let us reaffirm a fundamental truth: All children—born and unborn—are made in the holy image of God."[4]

Of course Trump didn't address only the horrors of abortion. He called on Congress to protect America's workers, to end the human sex trafficking spread through illegal immigration, and to protect our freedom by rejecting the seductive evils of socialism. He once more reiterated his determination to build a wall on our southern border. But above all he called the country to unity—to work hard toward the common goal of growth and safety.

After the speech Franklin Graham tweeted: "Thank you @POTUS @realDonaldTrump for covering the priorities of our nation so clearly in tonight's State of the Union address. It is my prayer that all Americans would support working together in a bipartisan way to solve the problems we face."[5]

CBN's David Brody called the speech the most pro-life State of the Union address ever. "No other President...has ever been so bold in their words describing the national immoral horror and impact of late-term abortion," Brody tweeted.[6]

Paula White Cain believes Donald Trump is "absolutely the most pro-life president" because of his defunding all foreign abortions, defunding Planned Parenthood, and being the first sitting president to ever actually address the March for Life.

Mark Levin told Pastor John Hagee during an interview on *Life, Liberty & Levin* that Trump's position "on life versus abortion" has surprised him. "It has been very consistent. It's been solid." Another promise kept.

Hagee told Levin he appreciates Trump's stand because "in the Bible, killing a baby in the womb of the mother is murder. We don't consider it a woman's right to murder a child. And we, as Evangelicals, oppose abortion, and feel like that anyone that does…, if they do not repent of that sin, will face God in the judgment [and have] to account for that. Because that's a very, very serious evil."[7]

TRUMP PROMISED TO UPHOLD CONSERVATIVE VALUES

Many wondered if this businessman with no experience in government would lead as a conservative—after all, he had been a Democrat and considered running for president on a third-party ticket. In office President Trump has exceeded expectations. Instead of spouting conservative promises with no intention of keeping them—as many Republican candidates do nowadays—Trump has been true to his word.

For example, unlike every president since Bill Clinton, Trump fulfilled his promise to recognize Jerusalem as Israel's capital and moved the US Embassy from Tel Aviv to Jerusalem. That embassy move has led several other countries to promise to do the same.

I think part of the reason Trump has been such a change agent for America is the fact that he doesn't play according to the rules of politics. He refuses to muck around in the deep state. On the contrary, he seems as though he truly wants to make America great again. And for that, Americans can be grateful.

"Donald Trump might be the most conservative president in the last century," Christian historian David Barton told me. "There were a lot of things we didn't know about him. But it's been amazing to me to see how he's risen to the occasion and how he has actually become our champion [for Evangelicals] more than George W. Bush or Jimmy Carter, who had better evangelical credentials, and he's even done more than Reagan, in my opinion."

TRUMP PROMISED TO OPPOSE POLITICAL CORRECTNESS

Candidate Trump also promised to confront political correctness, including bringing back "Merry Christmas" and standing up to the PC Thought Police.

"I credit [Trump] with so many things," Barton said. "He, more than anyone in my lifetime, has broken the back of political correctness. He kept saying things that the [Left] got upset over, but he didn't care. He just kept saying it, and now we're all cheering and saying, 'Way to go. I've so wanted to say that, and I never felt I could.' There's the president saying [these things] and taking a beating, and his favorability numbers have been slowly increasing."

TRUMP PROMISED TO PUT CONSERVATIVE JUDGES ON THE BENCH

No matter how much the left attacks, Trump is committed to doing the right thing. He has worked hard to place conservatives on the Supreme Court, despite Democrats doing everything they could to impede his progress.

"The Democrats have slowed down the confirmation process so much that at the current pace, experts say, it will take him eleven years to get just the current nominees confirmed," Barton said. "We still have some Cabinet-level departments that don't have undersecretaries yet because we can't get them confirmed. They're using every trick in the book—particularly Senate Rule 22 [which is used to break a filibuster]—to slow down what he's trying to do."

Despite the opposition, Trump keeps pressing forward with his agenda for the nation. Because of that there are many things Christians can learn from him, Barton says. Some Christians have placed unrealistic and unbiblical standards of leadership on Trump that not even God placed on leaders in the Bible.

To me and many other conservative Christians the single reason they voted for Trump is that he promised to appoint only conservative judges to the bench. "If we can get a cadre of judges that are right thinking, conservative, constitutional judges, this country will benefit for forty to fifty years from the administration of Donald Trump," Pastor Hagee told Levin.

"Ten years from now we will really begin to have a deep appreciation, historically, of what the president has achieved—and showing how this is an answer to prayer to believers through prayer and works of faith and acting on that," Paula White Cain told me.

With the appointment of Neil Gorsuch in 2017 and Brett Kavanaugh in 2018, many conservatives believe their taking a chance on supporting Trump has paid off. But Amedia said, "We're still one justice short," adding that God showed him Trump would appoint three justices and "that the third one is coming sooner than we thought."

TRUMP PROMISED TO MAKE AMERICA ENERGY-SUFFICIENT

After years of being dependent on OPEC oil, the US became a net exporter of energy. Barton points to projections that in the coming decades the US will become one of the world's major exporters of oil. One of the reasons is that under the Trump administration and former secretary of energy Rick Perry the permit time to approve a new well has gone from as long as many months down to sometimes a matter of days, which means drilling new wells can occur very fast.

Barton was in Poland recently and met with a deputy prime minister a week after then secretary of energy Rick Perry had been there. He told Barton, "We explained to Secretary Perry that…we have to get our natural gas and oil from Russia, which puts us under Russia's thumb. It's the same with Ukraine and Crimea." The deputy prime minister told Barton that Perry asked how much gas they needed, and when he answered him, Perry replied, "The US just happens to have that much we can sell Poland every month!" Barton said. "Poland is now able to get its energy from America, and they can in turn sell it to Ukraine. America is literally helping keep nations free in Europe because we're exporting so much energy."

TRUMP PROMISED TO CUT REGULATIONS

Trump promised during the campaign that he would cut regulations. One of the first things he did was require that for every new governmental regulation passed, two existing regulations must be repealed.[8] That sounded like a pretty good ratio to me to bring less government. But the record so far is that for every significant new regulation the bureaucracy writes, they *repeal four significant regulations!*[9] That's extraordinarily good news, but you don't hear much about it from the media. Instead there's a steady drumbeat of how bad Trump is, and it seems to go on twenty-four hours a day, seven days a week. Yet the president continues to keep his promises, such as cutting regulations.

The entire economy has benefited from less regulation. And the Labor Department cutting the amount of employment paperwork my company must fill out benefits me directly! However, there's one reduction in regulations that in an indirect way benefits the spread of the gospel. How? A certain out-of-date FCC regulation has been lifted, so there's more money left for Christian broadcasters to pursue their mission. For Trinity Broadcasting Network, founded by the late Paul Crouch Sr., it means saving a whopping twenty million dollars a year.

This FCC regulation was written in the 1930s to regulate radio stations (the regulation applied to TV after it was introduced to the public at the 1939 World's Fair). There were no satellites back then, no prerecorded programs. Everything was live. So the regulation was written to require a studio next to every broadcast tower. It was called the main studio rule.

I had noticed that when I visited various Christian TV stations, the studios were usually in remote locations next to the tower. I vaguely knew it was tied somehow to governmental regulations, but I had no idea what a burden that was until I talked to Matt Crouch, son of TBN's founder, who now runs the massive television network.

"When the main studio rule was written in the 1930s, it made sense," Crouch told me. "You had to own a building next to your transmitter, or close enough to run a wire up the tower. And because there was no way to record then, you had to do live broadcasts of every kind— dramatic news, sports. Whatever you were doing, it was live. So, prior to recording devices, that rule made all the sense in the world. But it was obsolete by the fifties."

When Crouch's dad began buying studios in the 1970s, he had to build a studio in Santa Ana, California, then another in Phoenix, as well as one in Miami, Oklahoma City, and so forth, as the network expanded. Even though broadcast networks were beginning to use satellites to create programing in one studio to beam to their affiliates, each had to have a "main studio" next to each tower. As the cable industry developed during the same era, CNN, MSNBC, Fox, and the others were not bogged down by these regulations because they did not transmit their signal via broadcast towers.

For a massive network such as TBN, this was a huge financial drain.

Not only did TBN have to build the studios, but those studios had to be maintained and staffed. "It is literally a reduction in our budget by one stroke of the pen. It just happened that quickly," Crouch said.

This was a cost of governmental regulation that added no value to the broadcasting industry. Previous presidents could have ended this regulation, but they didn't. It took a businessman like Donald Trump to realize this regulation was a drain on the entire broadcasting industry because the reason for its existence was no longer valid.

Crouch met President Trump when Gov. Mike Huckabee interviewed him at the White House for Huckabee's TBN show. He remembers the president was in a good mood so they had a few minutes to chat. He thanked the president for having the FCC chairman reconsider these archaic regulations.

When Crouch told him that cutting the regulations saved TBN twenty million dollars a year, the president lit up. "He brings the wisdom of business and the private sector into government," Crouch said. "I can tell you that when he ran on the platform of deregulation, he jumped into the middle of the broadcast industry and made a very significant change, and maybe there will be more on the way. We'll see."

TRUMP PROMISED TO SUPPORT ISRAEL

One of the biggest promises kept for Evangelicals was when Trump moved the US embassy to Jerusalem, declaring it Israel's capital and opening the embassy on the seventieth anniversary in 2018 of the founding of the State of Israel. Fulfilling one of his campaign promises, the proclamation brought joy to many Evangelicals.

The evangelical community showed its appreciation when the founder of the Friends of Zion museum in Jerusalem, Dr. Mike Evans, presented President Trump with the Friends of Zion Award in a ceremony at the White House.

"No president in history has ever built such an alliance for the State of Israel and the Jewish people, and no president has courageously stood up for the State of Israel on the global stage as you had, Mr. President," Evans declared at the ceremony. "President Trump's historic recognition of Jerusalem will secure his place in history as the first American president to take that step since the founding of the State of Israel in 1948."[10]

John Hagee told Mark Levin that Trump's promise to support Israel is what prompted him to tell the five million members of Christians

United for Israel they should vote for Trump in 2016. "Everything he has promised to do, he did it," Hagee said. "And that's a very unusual thing for politicians in our generation. We think the president is doing a fabulous job even with a Congress that is fighting him every step of the way."[11]

Paula White Cain said Trump "not only recognized Jerusalem as the capital, but [his] recognizing the Golan Heights will [benefit] the long-term security of Israel." When it comes to his peace and economic plans for the Middle East, Paula believes he's looking at objectives that support the long-term security and best interest of Israel. All these, she said, were "promises made, promises kept."

Trump Promised to Free the Economy to Boom

In my book *Trump Aftershock*, I devoted an entire chapter to "Trump's Booming Economy." No matter how hard the liberal media may try to refocus the world's attention on other issues, the good news coming from President Trump's booming economy is impossible to ignore. Take, for example, this review of the blazing-hot economy from *U.S. News & World Report*: "Wall Street opened 2018 on a winning note Tuesday, bidding Nasdaq to its first-ever close above 7,000 points following a rally in technology shares. At the closing bell, the tech-rich Nasdaq Composite Index had jumped 1.5 percent to end the first session of the year at 7,006.90. The S&P 500 also notched a fresh record, gaining 0.8 percent to close at 2,695.79, while the Dow Jones Industrial Average rose 0.4 percent to 24,824.01, about 13 points below its all-time record."[12] All this is actually happening, and all at the same time.

As economics analyst Peter Roff explained in his special report, this means "America is up to its eyeballs in good economic news." The Dow broke 26,000 on the first trading day of 2018. Unemployment was down to 3.75 percent as of June 2018, the lowest since 1969, and black unemployment was the lowest it had been since the Bureau of Labor Statistics started keeping track in 1972.

Two years into Trump's term as president the independent newspaper *Epoch Times* published seventy ways President Trump changed the nation, including this glowing account of the US economy: "From sweeping tax reform to support for energy production, President Donald Trump's pro-business policies have boosted the job market, set records in the stock market, and helped individuals and companies to thrive," the newspaper reported. "The economy hit the Trump administration's 3 percent growth target in the second quarter of 2017 and in the second and third quarters of 2018."[13]

TRUMP "KEPT MORE PROMISES THAN HE MADE"

President Trump famously bragged several times in 2018 that he kept more promises than he had made. One time was right before the midterms when he was stumping for Josh Hawley of Missouri (who defeated Claire McKaskill for US Senate a few days later). Such an outrageous claim by the president set on fire the hair of the mainstream media, who screamed that such a thing was not possible.

Newsweek claimed: "Some may beg to differ on Trump's claims of promises kept. The *Washington Post* reported in September that of the 60 pledges made after he was elected, he had kept 14 and broken 16. Ones he had broken, according to the *Post*, included reducing tax brackets, fully repealing Obamacare and making Mexico pay the United States for the full cost of the proposed southern border wall."[14]

Research shows that many of the "promises," such as allowing Americans to deduct child care and elder care from their taxes, gave way to legislative compromise. When working on the GOP tax plan, "the White House abandoned [the child care and elder care provision] in the face of opposition and instead pressed for a larger tax credit." However, the *Washington Post* said it was a "promise broken." As someone who has responsibility for the care of my ninety-one-year-old mother, that deduction would have benefited me, but I was happy for the larger tax cut. I don't consider that a broken promise.

Here's another so-called broken promise reported by the *Washington Post*: "Trump says he will create 25 million jobs over ten years, so we will track a prorated figure of 10 million in four years, or 2.5 million a year. In his first year, job growth has not kept pace at a level for Trump to meet his goal."[15] Give me a break. Trump sets lofty goals. If he wanted 10 million new jobs and it came in at 9.9 million, would that be a promise broken? I don't think so. It reminds me of a famous saying I've repeated many times to "aim for the moon, and maybe you'll hit the tree."

There seems to be so much hatred of the president that if Trump found a cure for cancer, the leftist media would say he was putting doctors out of work. I realize this sentiment isn't unique to Trump, or even to Republicans. President Lyndon Johnson once famously quipped: "If one morning I walked on top of the water across the Potomac River, the headline that afternoon would read: 'President Can't Swim.'"[16]

It just goes to show that some of the problems have been around for a long time. Some are so complex they are not solved overnight. The point is Trump remembers his promises and keeps them the best he can. Has he made Mexico pay for the wall? No, but he has focused on the problem of immigration more than any president in thirty years. And through diplomacy and bullying Mexico, he has gotten them to cooperate to solve the problem to a greater degree than most of the Democrats.

The issue of immigration is so important I devoted chapter 4 to it. But it's an ongoing issue, as Dr. James Dobson knows. He wrote in a recent newsletter: "President Donald Trump's border wall is…urgently needed. He seems to be the only leader in America who comprehends this tragedy and is willing to address it. Those who oppose him do everything they can to impede his effort."

"This is the system set up by a liberal Congress and judges," Dobson noted. "It is a well-known fact that President Obama's administration established many of these unworkable policies, and Congress is steadfastly unwilling to change them. Every effort at reform has been overridden or ignored. It is set in stone. Democrats want massive numbers of immigrants who will someday become voters. Some Republicans support the policies because they want cheap labor for agricultural purposes. The border *could* be fixed, but there are very few in authority who seem to care."[17]

One vitally important reason to reelect the president (and the primary reason I wrote this book) is that come inauguration day 2021, if a Democrat is taking the oath of office, many of the changes Trump has made will be undone with a vengeance. I believe the Left, if given a chance to be in power again, will oppress and persecute their opponents—especially conservative Christians—to such a degree that we might never recover. And it's not just religious values at stake.

Dennis Prager is concerned leftist lawmakers will reinstate what the president calls the "terrible" Iran nuclear deal if Trump loses. "Donald Trump has done so much good—to the surprise of many of us, including those of us who supported him. But if he loses, much of it can be undone," the popular talk show host told me.

Prager explained that during the first Democratic debates, when the twenty candidates were asked about the Iran deal, every one was in favor of "going back to the deal, which enriched the Iranian government—the most dangerous government on earth—with billions of dollars and ultimately permission to make a nuclear weapon."

Prager continued: "That's just one example of what will be undone. Obviously, [we'd have to contend with] all of the [liberal] judges who would be appointed. [And] there would be zero movement on immigration."

My point in this chapter is not to give an exhaustive list of the promises he kept. In my book *Trump Aftershock* I list the president's accomplishments in his first five hundred days, and it takes six pages of small print! He had done even more by the time the book came out. That's because this president loves this country and he wants to make it great. So he is making good on his promises even though he is opposed at every turn by the Democratic Party and the media.

Trump Promised to Support Religious Freedom

One of the most important promises to me as a Christian is the president's pledge to fight for religious liberty and persecuted Christians around the world. The right of religious freedom is enshrined in the First Amendment before the other freedoms, including freedom of the press (which I also highly value). That's because God is the giver of our rights, and religious freedom is the foundation for all other rights.

When Turkey wrongly imprisoned Pastor Andrew Brunson for two years, President Trump worked diligently to free the persecuted pastor—even to the point of imposing sanctions on Turkey. But no one should be shocked about this. Trump promised during his presidential campaign that he would pursue religious freedom for America's citizens—from the Christian baker who feels convicted about baking a cake for a gay wedding to the falsely accused minister whose only crime is sharing the gospel.

When Brunson flew home to the United States, President Donald Trump met with him in the Oval Office. One of the first things Brunson did was drop to his knees and pray for Trump: "Lord God, I ask that You pour out Your Holy Spirit on President Trump, that you give him supernatural wisdom to accomplish all the plans You have for this country."[18]

There are so many examples of President Trump being an advocate for religious liberty. He promised he would change the so-called Johnson Amendment, which muzzles churches and nonprofits from speaking up when politics is involved, and he issued an executive order to the IRS to not enforce it. The deregulations he has put in place not only have helped businesses but have freed faith-based entities to be able to help more people in places such as Baltimore as well as along the border with Mexico.

When Paula White Cain started working on the immigration problem, she called churches near the border and found out they were hindered from helping the immigrants due to governmental regulations. "Immediately I called a senior adviser [to the president] and said, 'I think we've got a regulation problem perhaps,' so within twenty-four hours they changed the policy."

Donald Trump made it clear even before he entered the presidential sweepstakes that he would use the power and influence of the United States to defend the interests of men and women in the faith community. Since that time, he has taken an interest in the plight of Christians suffering from persecution around the world.

According to David Curry, the president of Open Doors USA, which works on behalf of persecuted Christians, religious liberty will be one of the most critical issues facing the Trump administration over the next several years. It is, he said, "the central issue that they're going to have to deal with, whether you're looking at it through the lens of immigration, whether you're looking at it through the lens of terrorism."

He added that "nearly 1 in every 12 Christians in the world today lives in an area or in a culture in which Christianity is illegal, forbidden, or punished. And yet today the world is largely silent on the shocking wave of religious intolerance."[19]

Evidence that the president has taken the challenge seriously was the appointment of former US senator and former Kansas governor Sam Brownback on July 26, 2017, as ambassador-at-large for International Religious Freedom. "Confirmation of Sam Brownback as the Ambassador-at-Large sends a message to the world," said Oklahoma senator James Lankford, "that religious freedom is a priority of the United States government."[20] And it signaled that the president would be an advocate for religious freedom around the world.

President Trump and Vice President Pence have made a priority of maintaining an open dialogue with America's churches and church leaders, and the vice president reaffirmed that commitment in his remarks to the more than nine thousand members of the Southern

Baptist Convention who attended the annual meeting in Dallas on June 13, 2018. He spoke first about the progress the administration has made, protecting life, preserving religious liberty, helping the persecuted church, and standing with Israel. But those gains, he said, cannot be sustained without engaged churchgoing Americans.[21]

For a president whose administration began with a monumental shock wave and whose words and deeds continue to set off aftershocks around the globe, it may come as a shock of even greater magnitude that his administration has become such a strong defender of religious liberty. But for people of faith, it's really no surprise.

If keeping his promises shows one good character trait in Donald Trump, what do people who know him personally say he is really like?

CHAPTER 8

WHAT IS DONALD TRUMP REALLY LIKE?

The truth is not being told in this country about President Trump...and that is a disservice to every single American.[1]
—BILL O'REILLY
BEST-SELLING AUTHOR AND TALK SHOW HOST

YOU KNOW THAT Donald Trump is a true cultural hero when he's the character of a children's book. *Donald Drains the Swamp* by Eric Metaxas is about a kingdom of cavemen whose king ignores their suffering because he's distracted by a large swamp made of money. So a caveman named Donald seeks to help by draining the swamp (the out-of-touch federal government) at the request of his fellow cave dwellers (the deplorables). Donald is a hero, and in this creative way Eric explains to six-year-olds what so many have come to understand: Donald Trump gets it and is a hero to middle-class Americans who are ignored by the political elite.

Metaxas, known for his serious and highly acclaimed biographies of Martin Luther and Dietrich Bonhoeffer, has also written thirty children's books. He loves to write comedy, and his daily radio show recorded in New York City is usually funny.

Donald Trump wasn't even on Eric's radar until a year before the 2016 election, when his close friend, children's book illustrator Tim Raglin, told him he needed to look into Trump's platform. But Eric wasn't too sure. "Being a New Yorker, I was kind of jaundiced about Trump," Eric told me. "He could be vulgar, and there were things about him that I didn't like. But I started watching him on the stump out there at these rallies. And I saw what my friend saw. I said, 'This guy is like an American folk hero. I've never seen anything like it.'" So when Trump was elected, Eric and Raglin decided to write a children's book together about Trump. The results were, as he put it, "magical."

Gary Varvel, a political cartoonist for the *Indianapolis Star* for twenty-four years, had a similar epiphany and stopped drawing Trump as a clown and started depicting him as being presidential when he began to understand what Donald Trump was really like.

"When Trump announced he was running for president, I admit that I didn't take this millionaire, hotel magnate, reality TV show celebrity as a serious candidate," he wrote in a 2018 op-ed in *USA Today*. "I doubted his ability to do the job. So I drew him as a clown. In fact, my cartoons were as critical of him as many of my liberal cartoonist friends."

But Gary changed his opinion when he realized Trump was not just criticizing the problems but proposing fixes. "His political promises were simple, repeated often and easily remembered. I admit that I was wrong about Trump. He's not a clown. He's a businessman, entertainer, and now the president that I didn't want but now think we need," he wrote.[2]

Those who know Trump personally say that behind the bombastic persona portrayed in the media is a genuinely nice man who cares about people and who generates fierce loyalty from others as a result. That's what struck me when I interviewed him in August 2016 for *Charisma* magazine. I expected him to be a pompous celebrity who was running for president. Instead I found him to be soft-spoken and respectful.

When I interviewed President George W. Bush in 2004 with some other journalists, it seemed the president was eager to move on to his next appointment. Not so with Trump. He focused on my interview. He even offered me a bottle of water—something he didn't need to do, but it showed me he was a nice guy.

Jim Garlow, the activist pastor from California, has a similar analysis of Trump's temperament. Even though he is up against the strongest institutions in our culture and attacked ferociously by Democrats who want him impeached or imprisoned, Trump keeps a gentle spirit. "Hollywood stars mock him. Academia is stacked against him. They slam him hard, and he doesn't mind pushing back," Garlow said. "But quite frankly the temperament that many people may not like about Trump is the only kind of temperament necessary to survive the constant pounding he takes and to keep marching forward."

Mike Evans, who gave Trump a Friends of Zion Award for his support of the Jewish state, says Trump is the most gracious president of any in our lifetime, including Ronald Reagan, who despite his warm public persona was said to be very cold behind the scenes. Trump is just the opposite. "Donald Trump is Donald Trump twenty-four hours a day. He's authentic," Evans said.

"Every other word Trump says is *thank you*," Evans told me. "Of course he demands excellence, and if he gets it, he's happy. If not, then you're on your way out the door."

Evans said the president's love of Israel, evidenced by his decision to move the US Embassy to Jerusalem and recognize the annexation of the Golan Heights, has made him so popular that if Trump ran for prime minister of Israel, he would win by a landslide.

While other presidents wanted to get Evangelicals' support at election time but kept them at arm's length the rest of the time, Trump has done the opposite. The president and First Lady Melania recently did something no other president has done—they honored the evangelical community by hosting a state dinner in August 2018 "for all the good work they do," Religion News Service reported at the time. Calling America "a nation of believers," President Trump said he hosted the event to "celebrate America's heritage of faith, family and freedom."

"As you know, in recent years the government tried to undermine religious freedom, but the attacks on communities of faith are over," the president said. "We've ended it. Unlike some before us, we are protecting your religious liberty."[3]

Televangelist Kenneth Copeland and his wife, Gloria, were among the hundred or so leaders who donned their formal best that night. He remembers that the president said, "I want to hear from you. I want to hear your heart. I want to hear what you have to say."

Jim Garlow also attended the event and couldn't believe it when the president opened up the mic. "In no political environment is that ever allowed," Garlow said. "The handlers are always worried that someone will say something embarrassing. But here was Trump, so secure in who he is that he could turn the microphone over to ninety-five or more pastors and Christian leaders."

Once Trump realized he was in a room full of preachers, he quickly reminded them not to take too long. The pastors laughed at Trump's humor, but the dinner was no joke; Copeland said he could sense the Spirit of God in that place.

Garlow said Trump watched closely and listened intently as the ministers came to the microphone to express their love and appreciation

for the president and First Lady or commented on something important to evangelical Christians.

"Some politicians need a four hundred–page summary to absorb
anything," Garlow said. "Not President Trump. He picks up on things
very quickly. High-level leaders are like that. You don't have to go very
far in explanation, and they can kind of look at you and say, 'I get it.'
He was absorbing it—taking it all in. I saw a teachable spirit."

Someone close to the president who has seen Trump's ability is his
counsel, attorney Jay Sekulow, whom I've known since 1990. "President
Trump is a very quick study, and for a non-lawyer he has a tremendous
understanding of both the legal system and the nuances of the law. He
is very astute."

Sekulow should know because he, along with former New York
mayor Rudy Giuliani, helped the president navigate the most intense,
politically motivated investigation in US history. As high pressure as
it was, Jay says the president "never lost it," emotionally or otherwise,
which is impressive considering the future of his presidency may have
hung in the balance. Sekulow said he can't say that for most clients in
high-stakes cases who *do lose it* at some point.

"Rudy and I would always have very frank and honest calls with him,
and he'd absorb the information [and] ask what the ramifications of a
particular move by Mueller or somebody else meant. He always wanted
to know what we were going to do," Sekulow explained. "I always tried
to go into meetings and calls (these were calls taking place multiple
times a day) with an answer, not just a question. He absorbed it. He
listened to our legal advice, he challenged it, which was appropriate,
and he pushed back. But he would follow the advice of his lawyers."

A prime example was when the president wanted to give an interview to Mueller, but Sekulow's team of lawyers thought that was a very
bad idea. "We went back and forth with him over many months on
that, and of course he ultimately followed our advice, and we got a
good conclusion."

At the state dinner for evangelical leaders, Garlow marveled at how
Trump seemed to know what to say and what policies and Christian
principles were important to Evangelicals, adding, "He seems to figure
it out intuitively. I think he wants to do what's right."

Chicago pastor Choco De Jesús, who at the time led the twenty-
two-thousand-member New Life Covenant Church, one of the largest
congregations in the Assemblies of God, was seated at the same table

as Secretary of Housing and Urban Development Ben Carson and megachurch pastor Robert Morris of Gateway Church outside Dallas. He told me he felt out of place that night as he watched leaders go to the mic, lavish love on the first couple, and praise the economy and Trump's other accomplishments. But being Hispanic, Choco had a different perspective.

"Inside of me I'm saying I have to say something. I heard so much praising, but no one was saying anything from our perspective. So I get the courage to get up, and I stand in line."

After the next speaker finished, Choco said: "Mr. President and First Lady, thank you for inviting me to this dinner and allowing me to break bread with you. It is biblical to break bread and get to know each other." Then he said, "I, unlike my other colleagues, don't love you the way they appear to because I don't even know who you are. But I've come here tonight because I want to get to know you."

Pastor Choco added, "One thing that I know for sure about you, Mr. President, is when you say something, it gets done, which is a rare commodity coming out of the White House. So I look forward to working with you for the situation in our city, Chicago, and I thank you once again for inviting me to break bread with you."

With that, he moved to return to where he had been seated with his wife. But as he walked past the president's table, Trump pushed back his chair, stood up, and gave Choco a bear hug. When Choco got to his table, he received a text from Paula White Cain, who had just witnessed what happened. "POTUS was very moved by your authenticity," she texted.

THE PRESIDENT WHO PRAYS

When someone in the room asked Trump what he wanted to be remembered for, Copeland said the president responded, "I want to be remembered as the president who prayed more than any other." Of course that's not the stereotype we see in the press. In fact the press likes to play up everything in his past that was irreligious.

"I'm telling you, the anointing was there," Copeland said. "It was like being in a really anointed church service. Just the flow of the Spirit of God was just all over that." Copeland told me another story about something Trump did long before he ran for president. In 2011 Trump called Paula White Cain and asked her to gather several preachers to pray about whether he should run for president. "They prayed for over six hours—just stayed on their knees and stayed before God for six hours," Copeland told me.

At the end of the prayer session Trump asked Paula what she thought. She replied that she and the pastors praying with her didn't believe it was the right time for him to run for president. Of course he waited until the 2016 election to run, and won. "This is the Donald Trump people don't know anything about," Copeland said.

Choco De Jesús next met the president when he was invited to the National Day of Prayer at the Rose Garden with a smaller group of clergy including John Hagee and Jentezen Franklin. "My view of the president is that he made some promises in this campaign, and he wants to make sure he fulfills them," Choco said. "I can respect somebody who says here's what I'm going to do and does it. Since then I've worked with his staff if they come to Chicago. We have discussed violence in our city, and we have a good line of communication."

Choco sees Trump as a visionary who can lead into the future despite people who try to tarnish his name. "I just wish people would just work together with the president," he said.

Pastor Mark Burns, the black pastor from South Carolina we met in chapter 3, also sees character traits in Trump that his opponents can't see. "I believe he's getting some real things done because the president truly loves all Americans," Burns said. "He hasn't changed. And this is why he's going to win reelection."

Burns said he's told other black pastors that it doesn't matter if people hate Trump because people hated Jesus. "It doesn't matter how many people in your congregation are Democrats. You are not a neutral place. How in the world can anyone support the killing of babies when God said in Jeremiah, 'I knew you before I formed you in your mother's womb.' That alone should turn off every Christian in this nation [to the Democratic Party]."

Burns believes Trump has accepted Christ as his Savior: "I'm telling from what I know from firsthand experience—not from what I've read. God's hand is upon his life. I'm saying he loves Jesus. And he loves the Holy Spirit. And he knows that he can't do this job without having the voice of God close to him," Burns said. "He is growing every day in his faith."

Coming from the world of business and real estate development, Donald Trump was not familiar with the language and customs of the evangelical community when he entered the White House. Although he had been a close friend and supporter of the late Dr. Norman Vincent Peale in New York and attended services at the historic Marble Collegiate Church, he was suddenly being exposed to a different perspective and a different kind of religious experience as he hobnobbed with Evangelicals. But through his friendships with evangelical leaders such as Paula White Cain, James Robison, Dr. Robert Jeffress, and a few others, he also was gaining a deeper appreciation for the concerns of the millions of evangelical voters who, when faced with a choice between Trump and Hillary Clinton, gave him the critical margin he needed for victory.

That appreciation turned into action. During the campaign Trump began assembling an advisory board of faith leaders with whom he could meet from time to time and who would be available by telephone to offer insight on issues of concern to the churches. Then, in mid-July 2017, he invited a group of two dozen evangelical leaders to meet with him for a few minutes in the Oval Office before a day-long listening session with the Office of Public Liaison (OPL). As CBN reported, the group discussed a wide variety of issues with the OPL, focusing especially on religious liberty, criminal justice reform, and America's support for the nation of Israel.[4]

EXCEEDING EXPECTATIONS

As I interviewed evangelical leaders for this chapter, I began to notice a theme. Many Americans (including me) did not like Trump initially but began to like him when they got to know him. Trump is who he is. And despite being portrayed as a buffoon, he has become not only presidential but a statesman, exceeding most people's expectations.

Early in his presidency, on one of his first overseas trip as commander in chief, Trump attended the G20 summit in Germany. The press emphasized how unpopular he was with other heads of state and predicted he would be marginalized. Instead a photo was taken of him surrounded by America's closest allies, who were hanging on his every word. So much for being marginalized.

Unless you just wanted to ignore the facts, it became clear early, as we look at the life of this man, that he is an extraordinary and remarkably capable individual. He hardly sleeps. His aides can barely keep up with him. He has never smoked, he doesn't drink alcohol, and he has never used drugs. He is driven to achieve great things, to build great buildings, and he is determined to keep America great. These are not small ambitions, and he is not a small man by any measure. He towers over almost everyone, and he is the center of attention whenever he enters the room. Yes, he's passionate, he's outspoken, and he's a dynamic achiever. But he is also smart, sincere, and a man of faith.

During my interview with Donald Trump in 2016 I asked him about his child-rearing priorities and his secret of having such a close relationship with his children and their obvious respect for him. He told me he worked hard to rear them right, including telling them: "No drugs, no alcohol, no cigarettes."

Many people have commented that one of the best endorsements of Donald Trump is the character of his children, who supported their father every step of the way in the campaign. His oldest son, Donald Jr., was an especially articulate spokesman. After Don Jr.'s remarks at Heritage Baptist Church in Woodbridge, Virginia, Pastor Mike Edwards told a reporter, "I felt like seeing him in person lets you know just how genuine a young man he is and tells me that his father was just as genuine in the way that he raised him."[5]

And the longer he has been president, the more Donald Trump's stature has seemed to grow—especially compared with the small-minded Democrats who lambast him at every turn. One time where this came into view was when he flew to France to be a part of the celebration of the seventy-fifth anniversary of D-Day. That week Newt Gingrich wrote an insightful op-ed that contrasted the stature gap between Trump and House Speaker Nancy Pelosi, as well as other Democratic blowhards.

"While the president was proving he was a world leader in Japan, Britain, France, Ireland and Mexico, Pelosi's House Democrats were ineffectually talking about subpoenas and investigations—and asserting that there is no border problem. The stature gap just kept growing," Gingrich wrote.[6]

Trump's standing as a statesman may be what history remembers him for, but to find out what the man is like now, I turned to two longtime friends of the president—Jay Sekulow, who serves as counsel to the president, quoted earlier, and Paula White Cain, his longtime spiritual adviser.

Sekulow sees the president at least weekly, and he witnesses something the public doesn't often see: "He's got a really good sense of humor." The president is also a good family man and protective of his wife and children, taking the attitude that "it's one thing to go after me but another to go after my kids," which Sekulow considers "a very admirable trait."

Paula met Donald Trump in 2002 and knew him when he first met Melania. She said, "Trump sang her praises," telling Paula that Melania was not only a beautiful model but a smart businesswoman who is wealthy in her own right and speaks five languages. Trump also told Paula that Melania is not wasteful or a big spender as some women with her means would be.

"He really adores Melania and his children," Paula told me. "He's very disciplined and plays chess with Barron whenever he gets the chance." Of course Paula has seen that Melania is a phenomenal mother, especially as she focused on Barron finishing school and making the transition to living in the White House.

Paula said: "A lot of people see the tough side. I've seen the tender side," adding that when her mother died last December, the president called to see how she was doing. "He didn't call to [tell me about a vote] and then say, 'By the way, how are you doing?' No, he just called me and talked to me as a person who lost someone very significant to me, my mother."

Katrina Pierson, who often represents Trump on TV, made a similar point at the kickoff event for the Women for Trump coalition led by his daughter-in-law, Lara Trump, and aimed at courting female voters to support Trump's reelection. At the rally in Pennsylvania, Pierson told the crowd: "He's keeping his promises to you…and he's going to continue to fight to keep those [campaign] promises because it is important for everyone. Donald Trump doesn't see color; he doesn't see race; he doesn't see gender; he just sees the people that he loves."[7]

One time the president told Paula, "They say no one has received the amount of attack I have, except for maybe President Lincoln." She reminded him that Lincoln is idealized much more now than in his lifetime. "And I think Trump will be very similar," she said.

"He's such a great president. He accomplishes so much," Paula added. "He has the courage to do things, and that's why some people call him a fighter. He is very courageous. He thinks legacy. He thinks lineage. He thinks down the road."

Regarding his personality, she also sees an attention to detail and a compassion that others don't see. She saw this when he showed her one of his new country clubs. As they walked through the dining hall,

Trump pointed out the sconces on the wall and said how much they cost.

"Here's a man who's a multibillionaire, yet he knows the price of the sconce on the wall. He is always so proud when he can get things done faster and under budget. Those are the two [things] I always hear him say: 'It was under budget, and it was before the deadline.' To him that is just fabulous."

One of my first memories of Trump in the news was when the Wollman Rink in Central Park had fallen into disrepair. In 1980 they estimated it would take two years to fix. Six years later, after wasting almost thirteen million dollars, a thirty-nine-year-old Trump said he could fix it for no profit and have it up in time for the next winter, six months away. Instead he finished in four months and 25 percent below budget, even after Mayor Ed Koch tried to torpedo the project because Trump made the city look incompetent. *Forbes* magazine said the incident "demonstrated Trump's mastery and command of public relations and how to attract massive amounts of free press."[8]

Trump said at the time it wasn't rocket science—rather common sense and "management." It is an example of how he focuses on the details of getting a job done. Since Paula has interacted closely with him in many settings, she knows his attention to detail also relates to people. Paula says he goes out of his way to know people's names— George, the guy who sells hot dogs outside Trump Tower, or his employees, many of whom stay with him for years. She's been in fancy restaurants with the family where Trump will stop to take photos with well-wishers who approach his table. "He genuinely cares about people," she said. And he likes the way his son Don Jr. described him in a speech as the "blue-collar billionaire."

More than that, Trump is a visionary, which should be obvious since he has said many times that he took one million dollars his father gave him to get started and parlayed that into more than three billion dollars, according to *Forbes*[9] (though he has said he's worth ten billion dollars). Paula says he also had the foresight to buy the air rights over buildings in New York, which have become extremely valuable as developers seek to build more high-rise buildings.

He's also a man of integrity. If he gives his word for something or has a handshake agreement, he will follow through, even if his close associates try to convince him after the fact that it was a bad deal and he should walk away.

Paula gave an example: "Somebody pitched an idea, and he shook the man's hand and said, 'We'll do it.' He wasn't getting paid very much for this deal. And to everyone around him, it looked like a bad deal. [Trump] simply said, 'But I shook his hand.' And that to him is like a gentleman's [agreement]—if I shake your hand, it is a deal. And I've seen that several times."

Trump is clearly a man of principle. But the thing I like about him is how he has disrupted the status quo—not only the push to the Left by the liberal establishment but also what we now call the deep state and the Republican establishment, which I deal with elsewhere in this book. Paula agrees that this is "not necessarily a bad thing. I think that some things need to be disrupted and shaken."

David Barton is glad that Trump keeps saying things that upset the politically correct crowd and doesn't seem to care. "When Trump says something politically incorrect and is attacked for it, he just doubles down. He keeps saying it, and we're cheering and saying, 'Way to go! I've so wanted to say that, and I never felt I could.' There's the president saying it and taking a beating, and his favorability numbers are gradually increasing. He's committed to doing the right thing, even when he gets beat up over it."

Barton also theorizes that Trump's tweets are part of a strategy to keep the other side off balance. Barton says that by "being flamboyant, obnoxious, and really over the top," Trump's tweets control the mainstream news cycle, and no one is paying attention to the enormous things he is accomplishing at the cabinet level. "Nobody's paid attention to Rick Perry in the Department of Energy, and what he is doing would have been national news all eight years of Obama, but nobody's talking about Perry," Barton said of the former energy secretary.

Anyone who's read his tweets or watched him beat sixteen fellow Republicans in 2016 for the nomination and then defeat the corrupt Clinton political machine for the presidency knows Trump is a fighter.

"He doesn't start a fight. But he will certainly finish one off. I wouldn't want to be in that boxing ring with him," Paula said, adding that "he is not like some people who hold long-term grudges. I've watched him privately be very forgiving. Once something is settled and done with, he's over it. He's not a bitter person."

Maybe that is why he hasn't seemed to age while he's been in office. It seems most presidents—even Clinton, George W. Bush, and Obama, who were a decade or two younger than Trump when they became president—seemed to age ten years right away. Maybe one of the keys is that Trump has held on to things that are important to him like his family and golf—things Paula said bring him tremendous peace and joy.

Since Paula has become his spiritual adviser over the years, she has seen Trump's spiritual journey. He can recount sermons by his beloved pastor Norman Vincent Peale, and he grieved when Peale died in 1993 at age ninety-five. She knows he watches Christian TV, especially David Jeremiah. She knows that even though he was raised a Presbyterian, he "loves what Charismatics call the 'move of the Spirit'; he loves worship and the preaching of the Word."

Paula is careful of what she says. She knows some ministers in the past have not really ministered to him but seemed to just want money from him. So she has been careful never to take a dollar, and she's cautious of what she says about his religious faith. But it's clear to those around her that she believes the president has a genuine relationship with Christ and is open to what Pentecostals call "the things of the Spirit."

Trump's faith motivates him in many ways, Paula says, from the generous donations to all sorts of charities (which he doesn't like to talk about) to his consideration of a person who faints at one of his rallies. One example of this happened at a rally I mentioned in chapter 7 in Cape Girardeau, Missouri, for Josh Hawley (who defeated Claire McCaskill for US Senate a few days later). When an elderly woman fainted, Trump stopped the rally for about ten minutes until medical personnel could help her. Meanwhile, the crowd spontaneously broke into "Amazing Grace" during the wait.

"I know he called some of the people around to make sure she was OK. And he just sat there and waited at the podium until she was doing OK. That's what I call typical Trump. He really cares," Paula said. "You see how much Christian values mean to him."

The president clearly knows his own mind and doesn't let the opinions, criticisms, and outright attacks of others sway him from his chosen path. Perhaps it's because he senses a calling and purpose in his life that are higher than human aspirations and achievements. However, there is no better way to understand Donald J. Trump than to let him speak in his own words, which is the focus of the next chapter.

CHAPTER 9

DONALD TRUMP IN HIS OWN WORDS

Sadly, the American dream is dead. But if I get elected presi-
dent I will bring it back bigger and better and stronger than
ever before, and we will make America great again.[1]
—DONALD J. TRUMP IN HIS ANNOUNCEMENT
OF HIS PRESIDENTIAL BID
NEW YORK, JUNE 15, 2015

ONALD J. TRUMP may be the most covered president in history. This is partly due to the way he dominates the news
cycle with his tweets and his larger-than-life personality. The
"fake news media" hate him, yet they report his every move. On top of
the news coverage, he uses Twitter to accomplish his agenda. David
Barton says he tweets to get the media to focus on the tweet and not
pay any attention to the changes he is making in bureaucratic Washington. Whether or not that is the case, because the president's comments are constantly making headlines, everyone knows what Donald
Trump is thinking. Or do we?

As the election looms, I have filled this book with tens of thousands
of words of my opinion and those of several dozen news sources. I have
tried to be objective, although it's clear how much I respect the president and believe he is doing a good job and must be reelected. But what
does the president think is important as we approach the next election?
What does he think about the issues that will affect not only the United
States and the world but also your life and mine? There's only one way
to know. To find out what he thinks, we must look to what he has said.

I interviewed the president during his campaign in 2016, as I've mentioned previously. I have interviewed a number of presidential candidates, governors, and other politicians in my forty-five-year media career.
But interviewing Donald Trump in the midst of his unlikely campaign
was markedly different. With Trump what you see on television is not

what you get behind the scenes. The Republican nominee demonstrated a humility we don't see in the liberal media sound bites. He was still a straight shooter, but his sincerity was far more striking than I would have expected. I asked the kinds of questions I thought most of my readers would want to ask. His answers revealed a confident, determined man who is truly committed to making America great again through principles that honor God rather than defy Him.

After that interview I understood that Donald Trump believes America remains a great country even though we've drifted away from the clear vision of the Founders. I saw that he possesses an undeniable faith in America, and I realized a big reason for that is his lifelong faith in God.

His first term proved my initial impression to be true. During that time Democrats did everything to bring down his presidency, including what many conservatives believe was an attempt at a bloodless coup by declaring him mentally incompetent and invoking the Twenty-Fifth Amendment to remove him from office. Of course the effort failed, but it's evidence of how dishonest the other side is. They also tried to discredit him through the Mueller probe, but fortunately that also is now behind him, and he has survived.

As I've said before, this election is one of the most important in recent history. And the best way to understand the issues addressed in this book—what's at stake, Donald Trump himself, and even the spiritual dimension I deal with in part 3—is to hear Trump in his own words.

WHAT'S AT STAKE IN 2020

When I first interviewed Trump in 2016, he made clear there was a lot at stake, and I believe the same is true four years later.[2] One of the biggest issues to born-again Christians is preserving the religious liberty we have always taken for granted. So I asked him how he would respect religious liberty at a time Evangelicals and Catholics have felt under attack for their pro-life convictions and biblical views on marriage. Trump told me:

> Religious liberty is the foundation. Without religious liberty you don't have liberty. I feel that so strongly, and so many other people do, and plenty of politicians do, but they don't express it. Religious liberty is something that I cherish, and you will never be disappointed.

In July 2019 the president met at the White House with survivors of religious persecution from around the world. A few months later, in September 2019, he became the first US president to host a meeting at the United Nations on religious freedom. In his speech[3] (see appendix A) he said:

> Today, with one clear voice, the United States of America calls upon the nations of the world to end religious persecution. To stop the crimes against people of faith, release prisoners of conscience, repeal laws restricting freedom of religion and belief, protect the vulnerable, the defenseless, and the oppressed, America stands with believers in every country who ask only for the freedom to live according to the faith that is within their own hearts. As President, protecting religious freedom is one of my highest priorities and always has been.

During my interview with him in 2016 I asked him about his support of repealing the Johnson Amendment so churches and ministries would not have their free speech muzzled by the government (which he has articulated in other ways, including his speech at the UN in September 2019, included in appendix B). In 2016 he told me:

> How did this happen in the first place? It's shocking how they were able to take it away. So this is not something that was written from the beginning. This was something written by a strong politician; that's all it is. It silences people we want to hear. They are afraid to talk about it because they could lose everything. [I will] lobby very strongly to have this terminated....I have absolute confidence that I'll be able to get it done.

Along those lines I wanted to know when I interviewed him in 2016 if he personally agreed that our nation was founded on Judeo-Christian values and principles. He said:

> I think it was. When I look at football coaches who were fired because they held a prayer on the field, it's absolutely terrible. I think it is terrible to see so many things happening that are different from what our country used to be. So our religion is

a very important part of me, and I also think it's a very important part of the country.

He later said this during his 2019 UN address on religious liberty:

The United States is founded on the principle that our rights do not come from government; they come from God. This immortal truth is proclaimed in our Declaration of Independence and enshrined in the First Amendment to our Constitution's Bill of Rights. Our Founders understood that no right is more fundamental to a peaceful, prosperous, and virtuous society than the right to follow one's religious convictions.

A huge issue to Christians is our attitude toward Israel and how we deal with the threats in the Middle East. When I interviewed him in 2016, Trump promised Israel would always be a priority in his administration.

Well, for one thing, I support Israel. I don't think Obama supports Israel. I think he's the worst thing that's ever happened to Israel. The Iran deal is a disaster for Israel, and I'm very supportive of Israel and have tremendous relationships in Israel and have a son-in-law who's Jewish, married to my daughter. I will be very strongly in favor of Israel.

Since immigration is such a huge issue and Trump promised to build a wall, I quoted the Book of Deuteronomy, which says to be kind to the stranger in the land, and asked him how that scripture would guide policy in his administration. He said:

Well, I think that's good, but I think we have to be careful at the same time. We are allowing people to come into the country, and we don't know anything about them. There is no paperwork; there's no documentation. You see what's going on in Germany, France, and many other places where they have an open-door policy, and it could go on here too. We've allowed thousands and thousands of people into our country, and we have no idea who they are.

At the same time, we want to build safe havens, and we want to get the Gulf states to fund the money because it's a tremendous amount of money. So we want to take care of people, but we can't allow them in because we just don't know who they are. You see what happened in San Bernardino; you see what happened in Orlando…you see what happened with the World Trade Center. We can look all over to see what has happened in France (Nice), [in] Germany. We have enough problems. We can't do that.

During his speech in September 2019 before the UN General Assembly, he said, "Mass illegal immigration is unfair, unsafe, and unsustainable for everyone involved." And he had a strong message for "those open border activists who cloak themselves in the rhetoric of social justice: Your policies are not just. Your policies are cruel and evil. You are empowering criminal organizations that prey on innocent men, women, and children. You put your own false sense of virtue before the lives, wellbeing…[of] countless innocent people. When you undermine border security, you are undermining human rights and human dignity."

He said each nation has a right to protect its borders, including the United States: "As long as I am president of the United States, we will enforce our laws and protect our borders."[4]

UNDERSTANDING TRUMP

To understand the man, I asked him what is the most important thing in his life. He answered:

> Well, you always have to say family. Family is the most important thing from that standpoint. Religion is very important, but I'm assuming you are not talking about religion or family, but those two things are very important. Belief is very important, but you would always have to put family as number one.

Next I asked: "You have a very strong bond with your children. What has been the secret of your having such a close relationship with your children and their obvious respect for you?"

> I worked very hard when it came to my children, and one of the things I would tell them all the time is, 'No drugs, no alcohol, no cigarettes.' I have friends who have very smart children. But their children are hooked on drugs or alcohol. I added cigarettes because of the health thing. It's just easier if you don't

smoke. I was lucky enough not to smoke. I have friends that can't get off, and they're strong people, but if you've never started, it's not a problem. That's a big factor, the fact that they're not hooked, but you never know; it's a fragile world, so who knows what happened.

Trump had said the rough-and-tumble campaign and his connecting with Evangelicals had an effect on him, so I asked how the whole political process had changed him spiritually.

Well, I can tell you I've always been spiritual, but I really appreciate the Evangelicals because they really support me. When somebody supports you, you feel pretty good about it.... So I think the fact that I had the tremendous support from the Evangelicals meant a lot to me and will mean a lot to me in the future.

One question asking him what he would say to a Christian crowd showed the confidence we have seen in his first term and how he sees himself. He responded this way:

Well, I'm going to do a great job. I'm going to get the job done. I'm going to do a great job for religion and for Evangelicals. I am going to do a great job, and that's why we got a standing ovation from the pastors who don't give much for standing ovations because they've heard a lot of people speak, so that was a great honor, but I will do a great job. I will get the job done, and I'll get it done properly, and it will be a great thing for the Evangelicals.

THE SPIRITUAL DIMENSION

In my interview I asked a question every Christian believes is important: Does he feel the president needs God's wisdom and guidance, and to whom does he reach out for spiritual counsel?

I have many friends within the community. One of them who's been so incredible is Franklin Graham—he's been amazing, really terrific. So we're close to Franklin. Pastor [Robert] Jeffress has been terrific. Paula White [Cain] has been incredible. So many, so many.

I really like to stay with people who have been loyal because they were here at the beginning when this was very, very little, tiny flame, and they were here when everyone else was saying, "Well, you can't beat seventeen [Republican candidates]."

TRUMP ACCORDING TO TWITTER

If my interview in 2016 wasn't a foreshadowing of the president we would see in the next four years, we got to know him in the tweets he sent out at an average of sixteen a day. I culled through his tweets, which are considered official pronouncements from the president of the United States, to show what he says about several important topics. I am letting what Donald Trump said speak for itself:

His love for the American people

I don't want to Win for myself, I only want to Win for the people. (@realDonaldTrump, August 28, 2019)

Fighting for all Americans

I am doing exactly what I pledged to do, and what I was elected to do by the citizens of our great Country. Just as I promised, I am fighting for YOU! (@realDonaldTrump, January 14, 2019)

Keeping his promises

Together, we are breaking the most sacred rule in Washington Politics: we are KEEPING our promises to the American People. Because my only special interest is YOU! #Trump2020 (@realDonaldTrump, June 18, 2019)

Creating jobs

BIG NEWS! As I promised two weeks ago, the first shipment of LNG has just left the Cameron LNG Export Facility in Louisiana. Not only have thousands of JOBS been created in USA, we're shipping freedom and opportunity abroad! (@realDonaldTrump, June 2, 2019)

Moving the US embassy to Jerusalem

Today marks the one-year anniversary of the opening of the United States Embassy in Jerusalem, Israel. Our beautiful embassy stands as a proud reminder of our strong relationship with Israel and of the importance of keeping a promise and standing for the truth. (@realDonaldTrump, May 14, 2019)

Supporting farmers

Today I am making good on my promise to defend our Farmers & Ranchers from unjustified trade retaliation by foreign nations. I have authorized Secretary Perdue to implement the 2nd round of Market Facilitation Payments. Our economy is stronger than ever—we stand with our Farmers! (@realDonald Trump, December 17, 2018)

The Supreme Court

The Supreme Court is one of the main reasons I got elected President. I hope Republican Voters, and others, are watching, and studying, the Democrats Playbook (@realDonaldTrump, September 18, 2018)

The extremism of progressives

The Dems were trying to distance themselves from the four "progressives," but now they are forced to embrace them [Reps. Ilhan Omar of Minnesota, Alexandria Ocasio-Cortez of New York, Rashida Tlaib of Michigan, and Ayanna Pressley of Massachusetts]. That means they are endorsing Socialism, hate of Israel and the USA! Not good for the Democrats! (@realDonaldTrump, July 15, 2019)

Attacks on law enforcement

In recent days we have heard shameless attacks on our courageous law enforcement officers. Extremist Democrat politicians have called for the complete elimination of ICE. Leftwing Activists are trying to block ICE officers from doing their jobs and publicly posting their...home addresses—putting these selfless public servants in harm's way. These radical protesters want ANARCHY—but the only response they will find from our government is LAW AND ORDER! (@realDonaldTrump, June 27, 2018)

Immigration and the wall

My Administration is acting swiftly to address the illegal immigration crisis on the Southern Border. Loopholes in our immigration laws all supported by extremist open border Democrats...and that's what they are—they're extremist open border Democrats.... (@realDonaldTrump, June 21, 2018)

Protecting America

Democrats want Open Borders and Crime! So dangerous for our Country. But we are building a big, beautiful, NEW Wall! I will protect America, the Dems don't know where to start! (@realDonaldTrump, August 19, 2019)

Being a world leader

The G7 in France was so successful, and yet when I came back and read the Corrupt and Fake News, and watched numerous networks, it was not even recognizable from what actually took place at the Great G7 event! (@realDonaldTrump, August 27, 2019)

Criticism from the media

The question I was asked most today by fellow World Leaders, who think the USA is doing so well and is stronger than ever before, happens to be, "Mr. President, why does the American media hate your Country so much? Why are they rooting for it to fail?" (@realDonaldTrump, August 25, 2019)

Building a strong economy

In the "old days" if you were President and you had a good economy, you were basically immune from criticism. Remember, "It's the economy stupid." Today I have, as President, perhaps the greatest economy in history...and to the Mainstream

Media, it means NOTHING. But it will! (@realDonaldTrump, April 23, 2019)

Media working to create a recession

The Fake News LameStream Media is doing everything pos-sible…[to] "create" a U.S. recession, even though the num-bers & facts are working totally in the opposite direction. They would be willing to hurt many people, but that doesn't matter to them. Our Economy is sooo strong, sorry! (@realDonald Trump, August 21, 2019)

American diplomacy

I got severely criticized by the Fake News Media for being too nice to President Putin. In the Old Days they would call it Diplomacy. If I was loud & vicious, I would have been criticized for being too tough. Remember when they said I was too tough with Chairman Kim? Hypocrites! (@realDonaldTrump, July 20, 2018)

The black vote

So if African-American unemployment is now at the lowest number in history, median income the highest, and you then add all of the other things I have done, how do Democrats, who have done NOTHING for African-Americans but TALK, win the Black Vote? And it will only get better! (@realDonald Trump, September 30, 2018)

Creating opportunity zones

Under the Trump Administration, African American unem-ployment is the lowest (best) in the history of the United States. No President has come close to doing this before! I also created successful Opportunity Zones. Waiting for Nancy and Elijah to say, "Thank you, Mr. President!" (@realDonaldTrump, July 28, 2018)

Negotiating release of American missionary

Turkey has taken advantage of the United States for many years. They are now holding our wonderful Christian Pastor, who I must now ask to represent our Country as a great patriot hostage. We will pay nothing for the release of an innocent man, but we are cutting back on Turkey! (@realDonaldTrump, August 16, 2018)

Religious persecution

Christians in the Middle-East have been executed in large numbers. We cannot allow this horror to continue! (@real DonaldTrump, January 29, 2017)

Promoting religious freedom around the world

This week, my Administration is hosting the first-ever #IRFMinisterial. The U.S. will continue to promote #ReligiousFreedom around the world. Nations that support religious freedom are far more free, prosperous & peaceful. Great job, @VP, @SecPompeo, @IRF_Ambassador & @StateDept! (@realDonaldTrump, July 25, 2018)

Praying for the nation

On this day of prayer, we once again place our hopes in the hands of our Creator. We give thanks for this wondrous land of liberty, & we pray that THIS nation—OUR home—these United States—will forever be strengthened by the Goodness and the Grace & the eternal GLORY OF GOD! (@realDonald Trump, May 2, 2019)

Faith in public life

As we unite on this day of prayer, we renew our resolve to protect communities of faith—and ensure that ALL of our people can live, pray and worship IN PEACE. #NationalDayOfPrayer (@realDonaldTrump, May 2, 2019)

Tenacity in the face of adversity

Adversity is a fact of life. Be bigger than the problems, be ready to fight for your rights, & all will be well—Trump Never Give Up (@realDonaldTrump, July 17, 2014)

Millions of words have been written about the president. (And I've written a few of them myself!) But rarely is the spiritual dimension mentioned, though it is the most important dimension of all. The secular community doesn't understand it, and many Christians are oblivious to what God is saying. Yet in the next section we will look at prophecies about Donald Trump, analogies to him in Scripture, and even signs in the heavens—things the president himself may not even know—in order to understand the spiritual dimension of Trump's presidency.

PART III

UNDERSTANDING THE SPIRITUAL DIMENSION

CHAPTER 10

IS DONALD TRUMP FORESHADOWED IN THE BIBLE?

In the long sweep of Jewish history, there have been a handful of proclamations by non-Jewish leaders on behalf of our people in our land: Cyrus the Great, the great Persian King; Lord Balfour; President Harry S. Truman; and President Donald J. Trump.[1]
—BENJAMIN NETANYAHU
PRIME MINISTER OF ISRAEL

EVANGELICAL CHRISTIANS BELIEVE the Bible is God's plan for mankind. But is it possible that ancient figures in Scripture foreshadow leaders of our own day—revealing what they do and when they rise and fall, even down to the exact timing of dates?

Even more incredible, did a solar eclipse to be discussed in the next chapter herald the birth of Donald Trump and even foreshadow the founding of the State of Israel? I can't say for certain, but the evidence I gathered from Christian leaders may give us a peek into the spiritual dimension of what is happening in our day.

I was surprised when during the 2016 presidential campaign I began hearing comparisons between this political outsider named Donald Trump and Cyrus the ancient Persian king who, although never a true follower of the Hebrew God, declared that the Lord God of heaven charged him to build Him a house in Jerusalem—the temple.[2]

The Scripture says in Isaiah 45, "Thus says the LORD to Cyrus, His anointed…I have even called you by your name; I have named you, though you have not known Me."[3] In other words, God used a pagan king to accomplish His purposes.

Can the same be said of Donald Trump? Did God raise him up as He did King Cyrus to accomplish His purposes?

I've been following politics for a long time. I still remember going with my dad to see Richard Nixon speak at a rally in Tampa, Florida, during his 1968 presidential campaign. Years later I saw Jimmy Carter visit the newspaper where I worked in Orlando, and I was in the room when Reagan gave his famous "evil empire" speech at the National Association of Evangelicals conference in 1983. Yet in all the years I've been observing politics, I've never heard of any political candidates—Republican or Democratic—being compared to biblical figures. The one exception is Harry Truman, who referred to himself as Cyrus during a speech to a Jewish group after the United States recognized Israel as a sovereign nation.

But since his election Donald Trump has been compared to several biblical figures, not only to Cyrus. Why?

To understand whether God has raised up President Trump, you must first believe in God. Then you must understand that He has ruled over all the earth since the beginning of time and that He reveals Himself to mankind in His holy Word, which we call the Bible.

In the Bible and its stories of ancient people, there are mysteries that help unlock an understanding of how God is working. Of course this isn't always easy to see. There's a New Testament scripture that even says, "Now we see through a glass, darkly,"[4] meaning we don't always understand what we can't clearly see. But as I saw more and more parallels between Trump and certain biblical figures, I began to see more clearly their prophetic significance.

IS TRUMP A MODERN CYRUS?

As I've written before, it was helpful to me to hear other leaders use Cyrus, the pagan Persian king, as an example of how God raised up a nonbeliever to accomplish His plans and purposes in the Old Testament. One of those leaders was Israeli prime minister Benjamin Netanyahu, who likened the US president to Cyrus in 2019 before meeting Trump in the Oval Office.[5] In fact Netanyahu has made several statements associating Trump with King Cyrus, one of which I quoted at the beginning of this chapter.

The comparison was even solidified by the Mikdash Educational Center, a Jewish organization that minted a "temple coin" bearing an image of President Trump, alongside an image of King Cyrus, to honor Trump's recognition of Jerusalem as Israel's capital. One thousand copies of the coin, which also mentions the Balfour Declaration, were minted. A second coin in the Cyrus-Trump series has been released as well. The coins can't be used as currency, but you can buy one with a donation.

Jonathan Cahn, the author of *The Harbinger*, also sees a connection. He said, "Trump's proclamation concerning Jerusalem holds striking parallels to the decree of the Persian king Cyrus as recorded in the Bible." He went on to explain that "each proclamation recognizes the right of the Jewish people to the land of Israel. The result of Cyrus' decree was the rebuilding of Jerusalem after seventy years. The result of Trump's decree was the inauguration of the American embassy in Jerusalem after seventy years of Israel's existence—to the exact day."

Cahn also sees significance in Trump becoming president at age seventy. As we will see in the next chapter, many Christians perceive meaning in the pattern of the number seventy in Trump's presidency that correlates to scriptural passages. In his latest book, *The Oracle*, Cahn explains that Donald Trump moved the US embassy from Tel Aviv to Jerusalem exactly seventy years from when the Jewish state was formed. Seventy years was also the length of the Jewish exile foretold by Jeremiah, who wrote: "For thus says the LORD: *After seventy years* are completed at Babylon, I will…perform My good word toward you, and cause you to return."[6]

The prophecy was fulfilled when Cyrus became king of Persia exactly seventy years after the exile. And according to Cahn, the separation of the newborn Jewish state from Jerusalem and the world's refusal to grant Israel legal recognition of its ancient capital was a type of exile ended by Trump. As I mentioned previously, President Harry Truman, who recognized Israel soon after its birth was announced in 1948, even referred to himself as Cyrus because he encouraged the Jewish diaspora to return home.[7] Raised going to Sunday school, Truman knew the prophecies that the Jewish people would one day return to their homeland. So if Trump is also like Cyrus, the two Cyruses frame the seventy years of Israel's existence.

In *The Oracle*, Cahn elaborates:

> And when [President Trump] issued that declaration, he made special mention of another president. He spoke of the other Cyrus, Harry Truman. And his declaration contained the phrase that would link the modern declaration to the ancient—the phrase *seventy years*. He said this: "It was 70 years ago that the United States, under President Truman, recognized

the State of Israel." So the proclamation itself makes note that the proclamation is itself going forth at the end of a seventy-year period.[8]

The Oracle is one of the most amazing books I've ever read. As Cahn wrote in a recent *Charisma* article, the book reveals a three-thousand-year-old mystery that "lies behind the rise and fall of nations—including America—world wars, the resurrection of Israel, events that take place in the highest chambers of power, from ancient palaces to Capitol Hill, the changes and transformations that are taking place in our culture and much more. It has affected and continues to affect each of our lives."[9] I'd like to say more about the book, but to fully understand the mysteries it reveals, including the Jubilean mysteries around which the return and restoration of Israel have manifested, you must read it for yourself!

Cahn has an uncanny ability to see patterns in the Bible that have prophetic significance for today. His first book, *The Harbinger*, showed parallels between the disaster of 9/11 and Isaiah 9:10, an obscure scripture that says: "The bricks are fallen down, but we will build with hewn stones; the sycamores are cut down, but we will replace them with cedars." Revealing a pattern of God's judgment that was manifesting in the US, *The Harbinger* is an earth-shattering book that became an instant *New York Times* best seller and brought Cahn to national and international prominence.

Described as the prophetic voice of our generation, Cahn leads a large congregation in Wayne, New Jersey, called The Jerusalem Center/Beth Israel and speaks in diverse places, from the United Nations to Mar-a-Lago. I'm proud to call Cahn a close friend and to also be his publisher. *The Harbinger* has been the best-selling book my company has ever published, and it has spawned other popular books, including *The Paradigm*. Here, Cahn found in the Old Testament comparisons between contemporary and ancient leaders, including between two couples: the wicked King Ahab and his pagan wife, Jezebel, and Bill and Hillary Clinton. In Christian prophetic circles, preachers like to use Jezebel to represent any evil, but never before *The Paradigm* had anyone shown the parallels between Ahab and Jezebel and Bill and Hillary Clinton in such a detailed way.

But Cahn does not stop there. He goes on to show parallels between Bible characters and other leaders, including Barack Obama. The Clintons and Obama won't be running against Trump in 2020, so you might be asking yourself why this matters in a book about the upcoming election. It matters because the timing of each leader's emergence on the national stage and his or her rise to prominence matches the parallels from Israel's history that Cahn uncovers in his book. And all of it leads up to Donald Trump.

UNEARTHING ANCIENT MYSTERIES

Even for those who pay attention to prophecy and believe the Bible reveals God's plan for mankind, Cahn's insights are remarkable. In *The Paradigm*, Cahn unearths a "master blueprint" in the Old Testament that foreshadows modern events, even the rise and fall of leaders and governments. The interesting thing is that this ancient paradigm, as Cahn calls it, might have "determined not only the events of modern times but also their timing—even down to the exact dates." He believes this mystery has foretold "the outcomes of current events more accurately than any poll or expert—even the outcomes of presidential elections"— and that it may even reveal what will happen in the future. He says it holds "a warning critical for every person of this generation."

To understand what all this means, we must consider what Cahn writes in *The Paradigm*. Laying out his belief that the patterns he sees in the Bible are part of a larger picture that is much bigger than any comparisons to modern-day leaders, he writes that *The Paradigm* "is also the revealing of a warning to a nation and a civilization concerning its present course and the ultimate end of that course."

Cahn explains that the book deals with the political realm, but it is not a political message. Rather, he sees it as spiritual and prophetic. "If one is to see its revelations, one must, before going forward, put away all preconceptions and presumptions, all politics and related opinions and judgments. One must approach it with complete openness, especially if one is unfamiliar with or alien to that which is scriptural," he continued.[10]

The story of Israel in the Bible is the story of God revealing Himself to man, Israel following God, and then Israel falling away from God. After the time of Kings David and Solomon, it is a story of both righteous and apostate kings who led Israel to either follow or turn away from God.

By the time Ahab became king, Israel had divided into the northern kingdom of Israel, which included ten of the twelve tribes and was called Israel or sometimes Ephraim in Scripture, and the southern kingdom, which was called Judah, even though it also included the tribe of Benjamin.

If you follow the biblical account, Israel was carried into captivity first, and its ten tribes were ultimately "lost." Later Judah was carried into captivity in Babylon. Then, after seventy years, King Cyrus allowed them to return to Jerusalem to rebuild the temple. The term Jew comes from Judah and is used to this day.

But to understand Trump's significance in this hour of history, we must focus on wicked King Ahab, who married Jezebel, daughter of the king of the Sidonians. Because of Jezebel's influence, Ahab built a house to Baal, the god of his wife's people, in the capital city of Samaria and made an Asherah pole to use for pagan worship. Scripture says, Ahab "did more to provoke the LORD, God of Israel to anger than all the kings of Israel who preceded him."[11]

So how does this relate to Bill and Hillary Clinton? Cahn wrote that just as King Ahab rose to power during a time of deep national apostasy and stood at the front of a culture war that championed anti-biblical values, so did Bill Clinton, who became the first US president to champion abortion and homosexuality and led the nation at a time when the term *culture war* was just entering the public discourse.

Add to that the fact that Ahab was the first king in his nation's history to rule in a type of partnership with his wife, Jezebel. Cahn noted that Jezebel influenced her husband, was viewed as an opponent to traditional and biblical values, and was seen as having a harsher temperament than her husband. She was also ambitious to gain her own political power and was disliked by many in her nation. Sounds a lot like Hillary Clinton.

"Hillary Clinton has long been seen as an opponent of traditional and biblical values," Cahn wrote. "In terms of temperament, she was always viewed as the harder of the two. She would be unique in being the first presidential wife ambitious to acquire her own political power and would be distrusted by much of her nation."[12]

Jezebel was the first queen in Israel to share power with the king, and similarly Hillary Clinton is considered the most powerful first lady in history. After Ahab was removed from the throne by being killed in a battle with Syria (called the Arameans in some translations), Jezebel continued in power. Same with Hillary. She continued in power after her husband left the political scene, first as a US senator, then as secretary of state, and finally as a presidential candidate.

Jezebel's worship of Baal included child sacrifice, something completely abhorrent to Judaism, which values life and teaches that all life comes from God, the Creator of life. Hillary Clinton has been arguably the loudest advocate for abortion of any American politician. Conservative Christians who consider abortion murder have long compared it with the sacrifice of children, but in modern times these sacrifices are not made to a stone idol but for the convenience of the mother or on the altar of political correctness.

The Paradigm is fascinating reading because Cahn finds so many interesting parallels between ancient and modern times. For example, the length of Ahab's reign was twenty-two years. From the time Bill Clinton became governor of Arkansas to the end of his presidency is also twenty-two years. Jezebel's time on the public stage totaled thirty-six years. From the time Bill Clinton was governor until his wife bowed out of public life in 2017 (not including two she was a private citizen) was also thirty-six years. Like Jezebel, Hillary spent twenty-two years in power with her husband and fourteen years leading by herself.

Then there comes the story an outsider named Jehu, who fulfills prophecy and rids Israel of Jezebel and the House of Ahab. He is uncouth, yet he is the one who returns Israel to worship the one true God. Do you see any parallels to Donald Trump?

Jehu was a commander of King Ahab's army. His divine call, according to Scripture, was to be a reformer of sorts who was used by God to clean up the mess Ahab had made. Similarly, Trump is a fighter who promised to reform Washington and "drain the swamp" as president.

As ruthless as Jehu was, leaving things as they were would have meant the end of Israel because the Israelites would have abandoned the true God to worship pagan idols. Had Jehu not killed those who followed Baal, the Jewish people would have ceased to exist. The Bible would have been forgotten, Jesus would not have been born, and there would be no Christianity.

I believe Trump's presidency is just as critical to our nation's future. Yes, this president is unconventional. But like Jehu, he has brought needed reforms that have helped preserve our nation and our freedoms.

FORESHADOWING EVANGELICAL SUPPORT OF TRUMP

Cahn points out in *The Paradigm* that Trump could not have become president had it not been for the conservative Christian (evangelical) vote. Cahn sees in the biblical narrative a parallel to the Evangelicals—a holy man named Jehonadab, who was a mysterious figure Jehu encountered on his way to Samaria. Little is said of him. Then, hundreds of years later, we hear of Jehonadab in the Book of Jeremiah, where he is described as "a godly man, a leader, an ascetic, a holy man."[13] Here was a man who was remembered centuries after his lifetime because of his moral code.

Beyond connecting Evangelicals as a group to Jehonadab, Cahn writes that among the religious conservatives who joined Trump in his campaign, there was "one whom Trump asked to be his partner in the race, to ride with him to the throne. It was Mike Pence. Pence was a religious conservative. He defined himself as a Christian first, a conservative second, and a Republican third. He was well respected, a leader known for his virtue. Though of course imperfect, just as was Jehonadab, Pence had a reputation for piety and holiness."

Cahn goes on to write: "As Jehu knew that Jehonadab's partnership would help give legitimacy to his campaign and help convince the holy man's people to support him, so Trump knew that Pence's partnership would help give legitimacy to his campaign and help convince religious conservatives across the country to support him.

"As a man of God living in the midst of apostasy, [Jehonadab] would have been praying for his nation's revival," Cahn explained. "He would have hoped that in Jehu was a chance to stop or slow Israel's spiritual descent and perhaps even help turn the nation back to God." Can you see here the parallel with today's Evangelicals, who advocate holy living, and their embrace of Donald Trump, a man known for being uncouth? It's as Gov. Mike Huckabee wrote in his foreword to *God and Donald Trump*: there's no question Trump was never one of us.[14] For the past half century, Evangelicals have watched as the general Christian values we took for granted in America were stripped away. While America has never been truly godly by biblical standards, there was an underpinning of Judeo-Christian values, and even as these eroded in the general culture and later through Supreme Court decisions, there was still a facade that maybe things weren't as bad as they appeared. But as same-sex marriage was legalized and it seemed almost anything went in entertainment and online, these conservative Christians watched in horror as things seemed to go from bad to worse.

On top of that Hillary Clinton seemed to embody everything conservative Christians abhorred. Raised a Methodist, she shed those values for those of community organizer and socialist Saul Alinsky, whom she wrote about glowingly in a ninety-two-page senior thesis for Wellesley College. By the time she ran for president, she had become a proponent of same-sex marriage (something she opposed only a few years before) and also of abortion up to the time of birth. Both of these were the modern-day equivalent of Baal worship. And while Donald Trump was no saint, at least he opposed many of the things evangelical Christians opposed.

So it was with Jehu, who was used by God but was hardly godly. Cahn writes, "Those faithful to God will have to deal with the nature and ways of the warrior versus the promise of his reign. They will wonder if such a person could be used for the purposes of God. So too religious conservatives and evangelicals would be torn over Donald Trump. His actions and ways would prove troubling. They would wonder if someone who showed little evidence of having known God could be used for God's purposes."[15]

But with Jehu, the concerns of the people of God gave way to a hope that the warrior would be used as an instrument to stop or at least slow the nation's descent. They would see in him, even with all their concerns, the only alternative to a future of progressive apostasy and godlessness.

Trump was again likened to an Old Testament figure in March 2019 when US Secretary of State Mike Pompeo agreed with a comparison of Trump to the biblical Queen Esther. Chris Mitchell, CBN News Middle East bureau chief, asked Pompeo, "Could it be that President Trump right now has been sort of raised for such a time as this, just like Queen Esther, to help save the Jewish people from the Iranian menace?"

Pompeo, who was in Israel at the time, replied: "As a Christian, I certainly believe that's possible. It was remarkable—so we were down in the tunnels where we could see 3,000 years ago, and 2,000 years ago—if I have the history just right—to see the remarkable history of the faith in this place and the work that our administration's done to make sure that this democracy in the Middle East, that this Jewish state remains. I am confident that the Lord is at work here."[16]

I agree that just as Esther was put in the right place at the right time to save Israel from destruction, so might President Trump have been raised up to defend Israel and the Jewish people from the threat of Iran.

While most people reading this are Christians, even believers often don't understand that God can use someone who is not a Christian to accomplish His will.

R. T. Kendall, a respected theologian and pastor, once explained that God accomplishes this through what is called "common grace"—God's goodness to all humankind. Kendall explained that common grace was behind Cyrus' surprising decision to release the Jews from Babylonian captivity, and to Kendall this is a plausible explanation for why Donald Trump could also be used by God.[17] Kendall told me that God always raises up an unlikely leader and gives that person unmatched favor to stand against evil, conspiracy, and deceit in order to protect His people and provide unusual blessings during times of struggle.

THE DIVINE WRECKING BALL

Donald Trump is in many ways an enigma. His critics, even some Evangelicals, seem to dissect him in a way they did not scrutinize previous politicians. For example, no one generally noticed how often Barack Obama went to church; Trump is criticized for seldom attending a service, even though he has surrounded himself with Christian leaders who pray with him and speak to him about spiritual things.

Prolific author and radio show host Michael L. Brown, PhD, spoke out about the dilemma Evangelicals face with Donald Trump in a book titled *Donald Trump Is Not My Savior*. In my opinion Brown is one of the most articulate spokesmen for conservative Christianity, so I found it significant he put his name on such a book. The subtitle gives away what the book is all about: "An Evangelical Leader Speaks His Mind About the Man He Supports as President." It's his odyssey—documented in eighty-five op-eds written from August 2015 to August 2018—from being a strong supporter of Ted Cruz and a critic of Trump to reluctantly supporting him to being amazed at how he has kept his promises.

Yet he raises questions evangelical Christians must grapple with.

"First, Donald Trump did not die for our sins," he writes in the introduction. "Consequently, the allegiance we have to Jesus must be infinitely greater than the allegiance we have to the president. We cannot allow our loyalty to President Trump to compromise our loyalty to Jesus. Our greatest priority is to maintain our witness before a watching world."[18]

He goes on to say that at the same time, with important cultural issues, Trump will do a better job than the other side. And Brown is critical of the media who claim Franklin Graham is losing his credibility because he supports President Trump when they rejected Graham's moral and spiritual views in the past.

But mostly Brown points his pen at Evangelicals to say we must stand for biblical principles and support Trump when he backs those truths. But we must also be willing to criticize the president.

"I absolutely believe President Trump has been a divine wrecking ball. He is wreaking havoc on the political status quo. He is breaking the traditional rules. He is exposing the extraordinary bias of the liberal media and the radical core of the Democratic Party. Some would say he is [their] worst nightmare," Brown wrote.

"Yet a wrecking ball swings back and forth, and I believe President Trump has also exposed some weaknesses (and more) in our evangelical circles. Have we refrained from any criticism so we can keep our seat at the table? Have we ignored major character issues to preserve our political power? Have we become more identified publicly with our President than with our Savior? Have we confused patriotism with the kingdom of God?"[19]

I found Brown's book to be an interesting read because it was tied in real time to events as they happened since he wrote the chapters as blogs over a period of three years. He rushed the book out before the midterm elections in 2018, and it ends on a hopeful note: "When it comes to President Trump, I do believe he has been raised up as a significant 21st century leader, but as a divine wrecking ball, accomplishing much good (with the potential of even more good in the coming years) but with many unneeded casualties.

"We do well as evangelical followers of Jesus (and others of like mind) to respect [Trump's] office, to encourage him to do right, to support him however we can, but not to identify ourselves primarily as followers of (or defenders of) Trump.…He is our president, and as such, one of the most powerful men in the world. Let's not scorn him; let's not glorify him; and by all means, let's not give up on him," Brown wrote.

While most people's perceptions are informed by the media, academia, and pop culture, evangelical Christians must base their worldview on the Bible. Even with the spiritual divide in our nation that has lasted four decades, nearly a third of the nation shares my worldview. They might not express it as I do, but their Christian faith lets them know something is seriously wrong. On a daily basis they witness the craziness of a culture that seems to be spinning out of control, and they know there are unseen forces at work. Yet there is hope. We believe God is in control, and He still speaks today. And He sends us signs in the heavens, if only we have eyes to see, as I document in the next chapter.

CHAPTER 11

PROPHECIES AND SIGNS IN THE HEAVENS

*The longer I live, the more convincing proofs I see of this
truth—that God governs in the affairs of men.[1]*
—BENJAMIN FRANKLIN (1706–1790)
AMERICAN STATESMAN, REQUESTING PRAYER
AT CONSTITUTIONAL CONVENTION, 1787

A S WE APPROACH the 2020 election, there are Christian leaders who have prophesied that Donald Trump is going to win. It is an untold story of prophecies and spiritual signs that is off the radar screen of the secular media, which would never cover it except to ridicule. Yet many Christians believe God still actively guides us not only through the Bible, as we examined in the last chapter, but through the Holy Spirit and spiritual gifts.

As technology advances and the culture becomes more hedonistic and secular, the question of spirituality is increasingly left out of the public square. It's OK within the walls of the church, but even there the focus seems to be on personal faith and comfort, not understanding God's plans and purposes. Does God have a plan? And if so, whose god and what plan? No one seems to know, and when those who do dare to speak out disagree, confusion reigns and what they say is largely ignored.

Yet America is at a crossroads, not unlike the fledgling nation was when the Articles of Confederation failed and it seemed that forming a new constitution would be impossible. It was then that an aged Benjamin Franklin, one of the most influential Founding Fathers (who was also known to live a self-centered and hedonistic lifestyle), made one of the most memorable speeches in American history—the effects of which might have shifted the course of the Constitutional Convention.

When he saw the divisions that kept the delegates groping in the dark for a solution, he made the profound observation I quoted at the beginning of this chapter: "I have lived, Sir, a long time and the longer

I live, the more convincing proofs I see of this truth—*that God governs in the affairs of men.*"[2] Calling for daily prayers that the Constitutional Convention would be successful, Franklin went on to say:

> If a sparrow cannot fall to the ground without his notice, is it probable that an empire can rise without his aid? We have been assured, Sir, in the sacred writings, that "except the Lord build the House they labour in vain that build it." I firmly believe this; and I also believe that without his concurring aid we shall succeed in this political building no better, than the Builders of Babel: We shall be divided by our little partial local interests; our projects will be confounded, and we ourselves shall become a reproach and bye word down to future ages. And what is worse, mankind may hereafter from this unfortunate instance, despair of establishing Governments by Human Wisdom and leave it to chance, war and conquest.[3]

Franklin's imploring words remain eerily relevant in 2020 as the nation seems to struggle not only between Right and Left but between right and wrong. Does God govern in the affairs of men? For those who believe the Bible and think America was founded on Christian principles, the question takes on utmost importance. Outside of the public eye, and ignored by the media, academia, and government, many are praying things will change. To them it's a spiritual fight for the future of America.

Two hundred thirty-two years after Franklin's request an appeal from Franklin Graham and more than 250 evangelical leaders for Christians to pray in June 2019 reflected how many evangelical Christians felt about the state of American culture and about President Donald J. Trump. There's an awareness, the appeal noted, that "our nation is at a crossroads, at a dangerous precipice. The only one who can fix our nation's problems is God Himself, and we pray that God will bless our president and our nation for His glory."[4]

The son of the famous evangelist Billy Graham had written to Christian leaders asking them to help promote a Day of Prayer for President Donald J. Trump. "The onslaught from the President's enemies is unbelievable. In the history of our country, no president has been attacked as he has. The lies and the deceptions rage on," he wrote. "I want the President to know, and to feel, and to understand that the prayers of millions of people are behind him. My prayer is that President Trump will know and understand the power of God in a new way and that he will seek His face as he leads this nation to greatness with God's help."[5]

The appeal articulated what many Christians believe: "We know that God hears and answers prayer. God can soften hearts and change minds. He is all-powerful, and He rules over the affairs of nations. The Bible instructs us to pray for those in authority, 'that we may lead a quiet and peaceable life in all godliness and reverence. For this is good and acceptable in the sight of God our Savior' (1 Timothy 2:2–3, NKJV)."[6]

Most Americans are aware that our nation is deeply divided, and the campaign season for the 2020 election is bringing that to light as never before. Most pundits would say it's between conservatives and liberals or maybe between progressive leftists and constitutional conservatives on the right. But all see it in academic or secular terms.

Many Christians believe in the existence of modern-day prophets— people with a spiritual gift enabling them to tell others what God is saying. Therefore, it's no surprise that when various prophets have said God has raised up Donald Trump, many believe it's true. So what are these prophecies, and why should we even pay attention to them? Could God be speaking to us today, and does He still have plans and purposes for America?

Since I know many of these prophets and have reported on them and what they say from the Lord, I have tried to document them in various ways, including in the books I've written. I understand the reasons that some of you might be skeptical or totally disagree. For one, some prophecies are obscure or mostly symbolic. Add to this that the prophets sometimes seem to be wrong and that prophecies given in earlier times just weren't documented unless written down at the time.

I believe we can overcome these concerns, in part because of modern technology and the fact so many church services where prophetic words are given are now recorded and available online. This gives us a chance to evaluate them after the fact and to try to understand what's happening from a spiritual perspective. I believe there is a spiritual significance to the tumultuous times in which we live, because there were several prophecies spanning several years about Donald Trump's election. And they came to pass!

The number of prophecies about Donald Trump, many of which have gone viral, is one of the reasons Trump received so much

support from the Christian community, especially Charismatics and
Pentecostals. Not only is Trump a champion of religious freedom who
is keeping his promises, but there is also a sense that somehow, some
way, God is behind this real estate developer from Queens.

One of the most talked about prophecies on YouTube, viewed by
more than 1.2 million people (yet virtually ignored by the media), is by
the late Kim Clement. In 2007 he prophesied in a service in Redding,
California, that "Trump shall become a trumpet." Even more startling,
he said at a service in Scottsdale, Arizona: "God says, I will put at your
helm for two terms a president that will pray."

Other than the mention of the trumpet, there is no specific reference to Donald Trump. Only in hindsight have people latched on to
this video as a prophecy about Trump and passed it around.

I first met Kim Clement in the late 1990s, so I knew his story. He
moved to the United States from South Africa, where he had been
trained to be a classical pianist and later played in a rock band.
Surviving a heroin overdose caused him to become a Christian in 1974.
Gradually as he grew in his faith and ministry, he developed a reputation as a seer, a prophet. In Charismatic worship services he would
often accompany himself on the keyboards and sing or preach his
prophecies. (Unless you were raised a Pentecostal, this form of worship may seem odd.) A sort of mystic, Clement would often shake his
head of long, dark hair as he spoke or sang.

This resulted in a very heavy "atmosphere" in the service—an almost
palpable presence of God—and most people in the room seemed to
believe that God really was speaking through Clement.

In Scottsdale in 2007 Clement also prophesied: "There will be a
praying president, not a religious one. For I will fool the people, says
the Lord. I will fool the people. Yes, I will. God says, the one that is
chosen shall go in and they shall say, 'He has hot blood.' For the Spirit
of God says, yes, he may have hot blood, but he will bring the walls of
protection on this country in a greater way and the economy of this
country shall change rapidly, says the Lord of hosts."

Only in hindsight can we notice what he said about the president
having "hot blood" or building walls of protection or helping the
economy boom apply to Trump. But most interesting of all is that
Clement said, "Listen to the Word of the Lord, God says, I will put at
your helm *for two terms* a president that will pray, but he will not be a
praying president when he starts."[7]

Seven years later, on February 22, 2014, more than a year before Trump announced he would run for president, Clement prophesied that God had allowed a veil to be put on this nation, "for in darkness faith grows." He went on to say he found a man after his own heart like King David who would be singled out for the presidency of the United States. Clement continued: "I have searched for a man... who would stand in the Oval Office and pray... for the restoration of the fortunes of Zion [Israel].... Watch how I change everything, for there shall be those who are in justice, and there are those who are in a strong position (I am just hearing this now) in the highest court in the land. The highest court in the land. The Supreme Court. Two shall step down. For the embarrassment of what shall take place. But I wish to place in the highest court in the land, righteousness. And they shall attempt to put others in to reach their endeavors. But God says, 'Hear Me tonight. Hear Me today. I have this whole thing planned out, according to My will.'"[8]

For many conservative Christians who feel their nation is deteriorating before their eyes, such words bring hope. Even if they don't know whether to believe, they want to.

In the same meeting Clement shared a recent vision he'd had where he saw a group of people, and a man emerged from among them that he sensed God had singled out for the presidency of the United States: "And the Spirit of God... said, This man will throttle the enemies of Israel. This man will throttle the enemies of the West. And there are highly embarrassing moments that are about to occur for many, many politicians in this nation. There will be a shaking amongst, there will be a shaking amongst the Democrats in the upcoming elections, but unsettling for the Republicans."

Then he asks rhetorically, "Why is God doing this? For God said, I am dissatisfied with what emerges from both parties."

> And then there is a nation He showed me, He took me, itching for a new kind of war with America. They will shout, Impeach! Impeach, they say. But nay. This nation shall come very suddenly, but it shall not come in the time of President Obama. It shall come when this new one arises. My David, that I have set aside for this nation... They will shout, Impeach, impeach! But this shall not happen....
>
> God says, Once you recognize the man that I have raised up,

> pray. For the enemy will do everything in his power to put a witch in the White House....For Jezebel has chased away the prophets and even Elijah. Now I have said, Go back. For this shall be dismantled so that there will be no more corruption in the White House, says the Spirit.

Clement said more, and not all of it has come to pass. But to me it's interesting that between these two prophecies he touched on most of the significant issues at stake during Trump's presidency, and he uttered specific words about Trump that have come true.

For those who are wondering, Kim suffered a stroke in 2015 and passed away in November 2016, the same month Trump was elected. So there is no way someone could have recorded him saying these things after they played out during Trump's presidency and predated the prophecies to look as if he said them in advance. Both prophetic words were given before Trump had even announced he was running for office.

WHAT THE SPIRIT IS SAYING

Kim Clement is not the only prophet who predicted Trump would win. Chuck Pierce, a respected Charismatic prophet from Denton, Texas, prophesied in 2008 that America would have to learn to play "the Trump card." Only later did he begin to believe that the word from the Lord referred to Donald Trump.

Ohio Pastor Frank Amedia, who gave Trump a written "word" during the 2016 campaign that he would become president (which I describe in *God and Donald Trump*[9]), was the first one I remember saying strongly Trump would win.

Later, Lance Wallnau, a best-selling author, strategist, futurist, and communicator whom *USA Today* called one of three evangelical leaders to accurately predict Donald Trump's presidency from the moment he began his campaign, said in 2016 he believed Trump was the "chaos candidate" who would be "a wrecking ball to the spirit of political correctness."[10]

In 2011 a retired fireman from Central Florida named Mark Taylor was another one of the first to publicly say Trump would win. He later wrote a best-selling book with Mary Colbert titled *The Trump Prophecies*, which was made into a movie called *The Trump Prophecy*. Now he's predicting Trump will easily win reelection.

In the run-up to the 2016 election when it looked impossible Trump could beat Hillary Clinton, I knew about these prophecies, and because I believe God speaks today to those who will listen to His voice, I was hoping against hope they were right. Now, as we undergo another election cycle, it's comforting to hear people prophesy that God has a plan and that Trump will win a second term.

But as Taylor told me, that doesn't mean we can be complacent. "It doesn't mean we need to get lackadaisical with things, because we need to do our part. Go out and vote."

SIGNS IN THE HEAVENS

This November we will see whether Christians will get out and vote and whether these prophets were accurate. Meanwhile others have seen signs in the heavens that are too much of a coincidence to ignore. Again, these messages were broadcast on YouTube, this time from Steve Cioccolanti, a Charismatic pastor from Melbourne, Australia, who has written and preached about numerical patterns in the Bible and what they mean.[11]

Many Christians believe the Bible places a certain importance to the number seven—as in seven days for God to create the world. In Christian lingo it's the number of perfection. Cioccolanti sees numbers and patterns that correlate with Trump's life.

When Trump was born, on June 14, 1946, it was exactly *seven hundred* days later that Israel was reborn, on May 14, 1948. On Trump's first full day in office he was *seventy years, seven months, and seven days*. Not only that, he was inaugurated in the Hebrew year *5777*. And Trump beat Hillary Clinton by *seventy-seven* electoral votes (because seven electors defected).

Cioccolanti discovered that exactly seven months after Trump's first full day in office there was a total solar eclipse over the US continent. The path of totality was exclusively in the US, and that hasn't happened since 1776. On top of that, Trump's birth date, June 14, 1946, was a blood moon. And the midpoint of his first term, January 20, 2019, was a blood moon.

"These astronomical signs are just beyond coincidence," Cioccolanti said on my podcast, which is online. "The convergence of all these signs really tells us we're in a very special time of prophetic fulfillment. We have a special man in the White House, whom we should pray for." Then the pastor opined: "And that's why we see such darkness coming around him and trying to attack him in every way possible."[12]

I found out about Cioccolanti when my wife sent me a YouTube link to the sermon he preached about this that garnered more than a million views in just a few weeks. I contacted him to ask for a podcast interview about the prophetic connection between Trump and these blood moons. Cioccolanti sees such a significant connection between Trump's presidency and these lunar eclipses that he's actually started calling them "Trump blood moons." He says we as Christians must not pursue astrology, but God certainly uses astronomical signs at times to confirm prophecy, such as the Star of Bethlehem, which confirmed the timing of Messiah's birth.

Not only was there a blood moon the night of Trump's birth, but there was also one during his run for presidency and yet another one at the midpoint of his first term. "They're symmetric, and they keep pointing to Trump," he said.

Interestingly enough, Cioccolanti started talking about Trump before he even became the Republican nominee. The pastor noticed that in Old Testament prophecy, the Lord often played on words to communicate prophetic truths.

"So I said, 'Wouldn't it be poetic, wouldn't it be prophetic if God did that with Trump?'" Cioccolanti said. "First Corinthians 15 says that at the last *trump*, the dead in Christ will rise as a sign of the end times. I certainly never meant he would be a physical trumpet or that he would fulfill that sign, but I like to say that God drops hints like that."

As he continued to teach and think on this, Cioccolanti felt convinced it was God's will to vote for Trump, even though he is from Australia. In fact he made a prediction that Trump would win the presidency before he was even nominated as the Republican candidate.[13]

The secular mindset may not even understand or care what this means, but for those who are trying to see God's hand in the world today, such "coincidences" are huge and are talked about in Christian circles even if the larger culture is oblivious to them.

Since I had reported many of these prophecies in print and online and made them central in my previous two books, I expected some negative reactions, if not from the secular press, then from the Christians who believe prophecies ended when the Bible was written. Surprisingly I got very little pushback. When the left-leaning political website *Politico* reviewed *God and Donald Trump*, instead of ridiculing me for giving any credence to such things, the writer said the book was a glimpse into the evangelical subculture, where such things are accepted.[14]

Within the evangelical Christian community, we look for significance in a time when the Judeo-Christian values we took for granted are being relegated to the trash heap of historical irrelevance by secularists, many of whom don't even believe in God.

So it's powerful to hear of these documented examples of God speaking and to see examples in the Bible of how God raised up leaders, most of whom were imperfect, allowing Christians to rationalize how God would use an imperfect vessel like Donald Trump. This is the point I made when interviewed on CNN, MSNBC, and other secular outlets.

One story in the epilogue to my book *God and Donald Trump* took readers by surprise. I wrote about a Catholic "holy man" who made a prediction about Donald Trump in the 1980s. I was asked about the story many times by interviewers who wanted to know if it was true.

The Catholic holy man was Tom Zimmer, an American World War II vet who lived more than thirty years in Italy so he could pray and attend mass many times a day, first at the Vatican and later at the Holy House of Loreto, where the home of Mary the mother of Jesus is believed to be enshrined. Zimmer wrote a best-selling book called *The Pieta*, and he was said to have taken Mass one hundred thousand times in his over eighty years of life. In 2008 he returned home to Florida, and he died a year later.

The only person who can verify the story is a respected doctor named Claude Curran from Boston, who was a medical student at the University of Turin and later at the University of Rome in the 1980s.[15] A devout Catholic even as a young man, Curran met Tom Zimmer in St. Peter's Square. Curran said Zimmer told him various prophecies, including one in 1988 that the Berlin Wall would come down, and it did a year later.

In the same period, Zimmer told him, "Claude, there's a man in the United States right now who has the hand of God on him. He has a first-class education, a high IQ, and everything he addresses he attacks with a blinding efficiency. I'm telling you he has the hand of God on him."

Of course the young doctor wanted to know who he was. Zimmer said, "His name is Donald Trump." Curran had seen Trump on television. He considered him to be a jet-setter who dated actresses. So he asked, "You mean the New York playboy?" Tom answered, "God is going to work through him in the future, and I am so convinced of it that I bought a brick in the Vatican Holy Door with his name on it so that he will benefit from all the prayers and masses at St. Peter's."

When Trump ran for office and won in 2016, Curran told this story to his priest, Fr. Giacomo Capoverdi from Rhode Island, who made a video after the inauguration telling this story and also how he had once visited Loreto on a trip to Italy and had a nice conversation with the old man, and that as a result, he believed this story.[16] The video started making the rounds, which is how I found out about it. After interviewing Dr. Curran for an hour and a half, I also believe the story is true. All these years later it's obvious that God is working through Donald Trump, who has certainly reawakened the national conversation about faith, religious liberty, and the dangers of moral decline.

"I follow Trump's presidency as a spiritual journey for him and his family. I don't know what God tells him directly. But he must be going through something supernatural," Dr. Curran told me. "This is clearly a fight between good and evil."

Then he said something sobering. Tom Zimmer also told him that "the sinking of the Titanic was foreshadowing for what is going to happen to this country." And he said the old man had a favorite expression: "You can't kick God in the teeth for very long."

Those prophecies may sound ridiculous or impossible to some people, but Trump was elected—just as the prophets had said. That was one reason I had enough confidence to fly to New York for the election night party. I know it seems crazy, but somehow, some way, God intervened in that election and saved us from "corrupt Hillary" becoming president.

Any Christian trying to understand what God is saying doesn't rely solely on prophetic words. After all, they are fallible. Doesn't the Bible say, "We prophesy in part," and, "We see as through a glass, darkly"?[17]

God may have raised up President Trump, but there are bigger issues going on than just seeing God's hand on him. There are evil forces—and it isn't just his opponents or the fake news media. It's what the Bible calls spiritual warfare.

CHAPTER 12

SPIRITUAL WARFARE AND DONALD TRUMP

There is no neutral ground in the universe: every square inch, every split second is claimed by God and counterclaimed by Satan.[1]
—C. S. LEWIS (1898–1963)
PROLIFIC CHRISTIAN WRITER AND THINKER

WHEN PAULA WHITE Cain walked to the podium in Amway Arena in Orlando on June 18, 2019, the stands were filling up, and the crowd was teeming with excitement, though it would be another two hours before President Trump would announce he was running for reelection.

Wearing a bright red dress and looking more like a fashion model than a preacher, "Pastor Paula" positioned the mic, greeted the crowd, and called out: "Are you ready for a great night of victory?" The members of the crowd roared their approval as if they were attending a service at New Destiny Christian Center, a large Charismatic church she pastors in nearby Apopka, Florida, rather than a political rally.

Paula quoted President Trump as saying, "We worship God, not government," as a segue into her prayer, which she began after asking everyone to stand and join hands—a common way evangelical Christians pray. The media, cordoned off in a pen nearby, recorded every word as millions watched on TV.

After invoking the name of Jesus and thanking God for the "great United States," the president, and God's blessings, she prayed, "Father, You have raised President Trump up for such a time as this," and invoked blessings from Psalms and the Book of Daniel about revealing "the secrets and the deep things" to the president. Then Paula began to come against "principalities and powers"—terminology rarely heard or understood outside the walls of a Charismatic or Pentecostal church.

"Now I need you to really go with me here," she interjected as an appeal to her audience. Then she continued:

157

Let every evil veil of deception of the enemy be removed from people's eyes in the name which is above every name, the name of Jesus Christ.... You said in Your Word...in Ephesians 6:12, that, "We are not wrestling against flesh and blood but against principalities, powers, against rulers of darkness of this world, against spiritual wickedness in high places."

So right now, let every demonic network that has aligned itself against the purpose, against the calling of President Trump, let it be broken. Let it be torn down in the name of Jesus. Let the counsel of the wicked be spoiled right now, according to Job 12:17. I declare that President Trump will overcome every strategy from hell and every strategy of the enemy, every strategy. And he will fulfill his calling and his destiny. Destroy and divide their tongues, O Lord, according to Psalm 55:9. Give President Trump strength to bring forth his destiny, according to Isaiah 66:9. Let the secret counsel of wickedness be turned to foolishness right now, in Jesus' name. And I declare that no weapon formed against him, his family, his calling, his purpose, his council, will be able to be formed.

Now I declare that You will surround him and protect him from all destruction. That the angel of the Lord encamp around about him, around his family, according to Psalm 34:7. Establish him in righteousness, and let oppression be far from him, according to Isaiah 54:14. I deploy the hand of God to work for him in the name of Jesus. I secure his calling. I secure his purpose. I secure his family. And we secure victory in the name which is above every name, the name that has never failed for this nation and for my life, the name of Jesus Christ. And everybody said, "Amen."[2]

The respected Charismatic teacher Dutch Sheets was watching the livestream of the Orlando rally in Dallas. "I have never seen anything like that on TV," Dutch said. "I literally sat there with my mouth hanging open. I couldn't believe she had the boldness to do that or was allowed to do it. It was as if she drew a line in the sand spiritually."

Paula said many people "who are attuned spiritually" thanked her for not holding back in how she prayed just because of the huge public secular setting. "When I prayed, it was like taking a bat to a bee's nest," she told me. "The Holy Spirit was there."

But while the Christians who agreed with Paula were rejoicing, the secular press took her apart for her prayer, mostly because she used the phrase *demonic network,* which they misunderstood. I assume most of their readers never heard of taking authority over networks of evil forces and probably thought she meant news networks. Of course there were no news networks in New Testament times, and Paula was using scriptural terminology. As a Charismatic Christian, I'm used to hearing that wording, and it didn't register with me until later that the news media would assume she was bashing the fake media.

The Daily Beast twisted her words in its headline to say: "'Demonic' *News* Networks Aligning Themselves Against President" (emphasis mine).[3] At least the *Washington Post* was more accurate with this headline: "Trump's Spiritual Adviser Seeks His Protection From 'Demonic Networks' at Reelection Rally."[4]

Paula is no stranger to criticism. She has been on TV for years, had a very public divorce, and was even one of several ministries "investigated" by Sen. Chuck Grassley of Iowa about whether they misappropriated ministry money, although nothing ever came of it. But Paula told me that "absolutely nothing" compared to the twelve days of controversy her Orlando rally prayer brought. It was, she said, "both praise and accolades as well as controversy and consternation."

My Charismatic beliefs are similar to Paula's: believers have a spiritual authority to make "declarations and decrees." So I understood where she was coming from. But some thought she was calling the Democratic Party demonic.

"I was not," she told me in an interview for this book. "I was calling Satan, the enemy, and every principality [demonic]. Now anyone who operates in accordance with those principalities, I would [pray to] overturn...the same as I [prayed to] secure [President Trump's] purpose and all that God has for [him]. And so if it is the will of God, which I absolutely believe it is, he is walking that purpose out right now."

This is the mindset of many Christians: God has a plan for each of us, and we must walk in it while the enemy, Satan, comes to "steal and kill and destroy."[5] This is true not only of Charismatics and Pentecostals but also of non-Charismatic Evangelicals, including many who have backed Trump. While they may not identify with Charismatics, they understand the spiritual aspect. This is also true of Orthodox and Roman Catholic Christians, many of whom have contacted Paula and let her know they understood her prayer and agree.

She told me: "I know there are wonderful people and professing

Christians who might not be regular church attenders or Bible readers, etc., and who might not pray like that, but they understood. There was no pushback. The only pushback was from people who were, in my opinion, very blinded [by the truth]."

I know Paula well enough to know she did not mean that disrespectfully. It's biblical terminology that points to when Paul asked the "foolish Galatians" who "bewitched you that you should not obey the truth?"[6] Of course many who don't like Trump oppose anything associated with him, including Paula's prayer. If Paula had prayed a very traditional prayer such as the Lord's Prayer or recited some creed, she still would have been blasted.

No president in American history except for Abraham Lincoln has been attacked by more political enemies with less cause than Donald Trump. Most of the attacks are so vicious they go beyond partisan politics. Richard Land, the respected president of Southern Evangelical Seminary, said he doesn't know how President Trump holds up under the attacks. "I was at a dinner at the White House the night before the National Day of Prayer, and the president was ebullient. I mean, if I were the president and I'd gone through what he's gone through, I would be in a fetal position in the Oval Office with my thumb in my mouth."[7]

PUTTING THINGS INTO SPIRITUAL PERSPECTIVE

Light versus darkness. Good versus evil. God's plans and purposes versus the enemy's deceitful agenda. That is the binary way Bible-believing Christians see the world. An argument can be made that at one time most Americans would have understood this and seen it the same way. So the struggle politically isn't just between differing political philosophies but between good and evil. And I believe that behind the craziness manifested by Trump Derangement Syndrome are principalities and powers.

If you're Pentecostal or Charismatic, you are probably familiar with the phrase *spiritual warfare*. It's a phrase we use to describe the unseen battle between the kingdom of God and the kingdom of darkness. Everything we do has an effect on this spiritual battle, and spiritual forces have an effect on us as well. At times when we are under spiritual attack, we can feel an increased intensity or struggle to accomplish what we feel God has called us to do.

Many Christians see this increased resistance as a sign of spiritual warfare. It can happen in our personal lives or in our families, our churches, our communities, and even our country. There are spiritual beings assigned to oversee various realms and territories. This explains why Charismatics and even many evangelical Christians see what is going on in our country and in Trump's presidency as a spiritual battle. Even some mainline Protestants who usually avoid acknowledging such things as demonic spirits admit that the vitriol has gotten so extreme in America that maybe there is spiritual warfare behind it.

In biblical terms Christians are told they "wrestle not against flesh and blood, but against principalities, against powers...against spiritual wickedness in high places."[8] It's like in Frank Peretti's novel *This Present Darkness*, which allowed the reader to see the unseen evil forces influencing the fictional characters in the book.

I like the way Daniel Kolenda, international missionary and successor to world-renowned evangelist Reinhard Bonnke as president and CEO of Christ for All Nations, explains where we got the phrase *spiritual warfare*. He wrote in his book *Slaying Dragons*: "Like many useful terms the phrase *spiritual warfare* does not appear in Scripture as such. The wording is instead rooted in the use of scriptural military analogies to describe the manner in which Christ followers are to prepare for and repel evil." He then refers to Paul's instruction to put on spiritual armor in Ephesians chapter 6 as probably the most famous example of this type of military word picture. He says this illustrates to Christians that we are to treat the battle between good and evil as a matter of life and death.

In my attempt to explain what's happening spiritually in our nation, it was vitally important to dedicate a chapter to addressing these spiritually dark forces. Granted, I'm not a theologian. I'm a Christian journalist. And this is not a treatise on the supernatural. But as a Christian who is aware of this unseen world and someone who believes that we have authority over these powers through the name and blood of Jesus, I could not write a book about all that is at stake for our country without shedding light on the very real struggle in the spiritual realm. It's critical to look with spiritual eyes at America and our unlikely president, who stands strong for what I believe is right while experiencing unparalleled attacks that often defy reason.

In fact to me the vengeance with which some people hate Trump can *only* be understood if seen in spiritual terms. Of course there are many examples of unspeakable evil that at least make sense when seen in spiritual terms. Recognizing spiritual forces makes it easier to understand the actions of a Hitler or why there has been genocide in places such as Rwanda. Poverty, war, murder, hate, and many other sins make sense if you believe there are malevolent forces at work in the world. Even the hatred of brother against brother, horrible domestic violence, and nasty divorce fall into the same category.

You can understand these horrible things better when you realize that both God and Satan operate in the earth through people. Kolenda explains it this way:

> We glorify God most when we fulfill the purpose for which He made us. That is why He has constrained Himself in such a way that He will not act in the earth without us. We are His agents, His representatives, His gatekeepers in this world.
>
> God will not work without us. Likewise, Satan *cannot* work without us. Everything evil that happens in this world comes through evil people. Everything godly that happens in this world comes through godly people. This is why Satan tempts people to sin. He has no real power in this world except what we, the gatekeepers, give to him.[9]

So if we can accept that there is a devil and he influences humans to do his bidding, then we can conclude that people are subject to these spiritual authorities even if they don't understand what they are doing or why.

Even Christians can be Satan's tools. If you've ever lived through a bitter church split, you know the devil's influence on church politics. Or ask a Christian couple who survived a nasty divorce. Yes, Christians can be influenced by demons too. (I remember a preacher once was asked if a Christian could have a demon, and he responded somewhat tongue in cheek that "a Christian can have anything he wants!")

But my goal is not to open a debate about whether a Christian can be possessed or oppressed by a demon. My point is that even if *oppressed* is the more accurate term, if Christians aren't tuned in to God's voice, they too can fall prey to the lies of the enemy and be used for his purposes.

Other books about Trump's presidency or our country's current affairs will likely explain everything in political or cultural terms. I believe, however, that the only way to truly discern what's happening in our nation is through spiritual eyes. This is not a war between Left and Right or between Democrats and Republicans or even between President Trump and his political opponents. It's spiritual warfare.

A certain segment of Protestant Christians sees the world through this filter. That's why John C. Danforth wrote in his book *Resurrection* that the vile hatred that came out in 1991 against Supreme Court nominee Clarence Thomas was spiritual warfare.[10] The same thing happened again with the Brett Kavanaugh nomination in 2018. And there are many other examples. That's why Christians pray "against" such things. They aren't praying against the people but against the spirits behind what's happening. Many believe Trump has merely caused the evil that was already hidden in our government to show its face in public.

After the Mueller report came out in 2019, I dealt with this in an interview with Steve Johnson on KDOV-TV in Oregon. As I told Johnson, the Mueller report reveals a spiritual battle the enemy is waging against Trump—and Christians across the nation must be equipped to combat it. I wasn't surprised at Mueller's conclusions. In fact if there was any collusion at all, it would have been the Democrats and Hillary Clinton using Christopher Steele's dossier to defame Trump.

From my perspective the Left's incessant attack against our president reveals his role as a disrupter—as well as how deep corruption runs in our nation's politics. But just as Paula prayed the scripture in Ephesians 6:12, we Christians know we aren't fighting against people but "against principalities, against powers, against the rulers of the darkness of this world, and against spiritual forces of evil in the heavenly places." Spiritual warfare surrounds us all the time. It's a daily battle the enemy wages in our personal lives, in our homes, in our cities, and even in Washington.

Only those with spiritual discernment will understand this. And it explains why the Left went berserk when Trump was elected. You could see it in all the protests, some of which involved violence and many of which involved groups funded by socialist billionaire George Soros.

You also see it in the way the Left attacks Christianity in general. For example, some on the Left are actually introducing bills that would make it illegal for Christians to help people with same-sex attractions or who were uncertain about their gender identity.[11] Is the next step labeling the Bible a hate book because it condemns sins that people love and want to make legal? Thankfully that legislation has not passed, but it goes to show the extremes people will go to to oppose biblical principles.

If this kind of behavior goes unchecked, I believe we are only two or three elections away from extreme liberals getting a firm upper hand. And as Ronald Reagan once said, "Freedom is never more than one generation away from extinction. We didn't pass it on to our children in the bloodstream. The only way they can inherit the freedom we have known is if we fight for it, protect it, defend it and then hand it to them with the well thought lessons of how they in their lifetime must do the same."[12] We need to heed his words and fight harder because the Left already has the upper hand with the younger generations of voters through the news media, academia, and popular culture.

The Left gets the church to go along with its values by creating a false dichotomy between politics and spiritual matters. The Left has taken abortion—which is really a spiritual matter of defending life—and turned it into a purely political issue. It has taken same-sex marriage—a spiritual matter of biblical marriage—and turned it into a political issue of defending the rights of the LGBTQ community. Once leftists turn these spiritual matters into political issues, they tell the church to stand off with their false understanding of separation of church and state.

I don't believe this struggle in America is just about separation of church and state, and neither do most Christians. It's a battle between spiritual forces, but which ones?

IF IT IS SPIRITUAL, THEN WHICH SPIRITS ARE AT WORK?

On August 19, 2018, Pastor John Kilpatrick preached a sermon to his congregation at Church of His Presence in Daphne, Alabama, and told them that witchcraft had been unleashed against Donald Trump. He used the reference in 1 Kings 19 when Jezebel unleashed a spirit of witchcraft against the prophet Elijah—the most powerful Old Testament prophet—that left him running for his life and feeling totally discouraged. Someone posted on YouTube a clip of the end of the service, when Kilpatrick called on his congregation to pray for the president. Within a week almost a million people had watched it.[13]

When the sermon went viral, press from around the world began running stories. The *Newsweek* website blared: "Pastor Prays for Trump to Defeat Deep State 'Witchcraft,' Speaks in Tongues."[14]

Two days later, August 21, 2018, Paul Manafort was convicted on several counts in a case brought against him by the Mueller investiga-tion. The same day, Trump's former attorney Michael Cohen pleaded guilty to some minor charges. Suddenly the president was in even more hot water than usual. It seemed something had been unleashed. And two days before, this very thing had been predicted by this pastor in Alabama, who is best known in Christian circles as the pastor of the five-year-long revival at Brownsville Assembly of God, which drew four million people.

Somehow what Kilpatrick said resonated with Christians all over the country. They perceived something was very wrong, but they couldn't put their finger on it. So when Kilpatrick identified the attacks against Trump as spiritual warfare and told them to pray, they understood what they were supposed to do and why.

"Something's been unleashed in our nation," Kilpatrick told me when I interviewed him at the time. But he said only a few seem to see what is going on. "It's like everyone is in a spiritual stupor. It's time for America to turn and repent. This is more than just political differences. Spirits have been unleashed, but if we humble ourselves and pray, God will bring that spirit down."

When I interviewed Kilpatrick for my *In Depth With Stephen Strang* podcast a few months later, he told me, "The Spirit of God is going to begin to invade this nation. And it's time for us in the min-istry to begin preaching the word *repentance*. I have never seen people find it so hard to repent as they do today. And many in the ministry won't even give altar calls anymore and allow the people to come for-ward and repent of their sins and lead them in the sinner's prayer. It's like Satan has done everything he possibly can to keep a born-again experience away from this generation. It's going to take a moving of the Holy Spirit, and it's going to take revival [to turn things around]—and I believe we're getting close to it."

Although Kilpatrick says he's not a "Trump man," he prays for the president regularly and believes a coming revival depends on his being reelected. "Basically, this man God has given us right now is standing in the gap by himself in many cases, holding back the tide that would try to destroy this nation. This is spiritual warfare *for the soul of this nation*," he said. "When you go back and study revivals, national awak-enings, [these are] the very same kind of conditions that were preva-lent right before revivals or these national awakenings."

Dutch Sheets used the same terminology when discussing the way spiritual warfare for America is connected to Israel and the rest of the world. "We have to remember that this is a spiritual battle," Sheets said. "It's for the *soul of the nation*, but it's related to worldwide harvest. It's not just related to Israel."

In the same way Paula White Cain decreed over Trump at the rally, Chuck Pierce believes that when President Trump was following through with his promise to recognize Jerusalem as the capital of Israel, the words he uttered were actually a decree that was shifting the entire world into a new era. Dutch Sheets agreed.

"So we have to have [Trump] in there and be strong because this is a spiritual battle connected to Israel, but it's also connected to the harvest God is about to [bring] around the world....It's not Republican [versus] Democrat. But to me, it's a spiritual war for the soul of the nation connected to what God's going to do in the earth. And so we just have to...fight it spiritually," Dutch told me.

"That's our part....We do naturally [pray] and vote, but we're in a spiritual war probably unlike anything intensity-wise any of us have ever seen because the enemy knows if he doesn't stop this, then he's going to lose all the ground that he has gained."

Despite the spiritual battle, Trump continues to stand in defense of Christians, not only across America but around the world. In fact this is one reason I believe the Left is so bent on halting Trump's agenda. Just look at the way Trump has condemned murder in the womb. (His 2019 State of the Union address was one of the most pro-life speeches I have ever heard a president give.)

With all Trump is doing to advance conservative, biblical values, it's no surprise the enemy is trying to stop him and is using the Left to do so.

Kilpatrick is not the only Charismatic minister to prophesy the spirit of Jezebel was rising up to oppose President Trump. Dr. Michael L. Brown is one of the best thinkers and most prolific writers of our time. The author of more than thirty-five books and host of the nationally syndicated daily talk radio show *The Line of Fire*, he writes syndicated columns and scholarly publications ranging from biblical commentaries to articles in Semitic journals and theological dictionaries. He has served as an adjunct or visiting professor at seven leading seminaries and has debated gay activists, agnostic professors, and Orthodox rabbis on university campuses.

In 2019 Brown released a book called *Jezebel's War With America: The Plot to Destroy Our Country and What We Can Do to Turn the Tide*, which focuses on the fact that the spirit of the biblical figure

Jezebel is at work today and attempting to destroy America through a host of spiritual and cultural forces, including radical feminism, the extreme pro-abortion movement, and even a fascination with witchcraft and sorcery.

"This has Jezebel's name written all over it in all caps, boldly and clearly," he said of the current fascination with witchcraft, noting that Jezebel was known for her sorcery. "In early 2018, it was announced that 500 million Harry Potter books—books glorifying sorcery and wizardry—have now been sold worldwide....Just watch the children participating at the massive Wizarding World of Harry Potter area in a theme park in Orlando. They too want to be wizards and sorcerers."[15]

Want proof that interest in witchcraft is increasing? Brown did a Google search for "the rise of witchcraft in America." These headlines were among the results:

- "The US Witch Population Has Seen an Astronomical Rise"[16]
- "Report: Witchcraft Rising in US as Christianity Declines"[17]
- "There Are Now More Practicing Witches in the U.S. Than Ever Before"[18]
- "The Fastest Growing Religion in America Is Witchcraft" (posted October 2013, indicating that this has been going on for some time)[19]

Recently I found this May 2019 article from *Time* magazine: "Yes, Witches Are Real. I Know Because I Am One."[20]

For further confirmation Brown looked to his Twitter account, where his colleague Dr. James White said, "It is very hard not to see a strong spirit of deception and delusion working in this culture—we murder our babies, destroy the gift of marriage, even mutilate young children all in service to the god of human autonomy. But, the judgment is just."[21]

Fortunately Brown's eye-opening book not only unveils Jezebel's satanic plot, beginning with an all-out assault on the church, but also equips believers with tools to defeat the enemy in their own lives as well as in the nation.

FROM POLITICAL TO PERSONAL

So our discussion has been how, from the Christian perspective, Satan is attacking our nation and its institutions, including the presidency.

But it's also important to understand spiritual warfare and how it affects not just politics but people, including Donald Trump. To talk about the effect of spiritual attacks on Donald Trump the person, not the politician, I turned to someone who created the number one spiritual warfare app, called "Shut Up Devil!" Kyle Winkler is a practical Bible teacher and author who wrote a book called *Silence Satan*, which he claims "has helped thousands shut down the enemy's attacks, threats, lies, and accusations."[22]

Toward the end of Trump's campaign for president there was an "October surprise" in which an old audiotape from an *Access Hollywood* interview revealed the president saying some pretty disgusting things about women. When Winkler wrote an op-ed for Charisma News shortly after the audiotape came to light, many Christians were questioning if they could even vote for Trump.

Winkler wrote that his article wasn't "a political persuasion piece, but it's a current-event case study in the strategies of Satan against us all." He went on to say: "The allegations [against Trump], if true, are the substance of nightmares. But that's precisely what sin is. Let's not be naïve. Whatever the infraction, when exposed, it's never rosy. But if you're a Christian, these October surprises shouldn't come as a surprise at all. Not because of what we know about Donald Trump's sordid past, but because this tactic being waged against him has the signature of Satan all over it."

Winkler continued: "None of us are exempt from the enemy's accusations. And the greater the impact of your destiny, the more you can count on them. While it's true that you can't change the past, you don't have to be ruled or shut down by it. The solution to overcome Satan's strategy against you is to shut him up with the truth of God's Word consistently flowing through your mind and your mouth. When you're convinced of who you are and what you have in Christ, you will keep Satan silenced in your life."[23]

What Can We Do?

But are all the attacks evil, and is there any good we can learn from them? Hank Kunneman, pastor of Lord of Hosts Church in Omaha, Nebraska, said Christians often misread signs as Jesus' disciples did in the story in the sixth chapter of Mark where Jesus walked on the water. When the disciples saw Jesus, they thought He was a ghost and almost failed to see the miracle happening right in front of them.

"Some Christians attribute everything to evil and don't see any good. They don't understand the nature of God. God knew same-sex marriage would be approved. He knows America is apostate in many ways," Kunneman said. "The same could be said of all nations. Yet He loves America and desires for America to once again be a beacon to the world. How can this be? He looks at America through Jesus on the cross. It is His grace."

Kunneman also has a remarkable prophetic gift. In 2006 he said God was raising up someone from New York to be president. Because Rudy Giuliani was running, I assumed Kunneman's prophecy was referring to him. In hindsight I realize Hank was seeing that Trump would win. Kunneman also started saying God was raising up America to be great again, long before Trump began using the slogan.

Hank is typical of many spiritually oriented Evangelicals who see everything through the lens of what God is doing. The need for America to be great isn't just so we can put an end to bad trade agreements or have a strong military. Rather, it is to bring in a harvest of souls, which he predicts will number a billion people who come to Christ. It will be a fulfillment of when Jesus quoted the prophet Isaiah: "The people who sat in darkness have seen a great light."[24] Those who are in darkness in America will see the light of the gospel.

So how should Spirit-filled Christians respond to the spiritual warfare facing the nation? I believe it's imperative that believers rise up in this hour and pray. God has a good plan for America, but He is also a God of righteousness and justice, and He will judge wickedness. We must realize that in all this God is in control. If we are faithful to pray according to God's will—not a political party's will or a friend's will—we will see Him do incredible things.

As our culture grows more and more sinful, I see Christians getting more and more serious about their faith. I believe that as things get worse, God is going to raise up the church to stand for righteousness in a way it hasn't before. If you have faith to see this happen, share this book with your friends and urge them to pray for our nation.

We need Christians praying now more than ever because unfortunately this spiritual attack, this all-out war against all things Christian, was brought on, I believe, by a weak church, which is the subject of the next chapter.

CHAPTER 13

COMPROMISE IN THE CHURCH

Secularization...is not just something that happens to the
church; it is something that happens in the church.[1]
—MICHAEL S. HORTON
THEOLOGY PROFESSOR, WESTMINSTER SEMINARY

I F THE ENEMY causes the extremists on the Left and others in culture to oppose the work of God, what role is the church supposed to play? The Bible says that "judgment [begins] at the house of God."[2] Is it possible then that the church is partly responsible for our nation's current condition because it has abdicated its prophetic role? And will this have an effect on the 2020 election?

While there has never been a perfect time since mankind sinned way back in the Garden of Eden, it seems things are getting worse—almost as if our cultural decline is happening at warp speed now. It's manifesting itself on a global scale but also through the cultural divide we see so plainly in our own nation.

The belief that what has happened in America over the last century has to do with the differences between Republicans and Democrats betrays serious confusion. As I explained in the previous chapter, the war is spiritual. It is a battle between evil and good, between darkness and light. To put it in other terms, two distinct religions are vying for control of America's public square: secularism and Christianity. They cannot coexist; one will ultimately cause the destruction of the other.

On one side are those like Fred Jackson of the American Family Association, who told Richard Land in an interview that he believes pastors are under an obligation to speak out about abortion and issues such as the homosexual agenda. But many pastors are reluctant to do that. "They don't realize...the stuff that goes on behind the scenes, where it's spiritual warfare," Land told him in a radio interview.[3] On top of that, studies have shown that many of the people in evangelical congregations have either had an abortion or paid for or encouraged an abortion.[4]

"I must tell you," Land said, "I first went into the ministry when I was sixteen, [and] the one thing that [has] shocked me over these intervening six decades is the lack of spine in so many preachers. Many preachers are like invertebrates. They're [seemingly] in it because they want to please people. When pastors have said to me, 'I really appreciate that strong stand, but I can't do that in my church,' I'd say, 'I'm more afraid of what God will do to me if I don't take a stand for truth than I am afraid of what deacons may do to me if I do stand for truth.'"[5]

FROM ANTI-RELIGIOUS TO ANTI-CHURCH

To claim, as many do, that liberals are anti-religious or anti-Christian is one thing, but to show statistically that Democrats believe churches have a negative impact on society is a couple of steps beyond mere suspicion. But that's precisely what the Pew Research Center's Politics & Policy department discovered when it examined liberal and conservative opinions of the church. In a July 2017 report Pew found that 44 percent of liberal Democrats view churches as a *negative influence*. (Just 14 percent of Republicans held that view.) The study also found that 46 percent of those unaffiliated with any religion (and 43 percent of those who seldom or never attend religious services) believe churches have a *negative* impact on society.[6]

To show how divided the worldviews of Republicans and Democrats are, the same study found that 85 percent of Republicans believe the national news media have a *negative* impact on society, but only 46 percent of Democrats held that view. (Note that 51 percent of liberal Democrats say the news media have a *positive* impact on the country.)[7]

Reacting to the report, Mark Tooley, president of the Institute on Religion and Democracy in Washington, DC, said he believes the Democratic Party is rapidly on its way to becoming the opposition party to the Christian church in America. "We've [never] really had a political party, as many European nations do, with an opposition to the church," he said, "and hopefully we never will, but the trend seems to be that much of the Democratic Party—a plurality—seems to be heading in that direction."

It would be a great historical irony if the nation were to end up with a two-party system that was essentially a pro-religion political party and an anti-religion political party going head to head in America—a salutary reminder of the English Civil War with the Protestant Roundheads versus the royalist Cavaliers. As Tooley said, such a scenario "would be potentially dangerous."

Tooley noted that "many liberals ideologically are very statist...so for them, the Church and other institutions in civil society may seem peripheral—or unneeded—as the government can do it all on its own." He added that many people hostile to religion fail to fully appreciate the impact religious institutions can have for good in society.[8] But a substantial number of Americans have apparently made up their minds, deciding that the label "No Religion" best describes their belief system.

Conservative activist David Lane, founder of the American Renewal Project, has been sounding this alarm for years. "'Western culture that at first drifted and is now rushing headlong into apostasy from the Triune God' is a direct result of the vacuum created as American Christendom relinquished the town square. The disengagement from the culture by Christians left a void in America that is now being filled by everything anti-Christ," Lane wrote in his weekly American Renewal Project newsletter.[9]

"Decisions have consequences. The gathering storm engendered by baby boomers and passed on to the Millennial and Gen Z generations to sort out, will come down hard on the weak-kneed and lily-livered," he wrote. "What Christian minister and cultural theologian P. Andrew Sandlin styled 'Sunday-go-to-meetin' Christianity' has been the prevailing attitude over the last century. Making no demands on the culture, this attitude exposed 'the entire West to the risk of a grave cultural and political crisis, and perhaps to a collapse of civilization.'... The last two generations of Americans handed down this attitude to their children and their children's children.

"To illustrate, corporate America became in 2015 the biggest promoters of same-sex intercourse and marriage. More than 350 companies, including Apple, AT&T, Staples and Target filed amicus curiae briefs urging the Supreme Court to strike down same-sex marriage bans. Yet citizens in 30 states had passed amendments opposing same-sex marriage, often by wide margins.... Shortly thereafter, five secularized United States Supreme Court Justices promoted themselves to be 'god and creator,' weaponizing the state, and foisting homosexual marriage on all 50 states."

Lane noted that an even more egregious distortion occurred in

San Antonio in 2019, when the city council banned Chick-fil-A from opening a restaurant in the San Antonio International Airport. The "reasons" given were that the corporation's foundation donates to groups such as the Fellowship of Christian Athletes, which defines marriage as the union of one man and one woman. A week later officials in Buffalo, New York, moved to block Chick-fil-A from opening a restaurant in their airport, raising the question whether it is "now contrary to the values of an American city to award contracts to companies owned by tithing Christians," Lane said.

"The Founders could not have fathomed what's happening in twenty-first-century America, let alone wrapped their minds around it," he wrote. "What likely political motivations could there be against Chick-fil-A? Destroying a business simply because the owners hold biblical moral beliefs is going down a rabbit hole. Where is Hillary Clinton with her pretentious charade from August 2016 of 'I've been fighting to defend religious freedom for years.'"

Lane predicts that a battle over freedom of conscience is coming, and it will be "with the secular and media luminaries who dominate the spiritual, intellectual, educational, economic, and vocational cultural mountains of influence in America. 'Big Business' has become allied with the secular Left, turning into active combatants attempting to put the final nail in the coffin of America's once biblically-based culture. Public education already did so about fifty years ago, bringing America's schooling down to the lowest common denominator."

Lane points to Russel Kirk, an American political theorist, historian, and moralist who a generation ago took the long view on where this kind of thinking leads. Yet he also offered hope.

> This is the bent world of Orwell's *1984*, and it is the actual state in many lands of what once was a civilized order. Will the wave of the future engulf the remaining islands of refuge? Will the American Republic go down to dusty death?
>
> Perhaps you fear that I am embarking upon a long tale of woe. But I mean to spare you that. Rather, my purpose it is to suggest that you and I are not the slaves of some impersonal force called Destiny or History. I come to you not as a gravedigger, but as a diagnostician. Indeed, our whole civilization is sorely afflicted by decadence; yet it need not follow that, already having passed the point of no return, we must

submit ourselves to total servitude and infinite boredom. Just as renewal of soul and body often is possible for the individual person, so whole societies may recover from follies and blunders.

In another newsletter Lane noted that "contemporary secular political leadership 'hates knowledge of the moral order and scorns correction.'...Expecting them to comprehend that moral relativism, state-enforced morality and political correctness embody the death knell to sustainable freedom is equally unlikely, and foolish altogether to them, as expecting natural man to dismiss that life and life's events are endowed with the Spirit of God."[10]

This is all the more reason to get behind a president like Donald Trump—and many are getting the message. David Barton the historian noticed an interesting trend among evangelical pastors, many of whom did not support Trump in 2016 probably because they didn't like his personality. Recent polls show 50 percent of these pastors are finally supporting the president. Still, it is likely that Trump has less support among evangelical pastors than he does among Evangelicals overall. In 2016 some 81 percent of white Evangelicals voted for the brash developer from Queens, and Evangelicals have continued to support him despite the constant stream of negative news by most of the mainstream media and their criticism of nearly everything he does.

Barton says that in the current anti-Christian environment many pastors have been able to finally get over not liking Trump's tweets or the way he is shaking things up and, like most lay evangelical Christians, see the president as their champion. But their members saw it first and in 2016 actually ignored the advice of many of their pastors and other Christian leaders who were active Never Trumpers.

The urgent call in present-day America is for Christians to expose the current idols active in the public square. Nonbelievers lack both the moral fiber and the will to fathom what the battle for the soul of America is about.

WHAT'S NEXT?

Over the last century secularized intellectuals have succeeded in replacing Western civilization's immutable measure for judging society—the Bible—with laws based increasingly on sentiments and preferences. As a result, America now finds itself in a quandary that is much more significant than whether Donald Trump will win in 2020. Assuming Trump gets reelected, as I argue he will, his term ends in 2025. Then what? Where is God in all of this?

I posed this question to David Barton, and he flipped it around: "When you look at where we are now, my question is not where is God, but it's, Where are His people?" Barton believes the answer is not too good.

He has worked closely with researcher George Barna, who has conducted numerous polls on Christian values, beliefs, and so on. They polled a sampling of the 384,000 churches and senior pastors in America and learned 70 percent of churches and senior pastors say they do not agree with the Bible in its most basic and orthodox teachings. Even so that means 30 percent[11] are what Barna and Barton call "theologically conservative churches." Those pastors were asked, "Do you think the Bible applies to all issues of life?" The survey then specifically asked them about fourteen areas, including immigration, education, unborn life, traditional marriage, and national economics.

An overwhelming majority (between 91 and 97 percent, depending on which one of the fourteen issues) agreed that the Bible did address these issues. However, most of them also admitted that they did not address those topics from the pulpit because they considered them "political issues."

"But wait a minute," Barton said rhetorically. "You just said the Bible teaches those issues, and then you say no, if it's in the news, that makes it political, and we won't talk about it. So only a small fraction of pastors are addressing issues in the culture that the Bible also addresses."

As I mentioned in the previous chapter, it's as if the secularists have convinced Christians that moral values in the Bible such as life or marriage are no longer the purview of the church once they become "political." Says Barton: "That's not God's problem. That's our problem."

But it's only part of the problem these statistics show. Only 14 percent of Christians read the Bible on a daily basis,[12] and only 10 percent of American adults have a biblical worldview. Even among Christians who say they are born-again, only 31 percent have a biblical worldview, and only 4 percent of millennials have a biblical worldview.[13] This means we're a nation that doesn't think biblically and doesn't even know what the Bible teaches.

"I talk to Christian university presidents, and they say that the kids coming out of youth group to their schools—even from Christian schools—don't know the difference between Jonah and Moses. They don't even know the basic Bible stories," Barton told me. "A good friend of mine was talking with a Christian young man, and the names Adam and Eve came up. The young man had no idea who they were— he'd never heard of them."

Several years ago, Barton and George Barna coauthored a book called *U-Turn*, which noted there are more than seventy different moral behaviors in which the authors could not find any statistical difference between Christians and non-Christians.[14] I certainly see this to be true:

- Many Evangelicals now drink,[15] where a century ago Prohibition was the big issue for those we now call Evangelicals.

- It's been well documented that five of ten evangelical men view pornography at least monthly.[16]

- And several studies indicate that many, if not most, singles in evangelical churches are having sex outside of marriage.[17] Maybe that's why hardly anyone teaches or preaches about being a virgin at marriage.

This being said, Barton believes "biblical literacy" is the biggest problem America faces right now. And a lot of that goes to secular education, where nationally on college campuses there are seventeen Democratic history professors to every one Republican professor. But it gets worse. In a survey of fifty-one top-ranked liberal arts colleges, the Democrat-to-Republican ratio was ten to one. But *there were no Republicans at all* at 39 percent of the colleges surveyed, and 78 percent of the academic departments in the sample have either zero Republicans or so few as to make no difference. The ratio in the religion department was seventy Democrats to every one Republican.[18]

Before you decide it's a leap to correlate the Bible literacy of the average American with the political party of the average college professor, take a look at how Barton connects them. "There is a huge difference between the way the two parties view America and evaluate our history," Barton said. "If you doubt that, read the platforms of both parties. It becomes very clear in those platforms." Barton believes that when we put our kids into an educational system that is skewed to be very anti-America and anti-Bible, the result is what we now see: many

Christians apparently believe there is no absolute moral truth. Barton concluded, "If you can't agree that certain basic things are morally wrong, then you can't get a nation moving in the right direction. That's where intense polarization comes from."

As a lifelong Pentecostal, I've seen the secularized liberal drift of the church even in circles once deemed to be biblically conservative. It starts with a lifestyle that is basically no different than the secular world. Then it progresses to liberal theology where they don't believe the Word of God anymore or even vote on important issues such as whether same-sex marriage should be legal.

Historically, Pentecostals have been different. The holiness background of most major Pentecostal denominations called for very strict guidelines of personal behavior (and dress) and belief. There was a lot of focus on church attendance every time the doors were open. Even though many modern-day Pentecostal churches shy away from these views, which are now often considered "legalistic," as a journalist who has covered this segment of the church for years, I haven't seen Pentecostals experience the same sort of liberal drift theologically. Perhaps we have that holiness background to thank for the fact that there have never been resolutions in the annual meetings of any mainline Pentecostal denominations over liberalizing the rules on same-sex marriage or abortion.

But another form of compromise, liberalism, or just plain apathy affects the Pentecostals maybe worst of all. Few Pentecostal or Charismatic pastors actually preach against sin, even if they don't change their theology to embrace it. They just leave it alone and focus on other things such as church growth, evangelizing or discipling new converts, or even missions giving. They like to preach on faith—and there's nothing wrong with that—but many of the sermons just make you feel good when you go home. Having a great church service where you feel the power of God is important, but today's services rarely mobilize the members to change culture or turn out the vote in crucial elections.

In one area, Pentecostals are ahead of most other Protestant groups because their churches are more integrated. In fact the Assemblies of God has grown in membership for the past seventeen years, mainly because of the growth of Hispanic and African American members. Latinos both in South America and in the US seem to embrace the passion and excitement of the Pentecostal experience.

If you know your history, you know Pentecostalism grew out of the Azusa Street Revival, which was led by a black preacher named William Seymour, the son of former slaves. At its start Pentecostalism was more integrated than other forms of Protestant Christianity, and racial diversity is still common in Pentecostal churches today. Pentecostal forms of worship where people shout, lift their hands, and praise God exuberantly came from the black church experience, not from the formalism of the denominations the European immigrants brought with them.

Many "white" Charismatic churches in America have a sizable percentage of black members who feel comfortable with the exuberant worship experience. But drill down, and you will find the same dichotomy within these integrated congregations as in the wider culture. The white congregants tend to be Republican, and the black members tend to be Democrat.

Why is this? As I mentioned in chapter 3, I've talked to close friends who are leaders in black churches. On a few key issues Democrats have for the past half century supported the policies important to black Americans, such as civil rights, the desire for prison reform, or governmental programs for the poor. As a result, the black community overlooks the "faults" of Democrats, such as their many liberal policies. In fact studies have shown that black Christians align with white conservative Christians on most moral issues, but they still vote Democrat by huge percentages. However, as I pointed out earlier in this book, that is beginning to change.

On the Republican side the party supports (or gives lip service at election time to) some policies important to these conservative Christians, such as on abortion and same-sex marriage. So the white Christians vote Republican and overlook the things they disagree with, such as the way the Republicans say one thing at election time and govern like liberals, supporting big business at the expense of the little guy and dragging the US into meaningless wars.

IT'S TIME TO FOCUS ON WHAT'S MOST IMPORTANT

So while many Charismatic pastors may oppose same-sex marriage and abortion when they vote, they won't preach about it. To find out why, Barton said Barna has drilled down to find what is important to these pastors. When asked how they measured whether their church was successful, the top five answers of theologically conservative pastors were: size of the offering, weekly attendance, number of staff members, number of programs the church offers, and square footage of the facilities.[19]

"Of the top answers we get from evangelical, theologically conservative pastors, not a single one comes out of the Bible," laments Barton. He points out that the problem with this is that you get what you measure. "If your number one issue is offerings, you're not going to say anything that will jeopardize offerings, which means you're not going to address a whole lot of [controversial] stuff. And you're not going to do anything that will jeopardize attendance—you won't talk about these things that might offend someone, even if the Bible talks about those things."

And it's not just pastors, but it's also evangelists and large parachurch television ministries that are often crusade- and revival-oriented. Again, there is nothing wrong with that, but if the focus is just getting people saved, and their behavior or beliefs are not that much different from those who are unbelievers, then no wonder the culture is becoming more ungodly.

Pentecostals who used to pray for the power of the Holy Spirit and emphasized speaking in tongues often relegate that to services later in the week or small groups or classes. And while Pentecostalism came out of the holiness movement of a century and a half ago, and was known for its holiness "do's and don'ts" when I was growing up, rarely will you hear a sermon on holiness these days. (The joke when I grew up was that it was wrong to "drink, smoke, or chew, or go with girls who do.")

Barton also grew up Pentecostal and bemoans that the emphasis seems to be on conversions but not discipleship. "Right now, it's all about converts and getting people to say the sinner's prayer. Well, I can have a parakeet recite the sinner's prayer. That doesn't mean the parakeet is a Christian," Barton told me.

"We've moved away from discipleship, and as a result, we no longer see people thinking or behaving the right way. We're not discipling them. The real question is, How are they living? What's their behavior? Are they producing fruit worthy of repentance? There is a big emphasis on converts rather than disciples, and the irony is that for two thousand years we have let the 'professionals' do the work of ministry. As a result, Christians now comprise 33 percent of the world's population (compared to 23 percent Muslim, 14 percent Hindu, and 7 percent Buddhist).[20]

"We've got missionaries, evangelists, and pastors, and they do the work of the ministry—but the Bible says they are to teach the ordinary saints to do the work of the ministry," Barton said. "So if every Christian made it their objective to bring one person to Christ this year and then disciple them to think biblically, at the end of this year, twice as much of the world—64 percent—would be Christian. And if we did that again the next year, we would have the entire world Christian in only two years—if every Christian just discipled one other person."

Discipleship means teaching and modeling how to live a life set apart from the secular, godless culture. That set-apart life is what we used to call holiness. "Be holy, for I am holy," the Bible says in 1 Peter 1:16. But I've observed, and Barton agrees, that few are teaching holiness anymore.

"We're not finding people confronting wrong behavior, saying this is morally right or morally wrong. Few pastors are doing this. And not only are we not hitting the holiness aspect, but we largely don't have the fear of God anymore. There is no sense of having to account to God for our behavior, our beliefs, our thoughts—all the things the Bible teaches. So we have now become a user-friendly kind of a church. We don't want you feeling bad about things—we don't want you to radically change your life," Barton said on my podcast.

"Look at John 6 where Jesus was offending the crowds. Many left Him. His disciples said to Him, 'This is a hard teaching; who can bear it.' He looked at them and asked, 'Are you guys leaving me too?' They answered, 'No, we'll stay with you. You've got the bread of life.' But man, this is really hard stuff!" Barton said. "No American church I know of today is being accused of teaching hard stuff and driving people away, with true disciples remaining in the church to be taught more."

I agree. And this is part of the problem we face. As the culture declines and becomes more hostile to Christians and biblical principles, it boils down to a failure of the church in that there's no teaching on holiness that would change people's lives and then motivate them to go out and change the culture.

The contemporary, self-effacing church culture hidden behind the walls of the meeting place is not up to Christianity's standards. A different type of church will be required for America to be born again. Budgets, buildings, and bodies in seats can't be the theological focal point if America is to survive. Christians operating in the public square must be empowered by wisdom from above.

Barton said, "Get involved where you live—with your family, business, schools, and local government—and let's look at how Christ applies to all of these areas. That's where I think the church is really failing."

It's as David Lane wrote once: "Jesus paid not only the price for our souls and eternal salvation, 'but to redeem everything that was lost: people, business, education, and government. And there is nothing the devil can do to reverse it.' That is, if believers will but engage."[21]

Getting the church to be the church is necessary if we are to turn the tide in the culture—and make a difference in 2020, because so much is at stake politically and spiritually in this election.

CHAPTER 14

WHAT'S AT STAKE IF CHRISTIANS DON'T VOTE FOR TRUMP

*No matter what label they use, a vote for any Democrat
in 2020 is a vote for the rise of radical socialism
and the destruction of the American dream.*[1]
—DONALD TRUMP, IN HIS 2020 CANDIDACY
ANNOUNCEMENT SPEECH
ORLANDO, JUNE 18, 2019

IN THIS BOOK I've made the case for why Donald Trump should win—and how bad things will be in America if he loses reelection in 2020. I also made the case in chapter 2 that the other side is so corrupt and so motivated that there are those who believe he will lose. I agree with Pastor Choco De Jesús from Chicago, who believes the Democrats have lost their way so much they will lose this election. But it's no certainty. A lot can happen before November 3, 2020.

In chapter 11, I quoted modern-day prophets who say Trump will win a second term. I've tried to explain why I believe God's hand is on him. Whether or not you like everything he tweets, he's keeping his promises and leading our country in the right direction. America has made strides in some very important areas and risks having things go in the opposite direction if he loses—with very serious consequences for our nation.

I've made the case that Trump has stood up to globalism and helped America regain its sovereignty. What happens, then, if he loses? Trump has made securing the border his top priority. Will we become like Venezuela if millions of immigrants flood our country? And what about the attacks on Christianity either by censorship or hate speech laws that violate our constitutional rights of free speech and religious liberty? Trump has held back the barrage, and we need him in office another four years. And don't forget, without a leader with his pro-life stance, the next step in the abortion debate is legalizing infanticide.

Our economy has boomed under Trump. The United States is the greatest capitalistic system in the world. Yet Democrats are advocating socialism. And if they get a permanent majority through millions of new immigrant voters, we may see socialism in our lifetime and the end of this great nation as we know it.

There are many other issues—from terrorism to environmentalism to the national debt to the dangers we face from those advocating for sharia law. But this is not a book on policy, and I'm a Christian journalist, not a policy wonk. I'm trying to show the Christian community and other Americans why I believe the 2020 election is so important. We need Trump now more than ever.

Dennis Prager agrees. He told me that 2016 was the most important election in modern American history since the Civil War. "Had Donald Trump not won—or had a Republican not won—I do believe we would have lost our country certainly in my lifetime and perhaps through the lifetime of my children. That is how important I consider the last election," he told me when I interviewed him in Los Angeles. Prager also considers the 2020 election the *second* most important of his lifetime, and I agree.

John Hagee, on the other hand, told conservative TV show host Mark Levin this "election may be more important" than the 2016 election. "If [Trump] is not…reelected in this next time…many of the good things he has done can be reversed. And the socialist voice that is rising up in Washington will take control. And we will lose contact with the America that we know. The Democrats are going left and hard left, away from anything the Democratic Party has held up for in times past….If this next election is not a reelection of President Trump, our country is going to go into a socialist tailspin," Hagee said.

Levin agreed: "This is an election now of capitalism versus socialism. The Constitution versus the anti-Constitution. Faithful judges versus activist judges. A secure national border or no national border. The most powerful military on the face of the earth or an eviscerated military. Is it that dire? Am I right about this?"

"Exactly right," Hagee replied. "All of those things—nationalism versus socialism—that is the issue. [If those things happen,] downhill we will go."[2]

Washington Post columnist George Will, who is no fan of President

Trump, wondered if the Democrats were trying to lose in 2020 because their policies are so out of touch with what Americans care about.[3] Referring to comments Will made in a recent interview, Marc Nuttle said the Democrats are "proposing policy that has no connection to the purpose and cause of the United States."

Among the illogical proposals were a national health care plan that would eliminate private health insurance, which is currently found satisfactory by 71 percent of the 180 million Americans who have employer-provided coverage,[4] as well as the elimination of the electoral college, which benefits states with smaller populations.[5] Nuttle pointed to several other policies the Democrats have proposed, including the Green New Deal, "which will eliminate or severely curtail the fossil fuel and cattle industries; free college tuition without demanding any reforms from university bureaucracies; more regulation of the financial industry [even without] any evidence of cause and effect; and reparations for minorities without formulas for calculating amounts or guidelines for distribution."[6]

Levin had these additions to what the Democrats want to do when he interviewed Hagee: "They want to eliminate ICE law enforcement. So in other words, they want to eliminate our border and any notion of rule of law when it comes to immigration. They constantly are undermining the United States military and cutting the military's budget every time they get a chance, every time they are in power. They want to appoint to the bench, particularly the Supreme Court, judicial activists who do not embrace our founding principles as a factual matter."[7]

From an evangelical Christian point of view, Donald Trump is doing a great job. Yet the question keeps coming up, especially from the media, on how morally conservative Christians can support him. Dennis Prager says the same charge is leveled at conservative Jews. "There are so many more Christians that they don't bother with the Jews," he said on his radio program, "but Orthodox Jews, like evangelical Christians, overwhelmingly support President Trump."

As discussed in chapter 6, Prager understands Christians get most of the flak from the Left, and he said: "I spend a good part of my life defending [Evangelicals]. As a Jew defending Christians it lends a certain credibility that doesn't happen when we defend our own. If a Jew defends Christians, or [a] Christian defends Jews, it's different."

The day I was on his radio show, Dennis asked me if God preordained what happens in the world. I told him I believe it is a mystery.

It's preordained, but also we have free will. Then the topic changed to, Does this excuse us from voting? "Of course not," I replied. Then Prager hammered a point he brought up several times. David Lane had told him many Christians are not even registered to vote. And of those who are, many stay home on Election Day. "It's hard for me to see why they would stay home given that everything is on the line in that election," Prager said.

Ralph Reed has an interesting perspective as a political consultant. He believes Evangelicals sometimes assume we are still "the silent majority" and our leaders can "anoint someone for office," such as when an overwhelming percentage of high-profile leaders backed Ted Cruz for president. Of course when Cruz dropped out, they quickly switched to supporting Trump.

But Ralph has watched how the Jewish community approaches elections since they don't have the numbers to get behind one candidate during the primaries. "In the Jewish community, there are no illusions about being a majority; they know they are outnumbered. So in the Jewish community, leaders survey the field and plug various key individuals into the campaigns of the candidates with whom they have a close relationship. That way, instead of trying to back a single candidate, they have access and relationships no matter who wins. That's smart, and it is a strategy the Christian community would be wise to adopt. Rather than pick one horse, make sure you have leaders in every campaign and surrounding every candidate."

He said it's well known Christians have stayed home in recent elections rather than vote for those whom they consider to be the lesser of two evils. Or they are just complacent and feel there is nothing they can do to affect the outcome of the election. In 2012 a lot of Christians were very much against Obama, but they weren't comfortable with the Republican nominee, Mitt Romney—probably due to not only his "liberal" record as a politician but also the fact he is a practicing Mormon. It's estimated three million to five million evangelical Christians stayed home that year, and that was about the margin by which Obama won a second term. So what's it going to take for conservatives and especially Christians to get motivated to get out the vote?

"I think part of it is the president's record," Reed told me, speaking of Trump's election in 2016. "I think there were some Evangelicals and some pro-life Roman Catholics who either stayed home or maybe voted for a third-party candidate or came to support the president very reluctantly at the end. That's probably because they had reservations about him as a person and questions about whether they could really trust his promises, both to the faith community and the broader electorate, that he would govern as a pro-life president."

Reed continued: "The good news is, after only a few years in office, I think that argument is over. Trump is the most pro-life president in American history. He has appointed over one hundred district [and] appellate [judges] and [two] Supreme Court justices, Neil Gorsuch and Brett Kavanaugh. He has moved the embassy from Tel Aviv to Jerusalem. He has withdrawn from the Iran nuclear deal. He has made it a major priority to protect Christians around the world where they're minorities, in particular. I can't imagine that given the possibility of a second term, there won't be intense support in the faith community based on all he's done for us."

Prager understands all the reasons to vote for Trump, so he asked me: "Is it true to the best of your knowledge that there are still Evangelicals who don't vote? Why? So, tell me about Christians who might say, 'God appoints the leaders anyway. Why should I vote?' What's your answer to them?"

I said voting is our responsibility as good Christian citizens, but I understand some people feel marginalized or have a feeling of "Why bother?" because they think it won't make a difference.

"There are Christians who think their eternal home is in heaven. So just kind of hold out until then," I replied. "And they don't realize how serious the moral crisis is in America, which, if not solved, will affect how they can live what the Bible calls 'quiet and peaceful lives.'"

Alerting these people to the dangers of what lies ahead is why I wrote this book.

Look at the twenty or so Democrats who tossed their hats into the ring well over a year before the election, hoping to be nominated by their party. They espouse a form of socialism that to me almost sounds like communism.

The leftward progression toward communism begins with "liberalism," moves to "progressivism," then becomes "socialism," and finally "communism." I heard someone say that a socialist is really a communist without a gun. These socialists on the left are trying to take over without guns! If they can get voted in, they will take over everything. Socialists will regulate every part of our lives. They'll take away our freedoms, and if they do, how will we ever get those freedoms back?

I admire Dennis Prager because he perceives that part of society's problem is that people don't understand ultimate issues. "That's why they create causes, like teaching children that there's no such thing as male and female," he said. "They make up causes to fill the 'meaning vacuum' caused by the secular society."[8] He believes this is so important he focuses on it in his "Ultimate Issues Hour" every Tuesday on his radio show.

The weirdness is not only political but cultural, which proves the point that "politics is downstream from culture," the Don Eberly quote often attributed to the late Andrew Breitbart because he quoted it so often.[9] And it seems to get worse and worse. As I was writing this, ABC's *Good Morning America* was featuring an eleven-year-old boy who was cross-dressing as a "drag queen." Instead of acknowledging how sad his behavior is, the program was treating the little boy (who didn't look as if he had hit puberty) as if he were a hero. The show invited three adult drag queens to appear, and they congratulated the confused little boy for helping mainstream this abnormal behavior.

Politics may indeed be downstream from culture, but some use this as an excuse to ignore the truth that elections have consequences. What is also true is that culture is downstream from the church. The hope of the world is Jesus, and as His bride, the church is supposed to transform the world into His image.

But unfortunately we now live in a world where the nonbiblical LGBTQ agenda has hijacked civil rights that were founded on the Word of God and fought for by pastors. We can turn this around if the church will stop hiding our light. Once we stand up and begin to shine the light of God's love to deliver those in the darkness, we will begin to reverse this moral decline.

Steve Deace, the Iowa talk show host who is now on Blaze TV, calls this moral decline a "progressive cancer." In a blog subtitled "The Progressive Left Seeks to Dismantle Our Culture," he quoted conservative pundit Jesse Kelly:

> For too long the people on the Right (myself included) have called the American Left "socialists" or some brand of that. But it's dawned on me they're something else entirely and I can't quite put my finger on it. Even the commies loved their country. This is something worse. The commies didn't want to flood their countries with illegal aliens and deport nobody.

The commies would never have allowed government schools to encourage young children to question their gender. Or allowed a young boy to dress in drag and dance for men. I can't stop thinking about that Gallup poll showing only 22 percent of Democrats are proud of their country. Something has really shifted. It's not UN-American. It is ANTI-American. That's not communism. That's an insurgency.

Deace noted that if conservatism is going to be an effective movement going forward, we must realize that its detractors aren't driven primarily by political ideology. "No, they are devout knee-benders to a 'spirit of the age cult,' whose iconoclastic goal is the dismantling of Western civilization, or Judeo-Christendom, for the purposes of installing a totally different culture."[10]

This is what we are facing and why it's crucial we reelect President Trump in 2020. While no politician alone can solve what ails America, I've made the case for how Trump is an answer to prayer who has at least given us a reprieve for a few years.

The stakes are high if the other side wins. Deace said at one time to share Jesse Kelly's beliefs simply meant you were an American, no matter your political party. Now such beliefs "qualify you as a bigot who must shut up and guzzle whatever [the Left spews] forth from their rancid firehose." He warns against laughing at the absurdity of the Left. "We are being surrounded by an orgy of nonsense that far too many people write off as just another political debate, instead of hearing it as the ominous and looming executioner's song that it is."[11]

It's this sort of craziness in the culture that makes Prager think conservatives are energized for the 2020 election. "The Left does so much bad that even if you don't want to be energized, you can't help but be energized," he said, adding that the issue of "Christians who don't vote is disturbing because I'm such a big Christian. . . . I tell this to Jewish audiences or secular audiences—if Christianity fails in America, it's over for America. It's as simple as that"—something so obvious he believes any honest atheist would even agree. "There are just constantly wake-up calls because of [the Left's] extreme positions such as being for open borders. They are essentially for the end of the nation-state as we know it."

WHAT ARE CHRISTIANS TO DO?

It seems our nation has been divided into voting blocs, and Christians, especially Evangelicals, are an influential one. But our strength is in our numbers, and as Prager expressed with concern, too many conservative Christians are tempted to disengage on Election Day. The fact is, whether liberal or conservative, not all Christians vote, and even conservative Christians who do go to the polls don't always vote based on biblical principles.

David Barton watches Christian voting trends with interest and says no one can know precisely what the actual numbers are; they are based only on generally identified percentages in the United States. There will be regions where these numbers will be higher or lower, but they all combine to form a national general picture.

- The current US population is 329.5 million.[12]

- The number of eligible voters (those at least eighteen years old) is 255.7 million (which is 77.6 percent of the total population).[13]

- Professing Christians are 70.6 percent of the population,[14] or 180.8 million eligible voters.

- 33.1 percent of eligible voters are not registered to vote,[15] including 59.8 million Christians.

- 36 percent of professing Christians are considered evangelical,[16] so 21.5 million Evangelicals are unregistered.

Short story: about 59.8 million professing Christians are not registered to vote, of whom about 21.5 million are professing Evangelicals also not registered to vote.

Earlier in the book I discussed how both Republicans and Democrats are trying to get more people to register who they believe will vote for their candidates. If we are concerned, as I am, that people "vote biblically," the situation becomes more complicated.

"Getting church people to register to vote will not necessarily result in improved candidates," Barton said. For example, despite efforts to get Christians to register and vote in the 2016 presidential election, 57 percent of all first-time voters supported Hillary Clinton.[17] "That is one of the highest levels of support she received from any group,"

Barton said. "Thus, just because church people get registered to vote does not mean they will vote in a biblical or conservative manner."

Barton points again to statistics discussed in chapter 13 that show only a small percentage of Christians have a biblical worldview, a fraction read the Bible on a daily basis, and many American pastors are unwilling to preach on issues they deem too political. So if Christians are not taught to view current issues through a biblical worldview, we should not be surprised if they do not necessarily vote according to Christian values.

Barton told me, however, Christians do get involved in political activities if their pastors are talking about what the Bible says about current moral and cultural issues. David Lane of the American Renewal Project, discussed in chapter 13, has been a leader in helping pastors understand their role in addressing cultural issues and getting their members to become politically active.

He has also seen the value of distributing voter guides that provide simple, but specific, information showing the difference between candidates on five to seven key cultural/moral issues.

"Generally, in an election, any candidate will address numerous issues, many of which are not of particular relevance to biblical faith. But when the cacophony of noise of those dozens of issues is narrowed to presenting a candidate's position on just the few issues of importance to Christian beliefs and values, participation increases," Lane said, adding that while he's heard of a few small programs that seem to move the needle in some areas, there is nothing overall nationally that seems to make a big difference. The reasons: the basic problem with Christians not voting is not a lack of programs but the overall biblical and historical illiteracy of most professing Christians and their pastors.

Arthelene Rippy, a Christian broadcaster, has been saying for years on the air that she's sick and tired of lazy Christians who don't vote. "To me, that is an absolute disgrace," she said. "That ability to vote is holy to me."

Although the upsurge in evangelical voters in the 2016 election was surprising to an extent, it also made sense. After all, the US had been going down a path of increasing wickedness and liberalization for years, and Trump seemed the only realistic hope of flipping that trend. Arthelene agrees and says as liberals get more liberal, the differences between the Left and the Right become more distinct.

"We're really getting to a place in America where the line is well-defined," she said. "And if you are on the side of abortion, where they dismember babies' bodies inside the mother's womb and they sell the parts, and people who promote same-sex marriage, which trashes how many thousands of years of marriage that God set up in the Garden of Eden—those lines are pretty plain. You're either on one side or the other."

Cindy Jacobs, founder of Generals International, leads the Reformation Prayer Network. About thirteen thousand intercessors pray with them, plus there are fifty state prayer networks, some of which mobilize, they say, about ten thousand intercessors in their state.

In 2016 Jacobs mobilized ten thousand intercessors to "prayer-walk" the seven critical states that helped Trump win in November. These men and women walked around courthouses or through the center of town praying for righteousness to prevail. In addition, a coalition of prayer leaders called As One also mobilized their networks two different times to prayer-walk for forty days. "It was an urgent, Pentecostal type of prayer," Cindy told me. They knew this was not just another election. There were "battles in the heavenlies" for the soul of America, and Cindy's prayer warriors were engaged in those battles, praying that God's will would reign in America once again.

Cindy says she and other leaders believe it's God's will for Trump to win, but she also feels it is up to Christians to "pray as we've never prayed. And not only pray but to act and go out to the polls and...vote. [I believe] voting is a spiritual exercise."

Like Hagee, Prager, and others I've quoted, Cindy believes this is a "pivotal election, such as we haven't seen. I can't overstate how critical this is. It will determine if we go down, down, down, and become more socialist. If that happens, I believe we will lose the liberties that we have. I know that sounds extreme, but it's my opinion. That's why we are mobilizing prayer."

She is also calling Christians to fast and pray. "If we don't fast and pray, things will turn out a way we don't want them to. They'll shift suddenly," she told me. "Every church needs to pray. They are commanded to pray for the president. I think we have to do everything we can to see the election shift to righteousness."

Another prayer network organizer, Pastor Frank Amedia, told me God is doing mighty things in the nation right now, but he believes the church must again become aware of the power of God. He tells the story of a well-known Korean pastor who visited the US at the request of one of the biggest denominations. When the pastor came to America, he was disheartened at the lack of zeal for the Lord. Just before he left to return to Korea, he told the pastors who invited him that the American church has a form of godliness but no power.

"I think we need to be a voice calling the body of Christ to get hot, to get on fire and not to be complacent or live on the laurels of an election that was won a couple years ago when we're losing so many battles day by day in the earth today," Amedia said.

Cindy Jacobs was surprised in 2016 by how many intercessors around the world were praying for our election. Since she has ministered across the globe, people she knows in Europe, China, and Latin America told her intercessors were praying fervently that Trump would be elected. Many took the election so seriously they told her they were fasting and praying for hours each day.

Cindy's close friend Lou Engle, a revivalist and cofounder of TheCall, a group that hosts twelve-hour prayer rallies, sent out a call to friends and supporters to begin a three-day Esther fast—meaning no food and no water—as a petition for God's mercy. He rallied thousands to join him because the situation looked so bleak. Conservative Christians believed that if Hillary Clinton won the election it would be "game over" for religious freedom. The stakes are again high in 2020. Cindy and other ministries are not only mobilizing intercessors in the US; they are asking their international prayer networks again to fast and pray for America in the run-up to the election.[18]

Charismatic prayer leader and Bible teacher Dutch Sheets is also good friends with Cindy Jacobs. He and Chuck Pierce (who had prophesied that Barack Obama would win two terms as well as saying as early as 2008 that God was going to use "the trump card"—a prophetic indication he came to understand meant Donald Trump would be elected) believe there will be a revival around the world.

Dutch believes this revival will be "like the Jesus movement of the late 1960s–70s except on steroids." He's been traveling the country announcing that God is "birthing the future," adding, "we've been having some of the most powerful, significant gatherings I have ever participated in. And it's not because there is a great explosion of power; it's because there is such incredible depth that has come to the remnant church—the praying church. In the past twenty-five years, millions have prayed and fasted, and we are seeing those prayers answered. It's been encouraging."

But at the same time, Dutch, like other leaders, is aware of the vitriolic hate and the attacks against Trump, which are exposing the Left for who they really are and what they really believe.

"I believe it's all demonically motivated because I believe the powers of darkness are so angry to be seeing the momentum they had gained for the last forty to fifty years being reversed," Dutch said. "Because if America becomes weak and loses these markers and loses our strength, we can no longer be the basis for [spreading] the gospel around the world that we need to be. The awakening that's coming in is going to impact America, but it's going to be around the world."

Dutch told me of a prophetic word he received from the Lord. "[God] told me this so clearly years ago, and He may have told me for America: 'I must have this nation to do what I'm going to do around the world, and Trump is a part of that,' and God is using him, and He's using him as some have said as a wrecking ball. The Left hates it. They want somebody in there they can 'get along with,' which means [someone who will] compromise a little, and Trump won't."

Dutch went on to make an even more sobering statement: "It's why we must pray for him so diligently, because they're going to try to kill him. They're going to try to silence him with persecution, slander, and with all these court cases. What strikes me as so amazing is there seems to be insulation around him that has to be spiritual that is keeping this from discouraging him or slowing him down. It's almost like the more they do it, the tougher he gets. It's almost like he is a John the Baptist, [saying], 'Bring it on! I don't care.'"

There have always been citizens, Christian or not, who have wanted to sit on the sidelines. In the American Revolution, about half of the country didn't care who won the conflict but just hoped it wouldn't affect them. Another 15 to 20 percent remained loyal to England. Only 40 to 45 percent supported American independence, and only about a third of those fought in the war, either in the Continental Army or in the militia.[19]

Most people don't realize that only 15 percent of Americans actually participated in winning our freedom during the American Revolution. "We all sit here and think, 'Oh, we beat the British!' No, just [a small fraction] of Americans beat the British," Barton noted. If we could get as little as 15 percent on board with applying biblical principles in the

US, "we could turn this nation around for the good," he said. I hope you're willing to be a part of that number.

One of the most articulate spokesmen for Christian values is Pastor Robert Jeffress of First Baptist Church of Dallas. He's a regular on Lou Dobbs' show on the Fox Business Network, and Dobbs asked him almost two years before the election to prognosticate on the political situation in this country.

"The Left has been doing everything they can to try to delegitimize this president since day one," Jeffress said. "First it was the 'collusion illusion.' That hasn't worked out. And now they created what I call the myth of the midterm massacre—this idea that somehow the GOP lost massive amounts because of Trump's unpopularity. That is complete fiction. First of all, President Trump did not have the shellacking that Obama did in losing sixty House seats and six Senate seats. Instead he had minimal losses in the House and picked up three Senate seats."

Let me pause to say I agree with Jeffress, and I believe the president came out ahead in the midterms because the senators from swing states who opposed him about Kavanaugh are gone. I can't say that surprises me. The debacle surrounding Kavanaugh was one of the most despicable things in Congress I've ever seen.

Jeffress continued: "I'm going to make this prediction…that the House flipping and being under the leadership of Maxine Waters and Nancy Pelosi is going to give President Trump an even larger re-election majority win in 2020. This is all going to work for good….I believe there is great momentum and support behind this president because he's focusing on results, and we are seeing those results every day of every week."

Lou asked him who will win in 2020, and Jeffress answered loud and clear: "Donald J. Trump."[20]

ONE NATION UNDER GOD

What happens if Jeffress is wrong and Trump loses, as I asked in chapter 2? What is at stake? Everything. That's why people must pray. There's an old axiom that says we need to pray as if everything depends upon God and act as if everything depends upon us—because it does! Never has this been truer than at this critical hour when our nation's future hangs in the balance. Because we know this is a spiritual battle, prayer is absolutely critical in winning the fight. But it won't mean much if you don't vote. If any of the current Democratic presidential candidates wins the election this November, America as we know it is certain to pass away in our lifetime.

As Christian Americans, you and I have enjoyed the traditions of freedom and religious liberty that we've inherited from generations before us—values that have defined the United States from its inception. President Trump has vowed that under his watch, we will continue to reap these blessings in our nation. He has vowed that America will never become a socialist country. He has vowed that we will be a nation that believes in the power of prayer. And he has vowed that we will remain one nation under God.

As people of faith, we cannot stand by and allow these rights and privileges to be erased. We must stand up and be counted, casting votes that protect the values we hold most dear. It is the only way we will preserve those rights and freedoms for the generations that follow.

I opened this book by talking about Donald Trump's 2020 candidacy rally in Orlando, and I close now by sharing the powerful words he shared with us that evening, on June 18, 2019. In some ways they feel like Donald Trump's contract with America.

> We will never stop fighting for the values that hold us together as one America. We believe in the American Constitution and the rule of law. We believe in the dignity of work and the sanctity of life. We believe that faith and family, not government and bureaucracy, are the true American way. We believe that our children should be taught to love our country, honor our history, and always respect our great American flag. And we will live by the words of our national motto: In God we trust. Powered by these values, we won a victory two and a half years ago; we won a victory...for American self-government, self-rule, and self-determination. We have been blessed by God with the greatest nation on the face of the earth, and we are going to keep it that way.[21]

A CALL TO PRAYER AND ACTION

God calls all of us to fill different roles at different times and I
think that He wanted Donald Trump to become president. And
that's why he's there, and I think he has done a tremendous job in
supporting a lot of the things that people of faith really care about.[1]
—SARAH HUCKABEE SANDERS
WHITE HOUSE PRESS SECRETARY, 2017–2019

A BOOK WITH GOD as part of its title—describing what is not just a political or cultural, but spiritual, war—must conclude with a spiritual point of view. The Bible says to pray for those in authority so we may live quiet and peaceful lives in all godliness.[2] Elsewhere it says to seek God first, and these things will be added to you.[3] In the Bible, God promises that "if My people…will…pray… and turn from their wicked ways, then I will hear from heaven, and will forgive their sin and will heal their land."[4] It's hard to document and measure spiritual things, but millions of people have been praying in groups large and small, believing for a shift in the very serious situation in America.

One prayer warrior named Mary Colbert started the daily National Prayer Call in 2016, making her one of the earliest voices urging believers to pray for Trump. The movement she started has not diminished since Trump's election. Her preelection prayer conference calls reached as many as one hundred thousand people, and frequently she had to turn away listeners because the conference call was too full. Now, to continue to bring as many people as possible together in prayer, Mary has set up a new system of having local spiritually vetted leaders run conference calls in their community. There are already twenty-five of these new hosts, called nation builders, setting up prayer calls, and the number continues to grow. The calls emphasize praying for those in leadership, whether here in the US or abroad.[5]

Recently Mary had a powerful insight ab[...]
believers to "turn from their wicked ways," as 2 [...]
so God would "hear from heaven, and…heal t[...]
came with the parable of the talents, in which [...]
their talents and were called "good and faithf[...]
was afraid he'd get in trouble if he lost what he'd [...] so he did
nothing. The master called him "wicked."[6] Mary believes Christians
who "do nothing" because they fear being ridiculed as politically
incorrect are "wicked" and must repent.

"The scripture says, 'You wicked, lazy servant,'[7] so literally in God's
eyes, the wicked and lazy are synonymous," Mary observed. As it is
often said, "The only thing necessary for the triumph of evil is that
good men do nothing."

Mary believes "everyone has a voice," and she is doing everything
she can to mobilize the church with this truth. It must be working,
because Mary says she is stopped in airports by people who recognize
her and feel they have been given back their voices as they have begun
to pray and to be involved in turning back the tide of evil in our nation.

I believe Mary's focus on the 2020 election is important, including
her new strategy to pray for the Democratic Party—a party many
Evangelicals have given up on, measured by the 81 percent of white
Evangelicals who voted for Donald Trump.

One day in prayer Mary said she felt the Lord tell her that He set
up a two-party system—Democrat and Republican—for a balance of
power. The reason, she believes, is that if one party had absolute power,
it would be absolutely corrupt. And while God favors neither party,
one has drifted from godly principles and gone so far as to even take
any mention of God out of its platform.

A century ago the Democrats were so conservative that William
Jennings Bryan, a strong Evangelical, ran for president on its ticket. I
personally know Democratic politicians who claim to be born-again
Christians. But why do they seem like anomalies? Where have the
others gone?

In 2019 Mary began to pray for righteous people in the Democratic
Party who will stand for biblical values. Impossible? It seems so, considering the way this book has documented that the Democratic Party
has almost gone off the rails. But Mary Colbert believes God wants
believers to pray for the Democratic Party.

When she began saying this on her prayer calls and in appearances

stian TV, she was accused of supporting Democratic Party
ions. She told people her political positions haven't changed.
ather, she sees herself as praying as Jesus said for those who persecute
you and say all manner of evil against you[8]—persecution that, unfortunately, happens too often against evangelical Christians because of
the positions we hold. But she also believes there are godly Democrats
who are intimidated and staying silent instead of trying to move their
party toward righteous principles and platforms.

"There must be Democrats who are God-fearing people, but they
haven't spoken up. They need to take that party and turn it around.
That's my prayer," Mary told me.

Choco De Jesús, the pastor from Chicago, says, "I tell people I'm
just a prophetic voice, neither Republican nor Democrat." But he
appreciates the stands President Trump has taken. He hates it when
people show their disrespect to the man and the office by calling him
Forty-Five.

What's going to happen Tuesday, November 3, 2020? It's too early
to know for sure, but Choco says the Democrats don't know what they
want. "They've lost their identity as Democrats. They've gone too far
to the left, advocating Democratic socialism. I don't care if you put
Democrat in front of it. It's still socialism, and so I see Trump winning." As much as I want to see Trump win in 2020, I also believe we
must pray for righteous Democrats to take back their party.

Pastor John Kilpatrick also believes Christians must pray to stop
"what the enemy is doing. It's as if Satan has done everything to keep
a born-again experience away from this generation. It's going to take
a moving of the Holy Spirit, and I believe we're getting close to it."
As I pointed out earlier, Kilpatrick says he's not a "Trump man," but
he prays for him regularly and believes a coming spiritual renewal
depends on his being reelected.

Kilpatrick believes we are experiencing "spiritual warfare for the
soul of this nation," and he says "it's time to quit discussing things
about the president. It's time to quit discussing what's going on in
Washington—it's time to start praying. The people of God need to pray
right now."

The Bible says, "Faith without works is dead."[9] So we can pray, but
we must work, and we must vote. God's people are called to be "wise
as serpents and harmless as doves."[10] We must be like the gentle Jesus
even as we fight battles for the soul of our nation.

So I encourage you to get registered to vote, if you haven't already, and encourage others to do so. Get involved in your local community, and help turn the tide. I believe with what I've outlined in this book, there is hope for the future. But we must act now. None of this matters if you don't vote.

I'll conclude by quoting Dennis Prager, who may be the best Jewish friend to Evangelicals in this country.

"So I don't understand when Christians don't vote. It's a puzzle to me. Doesn't God want you to promote good on this planet? It's so foreign to my understanding of what God wants us to do. I mean, it's almost like saying, 'Why should I build the hospital? We're all going to die and go to paradise if we believe properly, right?'" he asked rhetorically. "What is the difference between building a hospital and voting? Each is an act of doing good as you understand that in society. So why do anything?...Why not just, you know, pray all day?"

He continued: "I am told by my Christian friends that there [are] still Christians who just sit home on Election Day. So they benefit from all these people before them who fought for America and to have a country whose motto is 'In God we trust' [and] who maintained that motto. I mean, if you don't [trust God], how do you defend Normandy Beach? These people didn't just vote; they got blasted by Nazi machine guns. What would they have said? 'Why bother? Why bother fighting a war?' It's the same thing [with voting]."

That generation rose up to meet the challenge. The question is, Will we? We cannot assume that others will do it. Donald Trump can't win without our help. Each of us must do our part. God demands no less.

EPILOGUE

As THIS BOOK goes to press, calls to impeach Donald Trump are louder than ever. Of course this is nothing new. The week after a whistle-blower repeated secondhand information about President Trump's conversation with the president of Ukraine that eventually spawned an impeachment investigation, Gov. Mike Huckabee said in his monologue on his TV program, "I thought that's what we've had ever since he got sworn in."[1]

Democrats, angry that Trump won in 2016, have been trying to get him out of office almost since he was inaugurated, and this latest effort is more of the same. As Huckabee said on his show, "This is, frankly, window dressing so the Democrats can say they're trying to impeach the president. Now, don't get me wrong. They're going to do everything they can to do it. But you've got to have a reason. You can't just impeach a president because you don't like how the election turned out. And that's basically what we're dealing with."

Later in the same show, Judge Jeanine Pirro blamed the deep state for all the impeachment drama: "They're pretty much deciding how things should be handled. They don't care what the rules are. They know how to circumvent the rules. They know what the loopholes are. And they get together, and they decide what they're going to do. And a classic example was the effort to unseat a sitting president."[2]

While I want to be careful in predicting the future, I believe Donald Trump will survive this attack too. I think the Democrats know they can't beat him at the polls, but if they can create a "scandal" and make him damaged goods in the eyes of some voters, that may shift enough votes to steal the election from him. One of the reasons Trump could lose that I cited in chapter 2 is the dishonesty of the other side.

But let's be clear. This impeachment inquiry is not about what Donald Trump may have said in a phone call with the Ukrainian president. It's about the fact that this president, as imperfect as he may have been in the past, has been standing for religious liberty and righteousness. He has stood with Israel. He is strong. He can't be intimidated.

The attacks are, in my opinion, from the pit of hell. As a Christian I believe that Satan is behind this. He is trying to steal, kill, and destroy. And Donald Trump has been raised up by God to stop our nation's headlong plunge into total depravity. Trump's presidency is God's mercy to America since we deserve judgment.

I'm amazed at how many of my sincere Christian friends are surprised by all these demonic attacks against the president. Why should they be surprised? Satan hates it when America stands with Israel. He hates it when righteousness and religious freedom are championed. No wonder he and his minions have focused their hatred toward Donald Trump.

I purposely wrote this book months before the election in order to motivate Christians and conservatives to reelect Donald Trump. Because I wrote so far in advance, I knew things would change, depending on who ran on the Democratic ticket. So I have written practically nothing about those who are running for the nomination to oppose Trump in the general election. My feeling is that it doesn't matter which one of them wins the nomination—someone new could even jump into the race right before the primaries begin—they all will be equally bad. If a Democrat wins in 2020, all the good things Trump has done will be immediately undone. Plus, once the person is in power, he or she will try to take away our liberties as Christians and create hate-crime legislation that will actually make proclaiming the gospel illegal if it contradicts the Left's politically correct perception of reality.

As I've said before, even though I have included a chapter on why Trump might lose, I personally believe he will win. As you read this, you know things that I didn't know when I wrote this in 2019. That's because while Satan comes to steal, kill, and destroy, Jesus comes to give life and give it more abundantly. I believe God has a plan for America. And I believe He raised up Donald Trump to help accomplish that plan.

I believe God spoke to prophets over the years, telling them that He would play "the trump card." I outline this in chapter 11, but I document only a few of the prophecies that have declared Trump would win. The prophets were right in 2016, even if right up until the votes were counted, everyone else expected Hillary Clinton to win. I believe the prophets will be right again this time and that in 2020 Donald Trump will win a second term.

Of course the larger culture doesn't believe in prophecy, and they couldn't care less about God's will. Even many Christians look at political trends and often use many of the same tactics as their secular counterparts in order to win at the polls. But as a Charismatic Christian who believes in the work of the Holy Spirit and the gift of prophecy, I base my belief on what the prophets have said—not what the talking heads on cable TV or the reporters in the *New York Times* newsroom think is going to happen.

In his first three years as president, Trump has exposed that deep state operatives in the Department of Justice and the FBI have engaged in a blatant attempt to overthrow an elected president. Now, with the recent whistle-blower's report, it seems the CIA is also part of the coup against Trump. CIA director Gina Haspel has close ties with former CIA director John Brennan, who served during the Obama administration, so nothing that comes from the CIA against Trump surprises me.

Two years ago my friend Doug Wead, whom I quote extensively in this book, made comments in an interview with Lou Dobbs that in hindsight were prophetic, and a clip of that interview has been circulating recently on the internet. Back then he claimed that the deep state, which has successfully overthrown the governments of foreign countries, was going to continue to actively seek a coup d'état of the duly elected president of the United States.

He said if there was ever a time in history to be concerned about another rise in communism, now is that time. Wead added that the deep state is determined to overthrow Donald Trump. The presidential historian refused to mince words, saying: "We have very skilled, talented professionals [in the US government]. They've overthrown governments in Vietnam and the Philippines, in Iraq and Iran, in Egypt, in the Ukraine. Duly elected democratic governments. They created what they called 'popular uprisings.'"[3]

Of course we should expect nothing less from shadow governments. As Wead noted, the very same people—some of whom work in the State Department, intelligence, and the media—have successfully caused uprisings in several other countries. They've worked together to overthrow foreign governments, and Wead believes Trump is a thorn in their side preventing a global takeover.

As this book goes to press, the deep state coup against Trump will only continue. If the so-called CIA whistle-blower story is exposed as false and dies down, rest assured that the Washington dealmakers, along with the Democrats and the corporate-controlled press, will invent any story and false scandal to try to destroy Trump's chance of reelection. So dear reader, be prepared; there will be more to come. Only time will tell of the intrigue of the so-called "swamp."

So even if the Democrats find the 218 votes needed to pass articles of impeachment over trumped-up, nonsensical charges, I believe Donald Trump will be vindicated. At the risk of being redundant, I stand by the things I've written in this book about what is at stake in this election, the policies Trump has advocated, and the type of man he is. I especially stand by the spiritual perspective I have presented—that this is spiritual warfare and Christians must wake up. A passive church is part of the reason the country is in the mess it's in. But Christians also have been praying, and in 2016 God answered prayer in the form of a man with no experience in politics and a bellicose style that turns some people off.

God raised up this man to lead our nation, and I believe Donald Trump will win a second term to complete the work he started—because I believe God has spoken.

Appendix A

REMARKS BY PRESIDENT TRUMP
AT THE UNITED NATIONS EVENT
ON RELIGIOUS FREEDOM

O N September 23, 2019, Donald Trump became the first US president to host a meeting on religious freedom at the United Nations General Assembly. Not only was his speech at the event in New York historic; it was one of his best, which is why I wanted to include it in this book. In it he articulated the value he places on religious freedom—both in America and around the world.

The United States is founded on the principle that our rights do not come from government; they come from God. This immortal truth is proclaimed in our Declaration of Independence and enshrined in the First Amendment to our Constitution's Bill of Rights. Our Founders understood that no right is more fundamental to a peaceful, prosperous, and virtuous society than the right to follow one's religious convictions.

Regrettably the religious freedom enjoyed by American citizens is rare in the world. Approximately 80 percent of the world's population live in countries where religious liberty is threatened, restricted, or even banned. And when I heard that number, I said, "Please go back and check it because it can't possibly be correct." And, sadly, it was. Eighty percent.

As we speak, Jews, Christians, Muslims, Buddhists, Hindus, Sikhs, Yazidis, and many other people of faith are being jailed, sanctioned, tortured, and even murdered, often at the hands of their own government, simply for expressing their deeply held religious beliefs. So hard to believe.

Today, with one clear voice, the United States of America calls upon the nations of the world to end religious persecution.

To stop the crimes against people of faith, release prisoners of conscience, repeal laws restricting freedom of religion and belief, protect the vulnerable, the defenseless, and the oppressed, America stands with believers in every country who ask only for the freedom to live according to the faith that is within their own hearts.

As President, protecting religious freedom is one of my highest priorities and always has been. Last year, our Secretary of State, Mike Pompeo, hosted the first-ever Ministerial to Advance International Religious Freedom.

In this year's ministerial, Secretary Pompeo announced plans to create the International Religious Freedom Alliance—an alliance of like-minded nations devoted to confronting religious persecution all around the world.

I've appointed a special envoy to monitor and combat anti-Semitism. We're standing up for almost 250 million Christians around the world who are persecuted for their faith. It is estimated that 11 Christians are killed every day for the following—I mean, just think of this: Eleven Christians a day, for following the teachings of Christ. Who would even think that's possible in this day and age? Who would think it's possible?

With us today is Pastor Andrew Brunson, who was imprisoned in Turkey for a long period of time. Last year, my administration was thrilled to bring him back home after a very short and respectful negotiation with a very strong man—and a man who has become a friend of mine, fortunately—President Erdoğan of Turkey.

I called the President, and I said, "He's an innocent man." They've been trying to get Andrew out for a long time—previous administration. I don't think they tried too hard, unfortunately.

But I want to thank President Erdoğan, and I want to thank you, Pastor, for being here with us today.... We did a good job with that negotiation, Andrew. You got back. It wasn't easy. It wasn't pretty. But you got back. And we're proud of you. You have a great family. And the love—when Andrew came back, the love from so many people, it was—actually, I hadn't seen anything quite like it.

So, congratulations. And I understand you're doing fantastic work with your family. Thank you very much. Thank you, Andrew.

And I also want to thank Franklin Graham because he's been so instrumental in everything we're doing. He's done such an incredible job in so many different ways, including floods and hurricanes. And every time I go, I see Franklin there. He's always there before me. I don't know how he gets there before me. I'm going to beat him one day. But he's always at these places of—really, disaster areas. He's right there with an incredible, large staff of volunteers that are just amazing. Thank you very much. And, CeCe, thank you very much. Thank you very much. And, Paula White [Cain], thank you very much.

In July, I met with survivors of religious persecution at the White House. And we're honored that many of them could be here today as well. Some of these individuals suffered as a result of state-sponsored persecution; others, at the hands of terrorists and criminals. No matter the case, America will always be a voice for victims of religious persecution everywhere. No matter where you go, you have a place in the United States of America. Could I ask those folks to stand up, please? Please, stand up. Thank you. Thank you very much.

In recent times, the world has also witnessed devastating acts of violence in sacred places of worship. In 2016, an eighty-five-year-old Catholic priest was viciously killed while celebrating mass in Normandy, France. In the past year, the United States endured horrifying anti-Semitic attacks against Jewish Americans at synagogues in Pennsylvania and California. In March, Muslims praying with their families were sadistically murdered in New Zealand. On Easter Sunday this year, terrorists bombed Christian churches in Sri Lanka, killing hundreds of faithful worshippers. Who would believe this is even possible?

These evil attacks are a wound on all humanity. We must all work together to protect communities of every faith. We're also urging every nation to increase the prosecution and punishment of crimes against religious communities. There can be no greater crime than that. This includes measures to prevent the intentional destruction of religious sites and relics. Today, the Trump administration will dedicate an additional $25 million to protect religious freedom and religious sites and relics.

We're also pleased to be joined today by many of the partners from the business community, as we announce a very critical initiative.

The United States is forming a coalition of U.S. businesses for the protection of religious freedom. This is the first time this has been done. This initiative will encourage the private sector to protect people of all faiths in the workplace. And the private sector has brilliant leadership. And that's why some of the people in this room are among the most successful men and women on Earth. They know how things get done and they know how to take care of things. And they're with us now for the first time, to this extent. First time, ever. And we're really honored to have you in the room. Great business leaders, great people of strength.

Too often, people in positions of power preach diversity while silencing, shunning, or censoring the faithful. True tolerance means respecting the right of all people to express their deeply held religious beliefs.

Before I conclude, I want to once again thank all of the survivors in the room for their courage and resilience. You're an inspiration to the world. You remind us that no force on Earth is stronger than the faith of religious believers. The United States of America will forever remain at your side and the side of all who seek religious freedom.

Today, I ask all nations to join us in this urgent moral duty. We ask the governments of the world to honor the eternal right of every person to follow their conscience, live by their faith, and give glory to God. The United States has a vital role in this critical mission.

Secretary-General Guterres will now share a few words on the U.N.'s efforts to promote religious liberty for all. And he has been a champion of exactly what we're in this room for.

So I want to thank everybody for being here. God bless you. God bless the faithful. And God bless America.

REMARKS BY PRESIDENT TRUMP TO THE 74TH SESSION OF THE UNITED NATIONS GENERAL ASSEMBLY

THE DAY AFTER his address on religious freedom President Trump gave another powerful speech, before the UN General Assembly. In it he outlined what makes this nation so great and reiterated his commitment to building a strong economy, protecting our borders, promoting religious liberty, and standing firm against socialism. It was one of the clearest articulations of Trump's agenda and vision for the future of our nation that I've heard, and it proved to me yet again that we must reelect him in 2020.

Seven decades of history have passed through this hall, in all of their richness and drama. Where I stand, the world has heard from presidents and premiers at the height of the Cold War. We have seen the foundation of nations. We have seen the ringleaders of revolution. We have beheld saints who inspired us with hope, rebels who stirred us with passion, and heroes who emboldened us with courage—all here to share plans, proposals, visions, and ideas on the world's biggest stage.

Like those who met us before, our time is one of great contests, high stakes, and clear choices. The essential divide that runs all around the world and throughout history is once again thrown into stark relief. It is the divide between those whose thirst for control deludes them into thinking they are destined to rule over others and those people and nations who want only to rule themselves.

I have the immense privilege of addressing you today as the elected leader of a nation that prizes liberty, independence, and self-government above all. The United States, after having spent over two and a half trillion dollars since my election to completely rebuild our great military, is also, by far, the world's most powerful nation. Hopefully, it will never have to use this power.

Americans know that in a world where others seek conquest and domination, our nation must be strong in wealth, in might, and in spirit. That is why the United States vigorously defends the traditions and customs that have made us who we are.

Like my beloved country, each nation represented in this hall has a cherished history, culture, and heritage that is worth defending and celebrating, and which gives us our singular potential and strength.

The free world must embrace its national foundations. It must not attempt to erase them or replace them.

Looking around and all over this large, magnificent planet, the truth is plain to see: If you want freedom, take pride in your country. If you want democracy, hold on to your sovereignty. And if you want peace, love your nation. Wise leaders always put the good of their own people and their own country first.

The future does not belong to globalists. The future belongs to patriots. The future belongs to sovereign and independent nations who protect their citizens, respect their neighbors, and honor the differences that make each country special and unique.

It is why we in the United States have embarked on an exciting program of national renewal. In everything we do, we are focused on empowering the dreams and aspirations of our citizens.

Thanks to our pro-growth economic policies, our domestic unemployment rate reached its lowest level in over half a century. Fueled by massive tax cuts and regulations cuts, jobs are being produced at a historic rate. Six million Americans have been added to the employment rolls in under three years.

Last month, African American, Hispanic American, and Asian American unemployment reached their lowest rates ever recorded. We are marshaling our nation's vast energy abundance, and the United States is now the number one producer of oil and natural gas anywhere in the world. Wages are rising, incomes are soaring, and 2.5 million Americans have been lifted out of poverty in less than three years.

As we rebuild the unrivaled might of the American military, we are also revitalizing our alliances by making it very clear that all of our partners are expected to pay their fair share of the tremendous defense burden, which the United States has borne in the past.

At the center of our vision for national renewal is an ambitious campaign to reform international trade. For decades, the international trading system has been easily exploited by nations acting in very bad faith. As jobs were outsourced, a small handful grew wealthy at the expense of the middle class.

In America, the result was 4.2 million lost manufacturing jobs and $15 trillion in trade deficits over the last quarter century. The United States is now taking that decisive action to end this grave economic injustice. Our goal is simple: We want balanced trade that is both fair and reciprocal.

We have worked closely with our partners in Mexico and Canada to replace NAFTA with the brand new and hopefully bipartisan U.S.-Mexico-Canada Agreement.

Tomorrow, I will join Prime Minister Abe of Japan to continue our progress in finalizing a terrific new trade deal.

As the United Kingdom makes preparations to exit the European Union, I have made clear that we stand ready to complete an exceptional new trade agreement with the UK that will bring tremendous benefits to both of our countries. We are working closely with Prime Minister Boris Johnson on a magnificent new trade deal.

The most important difference in America's new approach on trade concerns our relationship with China. In 2001 China was admitted to the World Trade Organization. Our leaders then argued that this decision would compel China to liberalize its economy and strengthen protections to provide things that were unacceptable to us, and for private property and for the rule of law. Two decades later, this theory has been tested and proven completely wrong.

Not only has China declined to adopt promised reforms, it has embraced an economic model dependent on massive market barriers, heavy state subsidies, currency manipulation, product dumping, forced technology transfers, and the theft of intellectual property and also trade secrets on a grand scale.

As just one example, I recently met the CEO of a terrific American company, Micron Technology, at the White House. Micron produces memory chips used in countless electronics. To advance the Chinese government's five-year economic plan, a company owned by the Chinese state allegedly stole Micron's designs, valued at up to $8.7 billion. Soon, the Chinese company obtains patents for nearly an identical product, and Micron was banned from selling its own goods in China. But we are seeking justice.

The United States lost 60,000 factories after China entered the WTO. This is happening to other countries all over the globe.

The World Trade Organization needs drastic change. The second-largest economy in the world should not be permitted to declare itself a "developing country" in order to game the system at others' expense.

For years, these abuses were tolerated, ignored, or even encouraged. Globalism exerted a religious pull over past leaders, causing them to ignore their own national interests.

But as far as America is concerned, those days are over. To confront these unfair practices, I placed massive tariffs on more than $500 billion worth of Chinese-made goods. Already, as a result of these tariffs, supply chains are relocating back to America and to other nations, and billions of dollars are being paid to our Treasury.

The American people are absolutely committed to restoring balance to our relationship with China. Hopefully, we can reach an agreement that would be beneficial for both countries. But as I have made very clear, I will not accept a bad deal for the American people.

As we endeavor to stabilize our relationship, we're also carefully monitoring the situation in Hong Kong. The world fully expects that the Chinese government will honor its binding treaty, made with the British and registered with the United Nations, in which China commits to protect Hong Kong's freedom, legal system, and democratic ways of life. How China chooses to handle the situation will say a great deal about its role in the world in the future. We are all counting on President Xi as a great leader.

The United States does not seek conflict with any other nation. We desire peace, cooperation, and mutual gain with all. But I will never fail to defend America's interests.

One of the greatest security threats facing peace-loving nations today is the repressive regime in Iran. The regime's record of death and destruction is well known to us all. Not only is Iran the world's number one state sponsor of terrorism, but Iran's leaders are fueling the tragic wars in both Syria and Yemen.

At the same time, the regime is squandering the nation's wealth and future in a fanatical quest for nuclear weapons and the means to deliver them. We must never allow this to happen.

To stop Iran's path to nuclear weapons and missiles, I withdrew the United States from the terrible Iran nuclear deal, which has very little time remaining, did not allow inspection of important sites, and did not cover ballistic missiles.

Following our withdrawal, we have implemented severe economic sanctions on the country. Hoping to free itself from sanctions, the regime has escalated its violent and unprovoked aggression. In response to Iran's recent attack on Saudi Arabian oil facilities, we just imposed the highest level of sanctions on Iran's central bank and sovereign wealth fund.

All nations have a duty to act. No responsible government should subsidize Iran's bloodlust. As long as Iran's menacing behavior continues, sanctions will not be lifted; they will be tightened. Iran's leaders will have turned a proud nation into just another cautionary tale of what happens when a ruling class abandons its people and embarks on a crusade for personal power and riches.

For forty years, the world has listened to Iran's rulers as they lash out at everyone else for the problems they alone have created. They conduct ritual chants of "Death to America" and traffic in monstrous anti-Semitism. Last year the country's Supreme Leader stated, "Israel is a malignant cancerous tumor...that has to be removed and eradicated: it is possible and it will happen." America will never tolerate such anti-Semitic hate.

Fanatics have long used hatred of Israel to distract from their own failures. Thankfully, there is a growing recognition in the wider Middle East that the countries of the region share common interests in battling extremism and unleashing economic opportunity. That is why it is so important to have full, normalized relations between Israel and its neighbors. Only a relationship built on common interests, mutual respect, and religious tolerance can forge a better future.

Iran's citizens deserve a government that cares about reducing poverty, ending corruption, and increasing jobs—not stealing their money to fund a massacre abroad and at home.

After four decades of failure, it is time for Iran's leaders to step forward and to stop threatening other countries, and focus on building up their own country. It is time for Iran's leaders to finally put the Iranian people first.

America is ready to embrace friendship with all who genuinely seek peace and respect.

Many of America's closest friends today were once our gravest foes. The United States has never believed in permanent enemies. We want partners, not adversaries. America knows that while anyone can make war, only the most courageous can choose peace.

For this same reason, we have pursued bold diplomacy on the Korean Peninsula. I have told Kim Jong Un what I truly believe: that, like Iran, his country is full of tremendous untapped potential, but that to realize that promise, North Korea must denuclearize.

Around the world, our message is clear: America's goal is lasting, America's goal is harmony, and America's goal is not to go with these endless wars—wars that never end.

With that goal in mind, my administration is also pursuing the hope of a brighter future in Afghanistan. Unfortunately, the Taliban has chosen to continue their savage attacks. And we will continue to work with our coalition of Afghan partners to stamp out terrorism, and we will never stop working to make peace a reality.

Here in the Western Hemisphere, we are joining with our partners to ensure stability and opportunity all across the region. In that mission, one of our most critical challenges is illegal immigration, which undermines prosperity, rips apart societies, and empowers ruthless criminal cartels.

Mass illegal migration is unfair, unsafe, and unsustainable for everyone involved: the sending countries and the depleted countries. And they become depleted very fast, but their youth is not taken care of and human capital goes to waste.

The receiving countries are overburdened with more migrants than they can responsibly accept. And the migrants themselves are exploited, assaulted, and abused by vicious coyotes. Nearly one-third of women who make the journey north to our border are sexually assaulted along the way. Yet, here in the United States and around the world, there is a growing cottage industry of radical activists and non-governmental organizations that promote human smuggling. These groups encourage illegal migration and demand erasure of national borders.

Today, I have a message for those open border activists who cloak themselves in the rhetoric of social justice: Your policies are not just. Your policies are cruel and evil. You are empowering criminal organizations that prey on innocent men, women, and children. You put your own false sense of virtue before the lives, wellbeing... [of] countless innocent people. When you undermine border security, you are undermining human rights and human dignity.

Many of the countries here today are coping with the challenges of uncontrolled migration. Each of you has the absolute right to protect your borders, and so, of course, does our country. Today, we must resolve to work together to end human smuggling, end human trafficking, and put these criminal networks out of business for good.

To our country, I can tell you sincerely: We are working closely with our friends in the region—including Mexico, Canada, Guatemala, Honduras, El Salvador, and Panama—to uphold the integrity of borders and ensure safety and prosperity for our people. I would like to thank President López Obrador of Mexico for the great cooperation we are receiving and for right now putting 27,000 troops on our southern border. Mexico is showing us great respect, and I respect them in return.

The U.S., we have taken very unprecedented action to stop the flow of illegal immigration. To anyone considering crossings of our border illegally, please hear these words: Do not pay the smugglers. Do not pay the coyotes. Do not put yourself in danger. Do not put your children in danger. Because if you make it here, you will not be allowed in; you will be promptly returned home. You will not be released into our country. As long as I am president of the United States, we will enforce our laws and protect our borders.

For all of the countries of the Western Hemisphere, our goal is to help people invest in the bright futures of their own nation. Our region is full of such incredible promise: dreams waiting to be built and national destinies for all. And they are waiting also to be pursued.

Throughout the hemisphere, there are millions of hardworking, patriotic young people eager to build, innovate, and achieve. But these nations cannot reach their potential if a generation of youth abandon their homes in search of a life elsewhere. We want every nation in our region to flourish and its people to thrive in freedom and peace.

In that mission, we are also committed to supporting those people in the Western Hemisphere who live under brutal oppression, such as those in Cuba, Nicaragua, and Venezuela.

According to a recent report from the U.N. Human Rights Council, women in Venezuela stand in line for ten hours a day waiting for food. Over 15,000 people have been detained as political prisoners. Modern-day death squads are carrying out thousands of extrajudicial killings.

The dictator Maduro is a Cuban puppet, protected by Cuban bodyguards, hiding from his own people while Cuba plunders Venezuela's oil wealth to sustain its own corrupt communist rule.

Since I last spoke in this hall, the United States and our partners have built a historic coalition of fifty-five countries that recognize the legitimate government of Venezuela.

To the Venezuelans trapped in this nightmare: Please know that all of America is united behind you. The United States has vast quantities of humanitarian aid ready and waiting to be delivered. We are watching the Venezuela situation very closely. We await the day when democracy will be restored, when Venezuela will be free, and when liberty will prevail throughout this hemisphere.

One of the most serious challenges our countries face is the specter of socialism. It's the wrecker of nations and destroyer of societies.

Events in Venezuela remind us all that socialism and communism are not about justice, they are not about equality, they are not about lifting up the poor, and they are certainly not about the good of the nation. Socialism and communism are about one thing only: power for the ruling class.

Today, I repeat a message for the world that I have delivered at home: America will never be a socialist country.

In the last century, socialism and communism killed 100 million people. Sadly, as we see in Venezuela, the death toll continues in this country. These totalitarian ideologies, combined with modern technology, have the power to... [exercise] new and disturbing forms of suppression and domination.

For this reason, the United States is taking steps to better screen foreign technology and investments and to protect our data and our security. We urge every nation present to do the same.

Freedom and democracy must be constantly guarded and protected, both abroad and from within. We must always be skeptical of those who want conformity and control. Even in free nations, we see alarming signs and new challenges to liberty.

A small number of social media platforms are acquiring immense power over what we can see and over what we are allowed to say. A permanent political class is openly disdainful, dismissive, and defiant of the will of the people. A faceless bureaucracy operates in secret and weakens democratic rule. Media and academic institutions push flat-out assaults on our histories, traditions, and values.

In the United States, my administration has made clear to social media companies that we will uphold the right of free speech. A free society cannot allow social media giants to silence the voices of the people, and a free people must never, ever be enlisted in the cause of silencing, coercing, canceling, or blacklisting their own neighbors.

As we defend American values, we affirm the right of all people to live in dignity. For this reason, my administration is working with other nations to stop criminalizing of homosexuality, and we stand in solidarity with LGBTQ people who live in countries that punish, jail, or execute individuals based upon sexual orientation.

We are also championing the role of women in our societies. Nations that empower women are much wealthier, safer, and much more politically stable. It is therefore vital not only to a nation's prosperity, but also is vital to its national security, to pursue women's economic development.

Guided by these principles, my administration launched the Women's Global Development and Prosperity Initiatives. The W-GDP is [the] first-ever government-wide approach to women's economic empowerment, working to ensure that women all over the planet have the legal right to own and inherit property, work in the same industries as men, travel freely, and access credit and institutions.

Yesterday, I was also pleased to host leaders for a discussion about an ironclad American commitment: protecting religious leaders and also protecting religious freedom. This fundamental right is under growing threat around the world. Hard to believe, but 80 percent of the world's population lives in countries where religious liberty is in significant danger or even completely outlawed. Americans will never tire in our effort to defend and promote freedom of worship and religion. We want and support religious liberty for all.

Americans will also never tire of defending innocent life. We are aware that many United Nations projects have attempted to assert a global right to taxpayer-funded abortion on demand, right up until the moment of delivery. Global bureaucrats have absolutely no business attacking the sovereignty of nations that wish to protect innocent life. Like many nations here today, we in America believe that every child— born and unborn—is a sacred gift from God.

There is no circumstance under which the United States will allow international [entities] to trample on the rights of our citizens, including the right to self-defense. That is why, this year, I announced that we will never ratify the U.N. Arms Trade Treaty, which would threaten the liberties of law-abiding American citizens. The United States will always uphold our constitutional right to keep and bear arms. We will always uphold our Second Amendment.

The core rights and values America defends today were inscribed in America's founding documents. Our nation's Founders understood that there will always be those who believe they are entitled to wield power and control over others. Tyranny advances under many names and many theories, but it always comes down to the desire for domination. It protects not the interests of many, but the privilege of few.

Our Founders gave us a system designed to restrain this dangerous impulse. They chose to entrust American power to those most invested in the fate of our nation: a proud and fiercely independent people.

The true good of a nation can only be pursued by those who love it: by citizens who are rooted in its history, who are nourished by its culture, committed to its values, attached to its people, and who know that its future is theirs to build or theirs to lose. Patriots see a nation and its destiny in ways no one else can.

Liberty is only preserved, sovereignty is only secured, democracy is only sustained, greatness is only realized, by the will and devotion of patriots. In their spirit is found the strength to resist oppression, the inspiration to forge legacy, the goodwill to seek friendship, and the bravery to reach for peace. Love of our nations makes the world better for all nations.

So to all the leaders here today, join us in the most fulfilling mission a person could have, the most profound contribution anyone can make: Lift up your nations. Cherish your culture. Honor your histories. Treasure your citizens. Make your countries strong, and prosperous, and righteous. Honor the dignity of your people, and nothing will be outside of your reach.

When our nations are greater, the future will be brighter, our people will be happier, and our partnerships will be stronger.

With God's help, together we will cast off the enemies of liberty and overcome the oppressors of dignity. We will set new standards of living and reach new heights of human achievement. We will rediscover old truths, unravel old mysteries, and make thrilling new breakthroughs. And we will find more beautiful friendship and more harmony among nations than ever before.

My fellow leaders, the path to peace and progress, and freedom and justice, and a better world for all humanity, begins at home.

Thank you. God bless you. God bless the nations of the world. And God bless America.

ACKNOWLEDGMENTS

I COULD NOT HAVE written this book without the help of the many sources I interviewed, many of whom know President Trump personally or had insights on what is happening culturally and spiritually in America. (Of course I also gleaned from books and online sources, which are carefully documented in the endnotes.)

As I wrote, I found myself repeatedly identifying the individuals as "my friends." It is true that they are my friends. I've known many of them for decades, and I wanted the reader to know I can personally vouch for them and trust their opinions. But rather than bog down the narrative by saying that again and again, I decided this is where I could acknowledge their friendship and their help with the book.

Tom Ertl, a builder and publisher from Tallahassee, Florida, has been a friend since I met him in 2016 through the organization Christians for Donald Trump. We worked together encouraging the evangelical vote for Trump. Right after the inauguration, he gave me Roger Stone's *Making of the President 2016* because he knew I was interested in the election and had interviewed then candidate Trump. Stone's book barely mentioned the importance of the evangelical vote, and I felt there was an "untold story" that needed to be written, something that told not only of the evangelical support for Trump but also of the spiritual aspect of God's hand being on him. *God and Donald Trump* was the result.

When I began working on this book, predicting Trump will likely win a second term, Tom was the first to give me pause when he argued in an op-ed on the website News With Views that the president might actually lose. Later he gave me permission to quote many of the points he outlined in that article. Tom is the one who connected me to **Ray Moore**, a prayer and revival leader and Christian educator from South Carolina. Ray encouraged me to contact **Trevor Loudon**, a New Zealander now living in Florida who has become an expert on communists infiltrating our country, and **John Graves**, the Texas-based president of Vision America, which is doing amazing things using data

218

to turn out the evangelical vote. I appreciate the contributions of each of these men to chapter 2, titled "Why Trump Could Lose."

I became aware of **David Lane** of Westlake Village, California, when I was involved with Mike Huckabee's campaign for president in 2008. I've come to admire his keen insights into what is happening in our culture and his strategies to mobilize the church by activating pastors. His American Renewal Project newsletters are must-reading for me every week. One newsletter on compromise in the church being the cause of the spiritual mess we are in inspired me to include chapter 13 on that subject in this book.

I've known **Paula White Cain** of Apopka, Florida, for more than twenty-five years, ever since she was involved in starting a church in Tampa, Florida. Some of her first speaking engagements outside her church were at our *Charisma* women's events in the 1990s. Over the years, she has been on the covers of the magazines *Charisma* and *Ministries Today* (now known as *Charisma Leader*), and our book group, Charisma House, published her book *He Loves Me, He Loves Me Not* in 1998. My wife and I were having dinner with her in the early 2000s when she told us a celebrity named Donald Trump had watched her television show and contacted her office because he had some questions about God. At the time, I never imagined Paula would play such a pivotal role in his spiritual development or that Trump would become president.

Because she is so close to the president, Paula gave me valuable insight into what he is like as a man. She also told me how fierce the spiritual warfare has been around his presidency. I deeply appreciate her giving me a behind-the-scenes perspective so I could offer readers a view of Trump that is very different from the secular books that blast the president. She also went to bat for me to get an interview with the president.

I read all 493 pages of **Eric Metaxas'** biography of Martin Luther and enjoyed being on his radio program in New York City. (Recently he expanded with a new program on TBN.) I consider him a renaissance man who not only is a serious biographer but also has written humor since he was editor in chief of the Yale humor magazine. He also has had humor published in the *New York Times* and the *Atlantic*. When I learned he wrote a kids' book called *Donald Drains the Swamp*, I suggested we record a podcast about it and later decided it was the perfect way to introduce chapter 8, "What Is Donald Trump Really Like?"

(He's a hero to the deplorable cave dwellers!) Eric's newest kids' book about the president, *Donald Builds the Wall*, released in September.

Attorney **Jay Sekulow** of Washington, DC, is someone I've known since he won an important religious liberty case for Jews for Jesus before the US Supreme Court in 1987, which led to *Charisma* publishing a cover story about him in 1990. I have watched his career with admiration as he has become more prominent through the American Center for Law and Justice and more recently as the attorney who advised President Trump during the Mueller probe.

Doug Wead, also of Washington, DC, gave me insights for chapter 5 into how Washington insiders have despised Evangelicals going back to the Ford administration. After he helped George H. W. Bush get elected in 1988 by rallying the evangelical vote, Doug held a key position in the Bush White House and for several years was a gatekeeper for Evangelicals (including me) to be invited to meet the president. I make mention in the book that I've known Doug since my teen years when his uncle was my pastor. When I was in my twenties, as Doug's writing career was taking off and I was starting *Charisma*, he was a mentor.

David Barton, the historian from Aledo, Texas, was generous with his time to opine not only about the historical significance of our nation's founding and how we have strayed from those principles as a nation but also where he thinks the country is headed as we approach the 2020 election. I published his book *U-Turn*, which he coauthored with researcher George Barna.

Ralph Reed, the respected political strategist from Atlanta, was also generous with his time to help me figure out the political landscape and what will happen in this next election cycle. I quote both Barton and Reed throughout the book. Ralph shared with me the comment I included in chapter 6 from **Danny Ayalon**, the former Israeli Ambassador to America who has become a friend and gave me additional insight for that chapter.

Attorney **Marc Nuttle** of Oklahoma City is someone I also met through the Huckabee campaign for president in 2008. Marc is a brilliant thinker and strategist, and in 2008 I published his book, *Moment of Truth*, which laid out how devastating it would be if Barack Obama was elected. Sadly his warnings proved to be true. Marc was a valuable resource for this book regarding future trends as well as the immigration problem we face at the southern border.

As I was writing the book, I had an opportunity to be on **Dennis Prager**'s national radio show in Los Angeles. I jumped at the chance because I wanted his insight to add to this book. I've admired him from afar, but it was a delight to meet him in person. I have never met a committed Jew who is more of a friend to evangelical Christians. I am grateful to have been able to quote from our discussion on his "Ultimate Issues Hour" several times in this book.

Other broadcasters have been longtime friends, such as **Gordon Robertson** of CBN, who, along with his father, Pat, was a great supporter of my previous books. I was able to quote Gordon from our great interview on CBN. Another longtime friend, **Arthelene Rippy** of Christian Television Network in Clearwater, Florida, was such a delightful interviewer I pulled several quotes from our discussion, which added spice to the manuscript. It's obvious she's a big supporter of President Trump.

Pat Boone, the famous singer from California and someone I've been privileged to know since the 1980s, helped verify certain stories about Ronald Reagan, including being an eyewitness to the prophecy to then governor Reagan that he would someday live at 1600 Pennsylvania Avenue. **Dr. James Dobson** of Colorado Springs, Colorado, is someone I've respected for years and am thankful to be able to call a friend. He also was generous with his time to share information and vet what I wrote. The same is true of **Kenneth Copeland** from Fort Worth, Texas, who was among the first Christian leaders to back Donald Trump. He had valuable additions to the story on the state dinner for Christian leaders in chapter 8.

Dr. Claude Curran of Massachusetts is the only person who could verify the Hermit of Loreto's prophecy about Donald Trump in the 1980s that I wrote about in *God and Donald Trump*. He gave me important details this time that made the story even more interesting.

I met **Michael Sabga** at a Trump Club meeting in St. Augustine, Florida (where I went to write the manuscript). When I learned he was born in Venezuela, I asked him how a country could survive 10 million percent inflation, never thinking he would become a source for this book. He gave insight into how unlimited immigration was the first domino to fall that led that once prosperous South American country to become socialist and implode as a nation and economically.

In addition to Washington insiders and conservative political activists, I also drew from the wisdom of theologians and deep Christian thinkers. Of particular help was Messianic **Rabbi Jonathan Cahn**, whose insights from his book *The Paradigm* and his new book, *The Oracle*, help explain how ancient mysteries hold secrets behind the events of our times, including the rise of Donald Trump. Rabbi Cahn has become a good friend, and I am proud to have published his blockbuster best seller *The Harbinger* as well as his other best sellers, including *The Paradigm* and his newest book, *The Oracle*, both of which I quote from and are cited in the endnotes.

I also drew from longtime friend **Dr. R. T. Kendall** of Nashville, who helped explain common grace from the Reformed tradition. I'm proud to have published his most recent book, *Word and Spirit*, as well as thirty-five other books over the past fifteen years—each of them deeply spiritual.

I'm also proud to have published six books with **Dr. Michael L. Brown** of Charlotte, North Carolina, including *Jezebel's War With America*, which I cite in this book. I also quote from another of his books, *Trump Is Not My Savior.*

Whenever I do a podcast with **Pastor John Kilpatrick** of Church of His Presence in Alabama, the interview gets a lot of downloads. I interviewed him after his prophetic word went viral that a spirit of Jezebel was seeking to attack the president, and I drew from both the interview and the prophecy for this book. I appreciate his wisdom and his friendship.

Over the years, I have worked on issues of racial reconciliation and prison reform with **Bishop Harry Jackson** of Maryland and **Dr. Alveda King**, a passionate pro-life activist from Atlanta, who is also the niece of Dr. Martin Luther King Jr. and author of *King Truths*, which I published. Bishop Jackson coauthored *Personal Faith, Public Policy* with Tony Perkins of the Family Research Council, a book my company also published. He and Alveda not only are friends but have been valuable resources for each of my books on Trump, including this one.

Alveda sent me information written by **Nina May** of Virginia on the roots of the Republican Party that I found valuable. She and her husband, Colby, a prominent Christian attorney, have been friends for many years. Finally, Pastor **Mark Burns** of South Carolina played a big role in helping me understand the mindsets of black Americans concerning the Democratic Party and Donald Trump in chapter 3.

Because he knows the president, he also helped me to describe Donald Trump as a person in chapter 8.

Pastor **Choco De Jesús** of Chicago and **Tony Suarez** of the National Hispanic Christian Leadership Conference both told me their experiences visiting the border. Choco, a new author with our book group, Charisma House, who is releasing *Love Them Anyway* in June, also pastored the largest Assemblies of God church in the nation before becoming the treasurer of the General Council of the Assemblies of God, headquartered in Springfield, Missouri. He gave me one of the best anecdotes in the book about the president giving him a bear hug when he spoke truth to power. Longtime friend **Sam Rodriguez** is the founder and president of the National Hispanic Christian Leadership Conference and author of a book Charisma House published called *You Are Next*. He gave me permission to use some of his material and helped vet parts of the book.

I've known **Mike Evans** since the late 1970s when we both considered the late Jamie Buckingham a mentor. Founder of the Friends of Zion museum in Jerusalem, though he is based in Colleyville, Texas, Mike has also been a door opener for me in Israel and a true friend.

Pastor **Jim Garlow** of San Diego has been my buddy since the early 1990s through our friendship with Jack Hayford. In 2016 he wrote an op-ed about why Christians should vote for Trump even if they didn't like him. It was shared four million times, and Tom Ertl told me he believes it had an impact on the 2016 presidential election. It was our biggest viral op-ed on the Charisma News website, and I keep inviting Jim to write more articles, hoping lightning will strike again!

Mary Colbert also had an impact on the 2016 election through her prayer network and told the story in the book *The Trump Prophecies*, which was later made into a movie. I've known Mary for years because her husband, Dr. Don Colbert, has been publishing his best-selling health books under our Siloam imprint for two decades. The Colberts live in Lake Mary, Florida, which is not far from us, and they have become dear friends. I am proud to be publishing Mary's forthcoming book, *Prayer That Changes Everything*.

Other friends who influenced the election through prayer are prophetic ministers **Cindy Jacobs** of Generals International in Texas and **Dutch Sheets** of Colorado, whose book, *The Power of Hope*, I published in 2014. Each is a trusted friend, and both have helped mobilize the Charismatic movement and the wider Christian community to pray and get involved in the political scene to bring righteousness to the nation.

Pastor **Hank Kunneman** of Omaha, Nebraska, author of *Don't Leave God Alone*, which I published in 2008, has been a good friend since we attended the 2005 inauguration of George W. Bush's second term. His incredible prophetic gifting added to chapter 11, about prophecies about Donald Trump. Pastor **Steve Cioccolanti** from Australia let me record a podcast about interesting numbers related to Trump that may have spiritual significance, such as the fact that on his first full day in office he was exactly seventy years, seven months, and seven days old. And Pastor **Frank Amedia** of Ohio, who helped me on all three of my books about Trump, brings an interesting spiritual perspective and was the first person I heard prophesy that Donald Trump would be elected. At the time in the natural it looked as if that was impossible.

I felt a strong calling to write this book, and I was able to take time away from the office to work on it because I have a capable executive team at Charisma Media to keep things running smoothly. I appreciate each one, beginning with my wife and business partner, **Joy Strang**, who is also our CFO; **Dr. Steve Greene**, executive vice president of our Media Group; and **Marcos Perez**, the executive vice president of our Book Group, who took a personal interest in this book.

Debbie Marrie, our gifted vice president of product development, collaborated with me on the manuscript at the end of the writing process, and then **Adrienne Gaines** did the substantive edit, **Kimberly Overcast** did all the fact-checking, and **Melissa Bogdany** did the copyediting. Each is a consummate professional.

My able assistant, **Chris Schimbeno**, helped with transcribing interviews, communicating with sources as we vetted the manuscript, and a host of other duties. And **Justin Evans**, the executive design director, outdid himself on the cover for this book (which in my opinion was even better than the last two). I could go on and on about each of the team members at Charisma Media. So many in marketing, such as **Lucy Diaz Kurz**, in manufacturing, such as **Frank Hefeli**, and even in distribution were necessary for this book to be finished on time and to succeed in the marketplace. I appreciate each one even if they weren't individually named.

I appreciate input from a couple of friends who showed an interest in the book from the beginning and offered advice on chapter titles and other things when I needed a sounding board. Besides Tom Ertl mentioned previously, my thanks go out to **Evan Trinkle**, **Gary McCollough**, and **Josh Ford**.

Finally I give honor to God for answering our prayers to give us a leader like Donald Trump and for the inspiration and vision to write this book at just the right time.

And I thank you for reading the book, for recommending it to your friends, and for leaving a good review of it on Amazon.com.

But most of all I hope you will pray for and get active to reelect Donald Trump in 2020.

ABOUT THE AUTHOR

STEPHEN E. STRANG developed an interest in journalism while working on the newspaper, yearbook, and literary magazine staffs during junior high and high school. He went on to earn a journalism degree from the University of Florida in 1973, the same year he won the William Randolph Hearst Award and started working for the *Sentinel Star* in Orlando. In 1975 he started a church magazine called *Charisma* as a part-time job. The publication has since grown to become the leading Pentecostal-Charismatic magazine in the world.

In 1981 he and his wife, Joy, started from scratch what is now known as Charisma Media, which has become one of the leading Christian publishing houses. He estimates Charisma Media has published more than two thousand individual issues of its various magazines as well as nearly twenty-five hundred books in English, including fifteen *New York Times* best sellers, and roughly five hundred titles in Spanish. It also publishes the Modern English Version of the Bible. For two decades the company published children's curriculum that was used in thousands of churches. Today Charisma Media's many websites draw fifteen million unique visitors each year, and more than fifteen million podcasts have been downloaded from the Charisma Podcast Network.

The company has won awards from the state of Florida and was named Industry of the Year in 1993 in Seminole County, Florida. In addition, Strang was nominated for Entrepreneur of the Year, and in 2005 *Time* magazine listed him among the twenty-five most influential Evangelicals in America. Through the years he has won other awards from the Florida Magazine Association and the Evangelical Press Association.

He has been interested in politics since high school. As a journalist he covered Ronald Reagan's famous "evil empire" speech at the National Association of Evangelicals in 1984 in Orlando and in the ensuing years interviewed George H. W. Bush and later George W. Bush. When Barack Obama was running for office in 2008, he met with evangelical leaders in a press conference setting, and Strang asked the future president his stance on abortion. He was never invited to interview Obama again.

In 2016 he interviewed candidate Donald Trump; the conversation is included in his book *God and Donald Trump*, which tells the untold story that many Evangelicals believed God had His hand on Trump and they rallied to his support and made the difference in his surprising upset of Hillary Clinton.

In addition to the thousands of books he has published, he has written six of his own, including *Mountain Moving Motivation* (with Karl Strader); *Old Man, New Man*; *God and Donald Trump*; *Trump Aftershock*; and *How We Fit In*, about the histories of both his and his wife's families.

Joy Strang is CFO of Charisma Media. Their son Cameron started a separate company called Relevant Media, and their son Chandler is a musician and works on Relevant podcasts. Their grandson, Cohen, is in fourth grade.

ENDNOTES

FOREWORD

1. Abraham Lincoln, "Annual Message to Congress—Concluding Remarks," Abraham Lincoln Online, December 1, 1862, http://www. abrahamlincolnonline.org/lincoln/speeches/congress.htm.

INTRODUCTION

1. "President Trump Announces Second Term Run," C-SPAN, June 18, 2019, https://www.c-span.org/video/?461325-1/president-trump-launches-election-bid-orlando-rally.

CHAPTER 1

1. George Santayana, *The Life of Reason* (Cambridge, MA: MIT Press, 2011), 172, https://books.google.com/books?id=cz31jn9wSDkC&vq=con demned&source=gbs_navlinks_s.
2. "How to Win the Spiritual Battle for America's Soul in 2020," June 2019, in *In Depth With Stephen Strang*, podcast, https://www.charisma podcastnetwork.com/show/indepth/43135e6be9a445e5a88391e3f0 af0d19.
3. Emily Guskin, "An Early Look at the 2020 Class of Swing Voters," *Washington Post*, July 13, 2019, https://www.washingtonpost.com /politics/2019/07/13/an-early-look-class-swing-voters/.
4. "Voter Turnout by Demographics: General Election, November 6, 2018," and "Voter Turnout by Demographics: General Election, November 4, 2014," Georgia Secretary of State, accessed August 8, 2019, https://sos. ga.gov/index.php/Elections/voter_turn_out_by_demographics.
5. "2016 November General Election Turnout Rates," United States Elections Project, accessed August 9, 2019, http://www.electproject. org/2016g.
6. "How to Win the Spiritual Battle for America's Soul in 2020."
7. "Voter Turnout," United States Elections Project, accessed August 5, 2019, http://www.electproject.org/home/voter-turnout/voter-turnout-data.
8. "Heritage Explains the Equality Act," Heritage Foundation, accessed August 6, 2019, https://www.heritage.org/gender/heritage-explains/the-equality-act.
9. Franklin Graham, "A Battle for the Soul of This Nation," *Decision*, July–August 2019, https://billygraham.org/decision-magazine/july-august-2019/battle-for-soul-of-nation/.
10. Human Rights Campaign, "Watch Live: Vice President Joe Biden Delivers Remarks at the 2019 HRC Columbus Dinner," YouTube, June 1, 2019, https://www.youtube.com/watch?time_continue=12&v=y6Ak-E2Dh9s.

11. "The Employment Situation—July 2019," Bureau of Labor Statistics, news release, August 2, 2019, https://www.bls.gov/news.release/pdf/empsit.pdf; "United States GDP Growth Rate," Trading Economics, accessed August 6, 2019, https://tradingeconomics.com/united-states/gdp-growth; "Gross Domestic Income (01/01/2017 to 01/01/2019)," Federal Reserve Bank of St. Louis, accessed August 6, 2019, https://fred.stlouisfed.org/series/GDI.

12. "Resolution Recognizing the Duty of the Federal Government to Create a Green New Deal," Congresswoman Alexandria Ocasio-Cortez, accessed August 6, 2019, https://ocasio-cortez.house.gov/sites/ocasio-cortez.house.gov/files/Resolution%20on%20a%20Green%20New%20 Deal.pdf; Danielle Kurtzleben, "Rep. Alexandria Ocasio-Cortez Releases Green New Deal Outline," NPR, February 7, 2019, https://www.npr.org/2019/02/07/691997301/rep-alexandria-ocasio-cortez-releases-green-new-deal-outline.

13. "Dear Friend of Freedom," Faith & Freedom Coalition, November 9, 2016, http://fafc.convio.net/site/MessageViewer?em_id=2102.0&dlv_id=6384; "Record Evangelical Vote in 2018 Midterm Election," Faith & Freedom Coalition, November 7, 2018, https://www.ffcoalition.com/record-evangelical-vote-in-2018-midterm-election/.

14. "Exit Polls: Florida President," CNN, updated November 9, 2016, https://www.cnn.com/election/2016/results/exit-polls/florida/president; "Exit Polls: Florida Governor," CNN, accessed August 6, 2019, https://www.cnn.com/election/2018/exit-polls/florida/governor.

15. "House: Full Results (2014)," CNN, updated December 17, 2014, http://edition.cnn.com/election/2014/results/race/house/#exit-polls; "Exit Polls: National House," CNN, accessed August 6, 2019, https://www.cnn.com/election/2018/exit-polls.

16. David Horowitz, *Dark Agenda: The War to Destroy Christian America* (West Palm Beach, FL: Humanix Books, 2018), 164, https://books.google.com/books?id=FDxxDwAAQBAJ&q.

17. "Gender-Neutral Language: Berkeley Changes Manholes to 'Maintenance Holes,' Brother and Sister to 'Sibling,'" ABC, July 18, 2019, https://abc7news.com/society/berkeley-manholes-will-now-be-called-maintenance-holes/5403786/.

18. Horowitz, *Dark Agenda*, 167–170.

CHAPTER 2

1. Edmund Burke, *Thoughts on the Present Discontents* (London: Cassell & Company, 1886), Project Gutenberg, accessed September 10, 2019, http://www.gutenberg.org/files/2173/2173-h/2173-h.htm.

2. As quoted in J. Ma. Corredor, *Conversations With Casals* (New York: E. P. Dutton, 1957), preface, https://archive.org/stream/conversation-swit 1957casa/conversationswit1957casa_djvu.txt.

3. "Election 2020 Presidential Polls," RealClearPolitics, accessed August 7, 2019, https://www.realclearpolitics.com/epolls/latest_polls/president/#.

4. Chris Mills Rodrigo, "Trump Predicted to Lose Reelection in Model That Forecasted Democratic Takeover of House," *The Hill*, July 1, 2019, https://thehill.com/homenews/campaign/451218-trump-predicted-to-lose-reelection-in-model-that-forecast-dem-takeover-of.

5. Rachel Bitecofer, "With 16 Months to Go, Negative Partisanship Predicts the 2020 Presidential Election," Christopher Newport University, July 1, 2019, http://cnu.edu/wasoncenter/2019/07/01-2020-election-forecast/.

6. Bitecofer, "With 16 Months to Go, Negative Partisanship Predicts the 2020 Presidential Election."

7. Portions of this chapter have been adapted from Thomas Ertl, "Seven Reasons Why Trump Could Lose in 2020," NewsWithViews, June 22, 2019, https://newswithviews.com/seven-reasons-why-trump-could-lose-in-2020/. Used with permission.

8. "Lara Trump: Russia Investigation Has Put Our Country Through Hell, Ruined People's Lives," Fox News, June 10, 2019, https://www.foxnews.com/transcript/lara-trump-russia-investigation-has-put-our-country-through-hell-ruined-peoples-lives.

9. Kathryn Watson, "Trump Campaign Manager Says He'd Win in an 'Electoral Landslide' as of Today," CBS News, updated June 18, 2019, https://www.cbsnews.com/news/brad-parscale-interview-trump-2020-campaign-manager-major-garrett-cbs-news-exclusive-2019-06-18/.

10. *The Alex Jones Show*, June 11, 2019, hour 3, http://rss.gcnlive.com/alexJones/?name=2019-06-11_alexjones0611193.mp3.

11. Acts 20:28 Pastors, "Who We Are," accessed August 13, 2019, https://www.2028pastors.com/#.

12. Michael R. Blood and Stephen Ohlemacher, "Democratic Sweep in California Raises GOP Suspicion," Associated Press, November 30, 2018, https://www.apnews.com/3cfd93f7859149809949bd611287154e.

13. "Guest Host: Fred Jackson Discusses With Dr. Richard Land the Spiritual Warfare Against President Trump," June 4, 2019, in *Sandy Rios in the Morning*, podcast, https://afr.net/podcasts/sandy-rios-in-the-morning/2019/june/guest-host-fred-jackson-discusses-with-dr-richard-land-the-spiritual-warfare-against-president-trump/.

14. Sarah Eekhoff Zylstra, "Jerry Falwell Jr. Endorses Donald Trump; Here's How Other Evangelicals Compare," *Christianity Today*, January 26, 2016, https://www.christianitytoday.com/news/2016/january/jerry-falwell-jr-donald-trump-evangelicals-liberty-universi.html.

15. Michael Wear, "Why Did Obama Win More White Evangelical Votes Than Clinton? He Asked for Them," *Washington Post*, November 22, 2016, https://www.washingtonpost.com/posteverything/wp/2016/11/22/why-did-obama-win-more-white-evangelical-votes-than-clinton-he-asked-for-them/.

16. Franklin Graham, "A Different Gospel Is No Gospel," *Decision*, June 1, 2019, https://decisionmagazine.com/different-gospel-no-gospel/.

17. Ronald Reagan, "Address Before a Joint Session of the Tennessee State Legislature in Nashville," Reagan Foundation, March 15, 1982, https://www.reaganfoundation.org/media/128632/tennessee.pdf.

18. Trevor Loudon, "Pro-China Communists Working to Mobilize 40 Million New Voters Against Trump," *Epoch Times*, updated July 22, 2019, https://www.theepochtimes.com/pro-china-communists-working-to-mobilize-40-million-new-voters-against-trump_2983985.html.

19. US Department of Commerce, Bureau of the Census, "Voting and Registration in the Election of November 1984," Population Characteristics, Series P-20, No. 405, March 1986, https://www.census.gov/content/dam/Census/library/publications/1986/demo/p20-405.pdf.

20. "Voting and Registration in the Election of November 2018," United States Census Bureau, April 2019, https://www.census.gov/data/tables/time-series/demo/voting-and-registration/p20-583.html; "Exit Polls: National House," CNN.

21. Steve Phillips, *Brown Is the New White: How the Demographic Revolution Has Created a New American Majority* (New York: The New Press, 2016), chapter 1, https://books.google.com/books?id=_kc2DgAAQBAJ&vq.

22. Roy S. Johnson, "Alabamians 'Will Die' If Roy Moore Wins, Says Vote or Die Movement Leader at Birmingham Rally," AL.com, January 13, 2018, https://www.al.com/news/2017/11/alabamians_will_die_if_roy_moo.html.

23. Fox News, "Donald Trump Jr. Slams Burr Over His Senate Subpoena," *Fox & Friends*, YouTube, May 23, 2019, https://www.youtube.com/watch?v=FLxQ1Q2Kb48.

CHAPTER 3

1. Frederick Douglass, "I Speak to You as an American Citizen," October 15, 1870, Frederick Douglass Papers, https://frederickdouglass.infoset.io/islandora/object/islandora%3A2820#page/4/mode/1up.

2. Karen Grigsby Bates, "Why Did Black Voters Flee the Republican Party in the 1960s?," NPR, July 14, 2014, https://www.npr.org/sections/codeswitch/2014/07/14/331298996/why-did-black-voters-flee-the-republican-party-in-the-1960s.

3. Steven Levingston, "John F. Kennedy, Martin Luther King Jr., and the Phone Call That Changed History," *Time*, June 20, 2017, https://time.com/4817240/martin-luther-king-john-kennedy-phone-call/.

4. Levingston, "John F. Kennedy, Martin Luther King Jr., and the Phone Call That Changed History."

5. Library of Congress, "The Civil Rights Acts of 1964: A Long Struggle for Freedom," accessed August 14, 2019, https://www.loc.gov/exhibits/civil-rights-act/civil-rights-era.html.

6. FBI, "Record 124-10035-10236," April 17, 1964, https://www.archives.gov/files/research/jfk/releases/docid-32129399.pdf; "The JFK Files Drop An Explosive Charge Against LBJ and Democrats Aren't Going To Like," Conservative Fighters, accessed August 9, 2019, http://the

conservativefighters.com/news/jfk-files-drop-explosive-charge-lbj
-democrats-arent-going-like/.

7. David Emery, "Did LBJ Say 'I'll Have Those N*****s Voting Democratic for 200 Years'?," Snopes, July 27, 2016, https://www.snopes.com/fact-check/lbj-voting-democratic/.

8. Doris Kearns Goodwin, *Lyndon Johnson and the American Dream* (New York: Open Road Integrated Media, 2015), chapter 5, https://books.google.com/books?id=Tv8QCgAAQBAJ&pg.

9. Michael E. Miller, "Strippers, Surveillance and Assassination Plots: The Wildest JFK Files," *Washington Post*, October 27, 2017, https://www.washingtonpost.com/news/retropolis/wp/2017/10/27/strippers-surveillance-and-assassination-plots-the-jfk-files-wildest-documents/.

10. Bates, "Why Did Black Voters Flee the Republican Party in the 1960s?"

11. "Exit Polls: National President," CNN, updated November 23, 2016, https://www.cnn.com/election/2016/results/exit-polls; "Exit Polls 2012: How the Vote Has Shifted," *Washington Post*, November 6, 2012, http://www.washingtonpost.com/wp-srv/special/politics/2012-exit-polls/table.html.

12. Jeff Diamant and Gregory A. Smith, "Religiously, Nonwhite Democrats Are More Similar to Republicans Than to White Democrats," Pew Research Center, May 23, 2018, http://www.pewresearch.org/fact-tank/2018/05/23/religiously-nonwhitedemocrats-are-more-similar-to-republicans-than-to-white-democrats/.

13. "When Americans Say They Believe in God, What Do They Mean?," Pew Research Center, April 25, 2018, https://www.pewforum.org/2018/04/25/when-americans-say-they-believe-in-god-what-do-they-mean/.

14. Diamant and Smith, "Religiously, Nonwhite Democrats Are More Similar to Republicans Than to White Democrats."

15. Devan Cole, "Virginia Governor Faces Backlash Over Comments Supporting Late-Term Abortion Bill," CNN, January 31, 2019, https://www.cnn.com/2019/01/31/politics/ralph-northam-third-trimester-abortion/index.html.

16. Donald Trump, "State of the Union Address," February 6, 2019, https://www.whitehouse.gov/briefings-statements/remarks-president-trump-state-union-address-2/.

17. Caroline Kelly, "Virginia Governor Apologizes for 'Racist and Offensive' Costume in Photo Showing People in Blackface and KKK Garb," CNN, February 7, 2019, https://www.cnn.com/2019/02/01/politics/northam-blackface-photo/index.html.

18. Sean McElwee, Jesse H. Rhodes, Brian F. Schaffner, and Bernard L. Fraga, "The Missing Obama Millions," *New York Times*, March 10, 2018, https://www.nytimes.com/2018/03/10/opinion/sunday/obama-trump-voters-democrats.html.

19. Philip Wegmann, "Trump Bets on More Black Support in 2020. (He Might Need It.)," RealClearHoldings, LLC, June 7, 2019, https://www.realclearpolitics.com/articles/2019/06/07/trump_bets_on_more_black_support_in_2020_he_might_need_it.html; Asawin Suebsaeng, Sam

Stein, and Lachlan Markay, "Trump's Plan to Stop Biden: Turn Black Voters Against Him," Daily Beast, May 30, 2019, https://www.thedailybeast.com/trumps-plan-to-stop-joe-biden-turn-black-voters-against-him.

20. *The O'Reilly Factor*, Fox News, December 15, 2016, archived at https://archive.org/details/FOXNEWSW_20161216_010000_The_OReilly_Factor/start/360/end/420.

21. Candace Owens, "Candace Owens DESTROYS Leftist on Racism!," Facebook, August 9, 2018, https://www.facebook.com/watch/?v=1799065083475533.

22. "Kanye West Says Democrats Brainwash Black People, Encourage Abortion," TMZ, October 29, 2019, https://www.tmz.com/2019/10/29/kanye-west-democrats-brainwash-black-people-abortion/.

23. Gerren Keith Gaynor, "Kanye West Defends Support for Trump, Says Political Decisions Based on Race Is 'Mental Slavery,'" Fox News, October 7, 2019, https://www.foxnews.com/entertainment/kanye-west-trump-mental-slavery.

24. Tomarra Burns, "Dr. David Jeremiah calls for strong African American Pastors to stand with Donald Trump. Kenneth Copeland prays, Paula White Prays then Jewish Jesus Rabbi Schneider gives an Abrahamic Jewish Blessing," Facebook, September 29, 2015, https://www.facebook.com/story.php?story_fbid=10200880103162632&id=1766336939.

25. Wegmann, "Trump Bets on More Black Support in 2020."

26. Harry R. Jackson Jr., "Bishop Harry Jackson Interview on Cultural Impact in America," Facebook, October 16, 2018, https://www.facebook.com/harryrjacksonjr/videos/338059530286734/.

Chapter 4

1. Daniel Ghezelbash, *Refuge Lost: Asylum Law in an Interdependent World* (New York: Cambridge University Press, 2018), 30.

2. "This Is How Much of the Border Wall Has Been Built So Far," CNN, January 19, 2019, https://www.fox47news.com/news/national/this-is-how-much-of-the-border-wall-has-been-built-so-far.

3. Hagee Ministries, "The Blessing of a Border," YouTube, June 2, 2019, https://www.youtube.com/watch?v=3Kzq4EAA8Ic.

4. "China GDP," Trading Economics, accessed August 10, 2019, https://tradingeconomics.com/china/gdp.

5. Laura He, "China's Economic Growth Slumps to Lowest in 27 Years as the Trade War Hits," CNN, July 15, 2019, https://www.cnn.com/2019/07/15/economy/china-gdp-growth/index.html.

6. Francis Myles, "Francis Myles—Why God Hates Open Borders," YouTube, July 8, 2016, https://www.youtube.com/watch?v=edH5oOCwlWA.

7. Alveda King, "African-American Leaders Unite Around Wall to Help Avoid Looming Crisis," Newsmax, January 10, 2019, https://www.newsmax.com/dralvedacking/trump-border-wall-national-security/2019/01/10/id/897672/.

8. Michael McIntee, "Obama Immigration Reform-Full HQ video," YouTube, July 1, 2010, https://www.youtube.com/

watch?v=KWEfeyiwTP8, 29:48. See also "Remarks by the President on Comprehensive Immigration Reform," White House Office of the Press Secretary, July 1, 2010, https://obamawhitehouse.archives.gov/reality-check/the-press-office/remarks-president-comprehensive-immigration-reform.

9. Barack Obama, "Remarks by the President in the State of the Union Address," The White House, February 12, 2013, https://obamawhite house.archives.gov/the-press-office/2013/02/12/remarks-president-state-union-address.

10. Julio Ricardo Valera, "Clinton: 'You Have to Control Your Borders,'" Latino USA, November 9, 2015, https://www.latinousa.org/2015/11/09/clinton-you-have-to-control-your-borders-video/.

11. Bill Clinton, "III. New Community—Immigration," The White House, accessed November 5, 2019, https://clintonwhitehouse1.archives.gov/White_House/Publications/html/briefs/iii-7.html.

12. "What They Said," BorderFacts.com, accessed August 16, 2019, https://borderfacts.com/.

13. Charlie Kirk (@charliekirk11), "Chuck Schumer has been in office for 38 years…," Twitter, July 21, 2019, 5:12 p.m., https://twitter.com/charliekirk11/status/1153095310136270849.

14. Brigitte Gabriel, *Rise: In Defense of Judeo-Christian Values and Freedom* (Lake Mary, FL: FrontLine, 2018), 73, https://www.amazon.com/Rise-Defense-Judeo-Christian-Values-Freedom/dp/154590829X.

15. Marc Nuttle, "The Trumpet of Don Trump," The Nuttle Report, August 1, 2015, http://www.theoakinitiative.org/src/pdfs/ol_69_080115.pdf.

16. Michael Winter and Matthew Diebel, "Reports: Federal Agent's Gun Used in S.F. Pier Shooting," *USA Today*, updated July 8, 2015, https://www.usatoday.com/story/news/2015/07/07/man-charged--san-franciso-waterfront-shooting---arraigned/29811735/.

17. Marc Nuttle, "The Trumpet of Don Trump," The Nuttle Report, August 1, 2015, http://www.theoakinitiative.org/src/pdfs/ol_69_080115.pdf.

18. Oswald Chambers, "July 28: After Obedience—What?," My Utmost for His Highest, accessed August 10, 2019, https://utmost.org/classic/after-obedience-what-classic/.

19. Steve Deace, "Megan Rapinoe's Antics Spell Out Exactly the Type of Civil War We Are Up Against," The Blaze, July 12, 2019, https://www.theblaze.com/op-ed/megan-rapinoes-antics-spell-out-exactly-the-type-of-civil-war-we-are-up-against.

20. Tucker Carlson, "Tucker Carlson: US Rescued Ilhan Omar," Fox News, July 10, 2019, https://www.foxnews.com/opinion/tucker-carlson-america-rescued-ilhan-omar.

21. "Hispanic Pastor Disputes Ocasio-Cortez's Claims About Border Facilities," Fox News, July 2, 2019, https://video.foxnews.com/v/6054944880001/#sp=show-clips.

22. James Dobson, *Dr. Dobson's July Newsletter*, July 2019, https://www.drjamesdobson.org/about/july-newsletter-2019.

23. Valentina Sanchez, "Venezuela Hyperinflation Hits 10 Million Percent. 'Shock Therapy' May Be Only Chance to Undo the Economic Damage," CNBC, updated August 5, 2019, https://www.cnbc.com/2019/08/02/venezuela-inflation-at-10-million-percent-its-time-for-shock-therapy.html; Adriana Diaz, Brian Pascus, Luis Giraldo, "Scenes From Venezuela: People Suffer and Starve as Political and Economic Crisis Drags On," CBS Interactive, updated May 7, 2019, https://www.cbsnews.com/news/venezuela-crisis-caracas-citizens-starving-worthless-currency-infant-mortality-death-reported-adriana-diaz/.

24. David Brody, "Inside View: The Evangelical Whisperer With Access to Both Pelosi and Trump on Immigration," CBN News, July 12, 2019, https://www1.cbn.com/cbnnews/politics/2019/july/inside-view-the-evangelical-whisperer-with-access-to-both-pelosi-and-trump-on-immigration. Used with permission.

25. Nancy Pelosi, "House Speaker Weekly Briefing," July 11, 2019, https://www.c-span.org/video/?462516-1/speaker-pelosi-holds-weekly-news-conference.

26. Brody, "Inside View."

CHAPTER 5

1. John W. Dean, *Conservatives Without Conscience* (New York: Penguin Books, 2006), xxxiv, https://books.google.com/books?id=ynMJCgAAQBAJ&q=Mark+my+word#v=snippet&q=Mark%20my%20word&f=false.

2. "Billy Graham on the Election," *Christian Life*, November 1952, 15–18.

3. Lee Dembart, "Carter's Comments on Sex Cause Concern," *New York Times*, September 23, 1976, https://www.nytimes.com/1976/09/23/archives/carters-comments-on-sex-cause-concern.html.

4. Jon Meacham, "The Editor's Desk," *Newsweek*, November 12, 2006, https://www.newsweek.com/editors-desk-106637.

5. Howard Norton and Bob Slosser, *The Miracle of Jimmy Carter* (Plainfield, NJ: Logos International, 1976).

6. Rich DeVos, "Gerald R. Ford Oral History Project," interview by Richard Norton Smith, August 21, 2009, https://geraldrfordfoundation.org/centennial-docs/oralhistory/wp-content/uploads/2013/05/Rich-DeVos.pdf.

7. Andrew P. Hogue, "1980: Reagan, Carter, and the Politics of Religion in America" (PhD diss., Baylor University, 2009), 252, https://baylor-ir.tdl.org/bitstream/handle/2104/5525/andrew_hogue_phd.pdf?sequence=1&isAllowed=y.

8. Bob Slosser, "The Prophecy," CBN, accessed August 11, 2019, https://www1.cbn.com/biblestudy/the-prophecy.

9. See Karen Tumulty, "Ronald Reagan's Letter to His Dying Father-in-Law, Annotated," *Washington Post*, September 14, 2018, https://www.washingtonpost.com/news/opinions/wp/2018/09/14/ronald-reagans-letter-to-his-dying-father-in-law-annotated/.

10. David D. Kirkpatrick, "In Secretly Taped Conversations, Glimpses of the Future President," *New York Times*, February 20, 2005, https://

www.nytimes.com/2005/02/20/politics/in-secretly-taped-conversations
-glimpses-of-the-future-president.html.

11. David D. Kirkpatrick, "From Psst to Oops: Secret Taper of Bush Says History Can Wait," *New York Times*, February 24, 2005, https://www.nytimes.com/2005/02/24/politics/from-psst-to-oops-secret-taper-of-bush-says-history-can-wait.html.

12. "Secret Wead Tapes Reveal Bush Plan to Woo Religious Right," Americans United for Separation of Church and State, April 2005, https://www.au.org/church-state/april-2005-church-state/people-events/secret-wead-tapes-reveal-bush-plan-to-woo.

13. Doug Wead, "What Ronald Reagan Says About Doug Wead May Surprise You," YouTube, January 1, 2008, https://www.youtube.com/watch?time_continue=2&v=OkYKEdOTQN8.

CHAPTER 6

1. J. C. Ryle, "Commentary on Matthew 17," *J. C. Ryle's Expository Thoughts on the Gospels*, StudyLight.org, accessed September 10, 2019, https://www.studylight.org/commentaries/ryl/matthew-17.html.

2. Dennis Prager, "Ultimate Issues Hour: Christians and Politics," *The Dennis Prager Show*, July 2, 2019, https://pragertopia.com/2019/07/02/dennis-prager-20190702-3-ultimate-issues-hour-christians-and-politics/.

3. CNN, "Falwell Jr. on Trump: We're Not Electing a Pastor-in…," YouTube, June 1, 2016, https://www.youtube.com/watch?v=G42VEGGmliQ.

4. Lance Wallnau, "Why I Believe Trump Is the Prophesied President," Charisma News, October 5, 2016, http://www.charismanews.com/politics/opinion/60378-why-i-believe-trump-is-the-prophesied-president.

5. Jonathan Sandys and Wallace Henley, *God and Churchill: How the Great Leader's Sense of Divine Destiny Changed His Troubled World and Offers Hope for Ours* (Carol Stream, IL: Tyndale, 2015), 80–81.

6. Fox 10 Phoenix, "Trump 2020: President Trump Re-Election Campaign Rally—Full Speech," YouTube, June 18, 2019, https://www.youtube.com/watch?v=MEqINP-TuV8; see also Donald J. Trump (@realDonaldTrump), "Together, we are breaking the most sacred rule in Washington Politics: we are KEEPING our promises to the American People. Because my only special interest is YOU! #Trump2020," Twitter, June 18, 2019, 9:52 p.m., https://twitter.com/realDonaldTrump/status/1141161757819441152.

7. Robert G. Hays, "The Miracle of Bastogne," The Link, October 1969, https://archive.org/stream/link2710unse/link2710unse_djvu.txt; see also Robert Hays, *Patton's Oracle: Gen. Oscar Koch, as I Knew Him* (Savoy, IL: Lucidus Books, 2013), 149–153, https://www.amazon.com/Pattons-Oracle-Gen-Oscar-Koch/dp/1477629793.

8. James H. O'Neill, "The True Story of the Patton Prayer," *Review of the News*, October 6, 1971, http://pattonhq.com/prayer.html.

9. Marc A. Thiessen, "Why Conservative Christians Stick With Trump," *Washington Post*, March 23, 2018, https://www.washingtonpost.com

/opinions/why-conservative-christians-stick-with-trump/2018/03/23
/2766309a-2def-11e8-8688-e053ba58f1e4_story.html.

10. George W. Bush, *41: A Portrait of My Father* (New York: Crown
Publishers, 2014), 81, https://www.amazon.com/41-Portrait-Father-
Random-House/dp/0804194718.

11. Stephen E. Strang, *Trump Aftershock* (Lake Mary, FL: FrontLine, 2018),
xi–xii.

12. Jim Garlow, "okay…Here goes! Moments ago on private FB messaging,
I was asked 'THE question'… again regarding Trump or Hillary.
I am not demanding that anyone else share my view. But, I was
asked. Here is my best attempt at a response at this time," Facebook,
August 4, 2016, 8:33 p.m., https://www.facebook.com/jimgarlow/
posts/10209897534852304.

13. Jim Garlow, "If You're on the Fence About Your Vote, This Pastor
Clarifies How the Very Future of America Is at Stake," Charisma
News, August 11, 2016, https://www.charismanews.com/politics/
opinion/59206-if-you-re-on-the-fence-about-your-vote-this-pastor
-clarifies-how-the-very-future-of-america-is-at-stake.

14. Planned Parenthood of Greater Texas Family Planning and Preventa-
tive Health Services Inc. et al. v. Charles Smith and Sylvia Hernandez
Kauffman (5th Cir. 2019), https://www.texasattorneygeneral.gov/sites/
default/files/images/admin/2019/Press/PP%20Opinion.pdf.

15. "Abortion Policy in the Absence of Roe," Guttmacher Institute, August
1, 2019, https://www.guttmacher.org/state-policy/explore/abortion-
policy-absence-roe.

CHAPTER 7

1. Alexander Hamilton, "From Alexander Hamilton to Philip A. Hamilton, 5 December 1791," National Archives, accessed September 6,
2019, https://founders.archives.gov/documents/Hamilton/01-09
-02-0419.

2. Cas Mudde, "Four Reasons Why Trump Is Cruising Toward Reelection," *Guardian*, June 20, 2019, https://www.theguardian.com/
commentisfree/2019/jun/20/four-reasons-why-trump-is-cruising-
towards-re-election.

3. "Is America Great Again?," CBN, November 6, 2018, https://www1.cbn.
com/video/I7C110618_StephenStrang/is-america-great-again.

4. Donald Trump, "Remarks by President Trump in State of the Union
Address," White House, February 5, 2019, https://www.whitehouse.gov/
briefings-statements/remarks-president-trump-state-union-address-2/.

5. Franklin Graham (@Franklin_Graham), "Thank you @POTUS
@realDonaldTrump for covering the priorities of our nation so
clearly in tonight's State of the Union address…," Twitter, February 5, 2019, 11:39 p.m., https://twitter.com/Franklin_Graham/
status/1093006303499354112.

6. David Brody (@DavidBrodyCBN), "The most pro-life president just
delivered the most pro-life State of the Union speech EVER. Not even

close...," Twitter, February 6, 2019, 12:02 a.m., https://twitter.com/DavidBrodyCBN/status/1093012007845089280.

7. *Life, Liberty & Levin*, Fox News, July 14, 2019, https://video.foxnews.com/v/6059161669001/#sp=show-clips.

8. "Presidential Executive Order on Reducing Regulation and Controlling Regulatory Costs," White House, January 30, 2017, https://www.white house.gov/presidential-actions/presidential-executive-order-reducing-regulation-controlling-regulatory-costs/.

9. "Regulatory Reform Results for Fiscal Year 2018," Office of Information and Regulatory Affairs, accessed August 14, 2019, https://www.reginfo.gov/public/do/eAgendaEO13771; "Regulatory Reform: Completed Actions Fiscal Year 2017," Office of Information and Regulatory Affairs, accessed August 14, 2019, https://www.reginfo.gov/public/pdf/eo13771/FINAL_BU_20171207.pdf.

10. "President Donald Trump, Received the Friends of Zion Award From Dr. Mike Evans," Friends of Zion Museum, August 14, 2019, https://www.fozmuseum.com/news-events/washington-dc-president-donald-trump-received-friends-zion-award-dr-mike-evans/.

11. *Life, Liberty & Levin*, Fox News.

12. Peter Roff, "Good News Doesn't Always Travel Fast," *U.S. News & World Report*, January 16, 2018, https://www.usnews.com/opinion/thomas-jefferson-street/articles/2018-01-16/the-economy-is-booming-under-trump-but-mainstream-media-wont-tell-you-that.

13. Jasper Fakkert, "American Revival: 70 Ways President Trump Has Changed the Nation Over the Past Two Years," *Epoch Times*, updated April 2, 2019, https://www.theepochtimes.com/two-years-in-office-trumps-revival-of-america_2772117.html.

14. Brendan Cole, "Trump Tells Rally He's Kept More Promises Than He's Made," *Newsweek*, November 2, 2018, https://www.newsweek.com/trump-tells-rally-hes-kept-more-promises-hes-made-1198181.

15. "Trump Promise Tracker," *Washington Post*, updated August 11, 2019, https://www.washingtonpost.com/graphics/politics/trump-promise-tracker/.

16. "Today in American Presidents History," White House Gift Shop, January 22, 2017, https://www.whitehousegiftshop.com/Today-in-U-S-History-President-Trump-in-the-News-s/2401.htm.

17. Dobson, "Dr. Dobson's July Newsletter."

18. "Freed Pastor Prays for Trump in White House," CNN, October 13, 2018, https://www.cnn.com/videos/politics/2018/10/13/freed-pastor-andrew-brunson-prays-trump-labott-sot-vpx.cnn.

19. Lauren Markoe, "Trump Must Aid Persecuted Christians or His Presidency Will Fail, Says Open Doors," Religion News Service, January 11, 2017, https://religionnews.com/2017/01/11/trump-must-aid-persecuted-christians-or-his-presidency-will-fail-says-open-doors/.

20. Kate Shellnutt, "Sam Brownback Finally Confirmed as America's Religious Freedom Ambassador," *Christianity Today*, January 24, 2018, https://www.christianitytoday.com/news/2018/january/sam-brownback-is-ambassador-international-religious-freedom.html.

21. Mike Pence, "Remarks by Vice President Pence at the Southern Baptist Convention Annual Meeting," White House, June 13, 2018, https://www.whitehouse.gov/briefings-statements/remarks-vice-president-pence-southern-baptist-convention-annual-meeting/.

Chapter 8

1. Ian Schwartz, "O'Reilly: The Truth Is Not Being Told About Trump and That Is a Disservice to Every American," RealClearHoldings, May 16, 2019, https://www.realclearpolitics.com/video/2019/05/16/oreilly_the_truth_is_not_being_told_about_trump_and_that_is_a_disservice_to_every_american.html.

2. Gary Varvel, "Donald Trump Is the President I Didn't Want, but Now I Know We Need," *USA Today*, updated July 11, 2018, https://amp.usa-today.com/story/opinion/nation-now/2018/07/11/how-went-donald-trump-critic-president-trump-supporter-column/774925002/.

3. Emily McFarlan Miller, "White House Honors Evangelicals 'For All the Good Work They Do,'" Religion News Service, August 28, 2018, https://religionnews.com/2018/08/28/white-house-hosts-dinner-to-honor-evangelicals-for-all-the-good-work-they-do/.

4. Heather Sells, "Faith Leaders Pray for Trump in Oval Office, Enjoy 'Open Door' at White House," CBN News, July 12, 2017, http://www1.cbn.com/cbnnews/us/2017/july/faith-leaders-enjoy-open-door-at-white-house.

5. Elisa Cipollone, "Don Jr. Goes to Church," LifeZette, November 6, 2016, http://www.lifezette.com/faithzette/don-jr-goes-church/.

6. Newt Gingrich, "Newt Gingrich: Trump vs. Pelosi—Why the 2020 Election May Turn Out Completely Differently Than You Expect," Fox News, June 12, 2019, https://www.foxnews.com/opinion/newt-gingrich-president-trump-nancy-pelosi.

7. "Katrina Pierson Remarks on Trump," NBC News Archives, July 16, 2019, https://www.nbcnewsarchivesxpress.com/contentdetails/2174939.

8. Irwin Kula and Craig Hatkoff, "Donald Trump and the Wollman Rinking of American Politics," Forbes, August 24, 2015, https://www.forbes.com/sites/offwhitepapers/2015/08/24/donald-trump-and-the-wollman-rinking-of-american-politics/#100ec5002fc8.

9. Chase Peterson-Withorn, "No, Trump Is Not Losing '3 to 5 Billion' Dollars From Presidency," *Forbes*, August 16, 2019, https://www.forbes.com/sites/chasewithorn/2019/08/14/no-trump-is-not-losing-3-to-5-billion-from-presidency/#3a557c634a2d.

Chapter 9

1. C-SPAN, "Donald Trump Presidential Campaign Announcement Full Speech (C-SPAN)," YouTube, June 16, 2015, https://www.youtube.com/watch?v=apjNfkysjbM, 46:30.

2. Steve Strang, "Mr. Trump, I Have a Few Questions," *Charisma*, accessed October 28, 2019, https://www.charismamag.com/life/politics/27528-mr-trump-i-have-a-few-questions.

3. Donald J. Trump, "Remarks by President Trump at the United Nations Event on Religious Freedom | New York, NY," September 23, 2019, https://www.whitehouse.gov/briefings-statements/remarks-president-trump-united-nations-event-religious-freedom-new-york-ny/.

4. Donald J. Trump," Remarks by President Trump to the 74th Session of the United Nations General Assembly," September 24, 2019, https://www.whitehouse.gov/briefings-statements/remarks-president-trump-74th-session-united-nations-general-assembly.

Chapter 10

1. "Remarks by President Trump at Signing of Presidential Proclamation Recognizing Israel's Sovereign Right Over the Golan Heights," White House, March 25, 2019, https://www.whitehouse.gov/briefings -statements/remarks-president-trump-signing-presidential -proclamation-recognizing-israels-sovereign-right-golan-heights/.

2. Ezra 1:2.

3. Isaiah 45:1, 4.

4. 1 Corinthians 13:12, KJV.

5. "Remarks by President Trump at Signing of Presidential Proclamation Recognizing Israel's Sovereign Right Over the Golan Heights," White House.

6. Jeremiah 29:10, NKJV, emphasis added.

7. Michael T. Benson, *Harry S. Truman and the Founding of Israel* (Westport, CT: Praeger, 1997), 189, https://books.google.com/books?id=jmoab5xc9ogC&pg.

8. Jonathan Cahn, *The Oracle* (Lake Mary, FL: FrontLine, 2019), 209, quoting Donald J. Trump, "Statement by President Trump on Jerusalem," White House, December 6, 2017, https://www.whitehouse.gov/briefings-statements/statement-president-trump-jerusalem/.

9. Jonathan Cahn, "The Oracle Unveiled," *Charisma*, September 2019, 26.

10. Jonathan Cahn, *The Paradigm* (Lake Mary, FL: FrontLine, 2017), ix–x.

11. 1 Kings 16:33.

12. Jonathan Cahn, "The Paradigm," *Charisma*, September 2017, 23.

13. Cahn, *The Paradigm*, 190–192, 199.

14. Stephen E. Strang, *God and Donald Trump* (Lake Mary, FL: FrontLine, 2017), xi.

15. Cahn, *The Paradigm*, 195.

16. David Brody, "EXCLUSIVE Secretary of State Pompeo to CBN News: God May Have Raised Up Trump Like He Raised Up Queen Esther," CBN News, March 21, 2019, https://www1.cbn.com/cbnnews/israel/2019/march/exclusive-secretary-of-state-pompeo-to-news-god-raised-up-trump-like-he-raised-up-queen-esther.

17. R. T. Kendall, "Donald Trump and Toby," R. T. Kendall Ministries, accessed August 17, 2019, https://rtkendallministries.com/donald-trump-and-toby.

18. Michael L. Brown, *Donald Trump Is Not My Savior: An Evangelical Leader Speaks His Mind About the Man He Supports as President*

(Shippensburg, PA: Destiny Image, 2018), 21, https://www.amazon.com/Donald-Trump-Not-Savior-Evangelical/dp/0768449936.

19. Brown, *Donald Trump Is Not My Savior*, 20, 327–328.

CHAPTER 11

1. John R. Vile, *The Constitutional Convention of 1787* (Santa Barbara, CA: ABC-CLIO, 2005), 593.

2. Max Farrand, ed., *The Records of the Federal Convention of 1787*, vol. 1 (New Haven, CT: Yale University Press, 1911), 452, https://oll.libertyfund.org/titles/farrand-the-records-of-the-federal-convention-of-1787-vol-1.

3. Farrand, *The Records of the Federal Convention of 1787*, 452–453.

4. BGEA, "Statement From Faith Leaders Regarding Special Day of Prayer," Billy Graham Evangelical Association, May 26, 2019, https://billygraham.org/story/special-day-of-prayer/?fbclid=IwAR2oH0X1J5H-7Tc3cc_MrtxqlxkLw7tkq0x2nFcvR2WKnHFIyPvUgz0O2HU.

5. "Franklin Graham Wants You to Join Him to Pray for the President," Intercessors for America, May 24, 2019, https://www.ifapray.org/blog/franklin-graham-wants-you-to-join-him-to-pray-for-the-president/.

6. Franklin Graham, "Along with 250+ Christian leaders, I am asking followers of Christ across our nation to set aside next Sunday, June 2, as a special day of prayer for the President, Donald J. Trump," Facebook, May 26, 2019, 6:10 a.m., https://www.facebook.com/FranklinGraham/posts/2497135067009326?__tn__=-R.

7. Rob Poindexter, "Kim Clement Prophesying About Donald Trump 2007," YouTube, November 24, 2016, https://www.youtube.com/watch?v=eFfFtq1fljY, emphasis added.

8. Donné Clement Petruska, "Kim Clement Prophecy—Supreme Court, Drain the Swamp," YouTube, March 12, 2018, https://www.youtube.com/watch?v=Xqae12Otunk.

9. Strang, *God and Donald Trump*, 127–128.

10. Josh Hafner, "Meet the Evangelicals Who Prophesied a Trump Win," *USA Today*, updated November 11, 2016, https://www.usatoday.com/story/news/nation-now/2016/11/10/meet-evangelicals-prophesied-trump-win/93575144/; Lance Wallnau, "Why I Believe Trump Is the Prophesied President," Charisma News, October 5,2016, https://www.charismanews.com/politics/opinion/60378-why-i-believe-trump-is-the-prophesied-president.

11. Steve Cioccolanti & Discover Ministries, "The Trump Eclipse—President's List of Accomplishments & End Time Signs," YouTube, January 24, 2019, https://www.youtube.com/watch?v=HI1jKBDwsxE.

12. Stephen Strang, "'Trump Blood Moons' Reveal How God Is Fulfilling Prophecy With Steve Cioccolanti," *The Strang Report* (blog), *Charisma*, February 25, 2019, https://player.fm/series/strang-report/trump-blood-moons-reveal-how-god-is-fulfilling-prophecy-with-steve-ciccolanti.

13. Steve Cioccolanti & Discover Ministries, "The Donald Trump Prophecy | End-Time President Predicted," YouTube, April 18, 2016, https://www.youtube.com/watch?v=FsQG6WzmuE8.

14. Amy Sullivan, "Millions of Americans Believe God Made Trump President," *Politico*, January 27, 2018, https://www.politico.com/magazine/story/2018/01/27/millions-of-americans-believe-god-made-trump-president-216537.

15. Strang, *God and Donald Trump*, 179–181.

16. Giacomo Capoverdi, "Hermit of Loreto," YouTube, February 19, 2017, https://www.youtube.com/watch?v=lyV7kwMRzdo.

17. 1 Corinthians 13:9, 12, KJV.

CHAPTER 12

1. C. S. Lewis, *Christian Reflections* (Grand Rapids, MI: William B. Eerdmans Publishing Company, 1967), 33.

2. Right Side Broadcasting Network, "Full Rally: President Trump Holds Massive Rally in Orlando, FL," YouTube, June 18, 2019, https://www.youtube.com/watch?v=udSUXW2_OiI.

3. Julia Arciga, "Trump Spiritual Adviser: 'Demonic' News Networks Aligning Themselves Against President," Daily Beast, June 18, 2019, https://www.thedailybeast.com/paula-white-trumps-spiritual-adviser-demonic-news-networks-aligning-themselves-against-president.

4. Meagan Flynn, "Trump's Spiritual Adviser Seeks His Protection From 'Demonic Networks' at Reelection Rally," *Washington Post*, June 19, 2019, https://www.washingtonpost.com/nation/2019/06/19/paula-white-donald-trump-orlando-rally-demonic-networks/.

5. John 10:10.

6. Galatians 3:1.

7. "Guest Host," *Sandy Rios in the Morning*.

8. Ephesians 6:12, KJV.

9. Daniel Kolenda, *Slaying Dragons* (Lake Mary, FL: Charisma House, 2019), 80–89.

10. John C. Danforth, *Resurrection: The Confirmation of Clarence Thomas* (New York: Viking, 1994).

11. Jessilyn Justice, "Bethel Issues Rare Urgent Call to Action Over 'Troubling' Bills," Charisma News, March 26, 2018, https://www.charismanews.com/politics/press-releases/70247-bethel-issues-rare-urgent-call-to-action-over-troubling-bills; "California Lawmaker Drops Anti-Biblical Bill," Charisma News and CBN News, August 31, 2018, https://www.charismanews.com/politics/72957-california-lawmaker-drops-anti-biblical-bill.

12. Ronald Reagan, "Speech Before the Phoenix Chamber of Commerce," March 30, 1961, https://archive.org/details/RonaldReagan-Encroaching Control.

13. Pray Alabama, "Pray Against Witchcraft Coming Against President Trump," Facebook, August 20, 2018, 2:27 p.m., https://www.facebook.com/116678935084921/videos/241848136380412/.

14. Benjamin Fearnow, "Pastor Prays for Trump to Defeat Deep State 'Witchcraft,' Speaks in Tongues," *Newsweek*, August 23, 2018, https://www.newsweek.com/alabama-pastor-john-kilpatrick-witchcraft-trump-jezebel-speakingtongues-1087386.

15. Michael L. Brown, *Jezebel's War With America: The Plot to Destroy Our Country and What We Can Do to Turn the Tide* (Lake Mary, FL: FrontLine, 2019), 121.

16. Sangeeta Singh-Kurtz and Dan Kopf, "The US Witch Population Has Seen an Astronomical Rise," Quartzy, October 4, 2018, https://qz.com/quartzy/1411909/the-explosive-growth-of-witches-wiccans-and-pagans-in-the-us/.

17. Calvin Freiburger, "Report: Witchcraft Rising in US as Christianity Declines," Life Site News, October 11, 2018, https://www.lifesitenews.com/news/report-witchcraft-rising-in-us-as-christianity-declines.

18. Christina Marfice, "There Are Now More Practicing Witches in the U.S. Than Ever Before," Scary Mommy, November 19, 2018, https://www.scarymommy.com/witches-rising-numbers/.

19. Michael Snyder, "The Fastest Growing Religion in America Is Witchcraft," The Truth, October 30, 2013, http://thetruthwins.com/archives/the-fastest-growing-religion-in-america-is-witchcraft.

20. Pam Grossman, "Yes, Witches Are Real. I Know Because I Am One," *Time*, May 30, 2019, https://time.com/5597693/real-women-witches/.

21. Brown, *Jezebel's War With America*, 121, quoting James White (@DrOakley1689), "It is very hard not to see a strong spirit of deception and delusion working in this culture—we murder our babies, destroy the gift of marriage, even mutilate young children all in service to the god of human autonomy. But, the judgment is just," Twitter, December 16, 2018, 6:44 a.m., https://twitter.com/DrOakley1689/status/1074314225617559557.

22. Kyle Winkler, "The Accuser vs. Donald Trump—and Us All," Charisma News, October 22, 2016, https://www.charismanews.com/opinion/60691-the-accuser-vs-donald-trump-and-us-all.

23. Winkler, "The Accuser vs. Donald Trump—and Us All."

24. Matthew 4:16, NKJV. See also Isaiah 9:2.

CHAPTER 13

1. Michael Horton, *The Gospel Commission* (Grand Rapids, MI: Baker Books, 2011), 10–11.

2. 1 Peter 4:17.

3. "Guest Host," *Sandy Rios in the Morning*.

4. "Study of Women Who Have Had an Abortion and Their Views on Church," LifeWay Research, accessed August 20, 2019, https://lifeway research.com/wp-content/uploads/2015/11/Care-Net-Final -Presentation-Report-Revised.pdf.

5. "Guest Host," *Sandy Rios in the Morning*.

6. "Sharp Partisan Divisions in Views of National Institutions," Pew Research Center, July 10, 2017, http://www.people-press.org/2017/07/10/sharp-partisan-divisions-in-views-of-national-institutions/.

7. "Sharp Partisan Divisions in Views of National Institutions," Pew Research Center.

8. Bill Bumpas, "Poll: GOP vs. Dems Is Really Religion vs. Anti-Religion," American Family News Network, July 14, 2017, https://www.one newsnow.com/church/2017/07/14/poll-gop-vs-dems-is-really-religion-vs-anti-religion.

9. David Lane, "When Christians Disengaged Culture, the Antichrist Spirit Stepped In," Charisma News, April 15, 2019, https://www .charismanews.com/opinion/renewing-america/75949-when-christians-disengaged-culture-the-antichrist-spirit-stepped-in. Used with permission.

10. David Lane, "This Is What Happens When We Forget God," Charisma News, March 25, 2019, https://www.charismanews.com/opinion/renewing-america/75682-this-is-what-happens-when-we-forget-god.

11. James L. Garlow and David Barton, *This Precarious Moment* (Washington, DC: Salem Books, 2018), https://books.google.com/books?id=ZLZTDwAAQBAJ, and the source he provided in that book (https://web.archive.org/web/20160721024346/http://www.culturefaith.com/pastors-of-conservative-churches-say-they-wont-preach-what-the-bible-says-about-the-issues/).

12. "State of the Bible 2018: Seven Top Findings," Barna Group, July 10, 2018, https://www.barna.com/research/state-of-the-bible-2018-seven-top-findings/.

13. "Groundbreaking ACFI Survey Reveals How Many Adults Have a Biblical Worldview," American Culture & Faith Institute, February 27, 2017, https://web.archive.org/web/20170310194759/https://www .culturefaith.com/groundbreaking-survey-by-acfi-reveals-how-many-american-adults-have-a-biblical-worldview/.

14. George Barna and David Barton, *U-Turn* (Lake Mary, FL: FrontLine, 2014), 101.

15. Philip Schwadel, "Americans' Drinking Habits Vary by Faith," Pew Research Center, March 6, 2019, https://www.pewresearch.org/fact -tank/2019/03/06/americans-drinking-habits-vary-by-faith/.

16. "Pornography Survey Statistics," Proven Men Ministries, accessed August 21, 2019, https://www.provenmen.org/pornography-survey -statistics-2014/.

17. David J. Ayers, "Sex and the Single Evangelical," Institute for Family Studies, August 14, 2019, https://ifstudies.org/blog/sex-and-the-single-evangelical; Erik Cain, "Study Finds Majority of Young Evangelicals Have Premarital Sex," *Forbes*, October 1, 2011, https://www.forbes.com/sites/erikkain/2011/10/01/study-finds-majority-of-young -evangelicals-have-premarital-sex/#378e46c0739d; "'True Love Waits' Offers Christian Abstinence Program," *Christian Post*, March 11, 2004, https://www.christianpost.com/news/-true-love-waits-offers-christian-abstinence-program.html.

18. Mitchell Langbert, Anthony J. Quain, and Daniel B. Klein, "Faculty Voter Registration in Economics, History, Journalism, Law, and

Psychology," *Econ Journal Watch* 13, no. 3 (September 2016): 433, https://www.conservativecriminology.com/uploads/5/6/1/7/56173731 /langbertquainkleinsept2016.pdf.

19. Barna and Barton, *U-Turn*, 137.

20. Frank Jacobs, "These Are All the World's Major Religions in One Map," World Economic Forum, March 26, 2019, https://www.weforum.org /agenda/2019/03/this-is-the-best-and-simplest-world-map-of-religions/.

21. Lane, "When Christians Disengaged Culture, the Antichrist Spirit Stepped In."

CHAPTER 14

1. Fox 10 Phoenix, "Trump 2020: President Trump Re-election Campaign Rally—Full Speech," YouTube, June 18, 2019, https://www.youtube.com/ watch?v=MEqINP-TuV8.

2. *Life, Liberty & Levin*, Fox News.

3. George Will, "Are Some of the Democrats Trying to Lose," *Washington Post*, July 31, 2019, https://www.washingtonpost.com/opinions/ are-some-of-these-democrats-trying-to-lose/2019/07/31/fdcf5fda-b2f0- 11e9-951e-de024209545d_story.html.

4. Cathryn Donaldson, "Majority of Americans Satisfied With Their Employer's Health Plan, New Survey Shows," America's Health Insurance Plans, February 6, 2018, https://www.ahip.org/majority-of -americans-satisfied-with-their-employers-health-plan-new-survey- shows/.

5. Tim Hains, "George Will on 2020 Election: Will Voters Stick With the Doofus They Know or Pick the Doofus They Don't Know?," Real-ClearPolitics, June 5, 2019, https://www.realclearpolitics.com/ video/2019/06/05/george_will_on_2020_will_voters_pick_the_doofus_ they_know_or_the_doofus_they_dont_know.html.

6. Stephen Strang, "What the Left Totally Misses About What America Truly Represents," *The Strang Report* (blog), *Charisma*, accessed August 27, 2019, https://www.charismamag.com/blogs/the-strang- report/42222-what-the-left-totally-misses-about-what-america-truly- represents.

7. *Life, Liberty & Levin*, Fox News.

8. Prager, "Ultimate Issues Hour."

9. Don E. Eberly, *Building a Healthy Culture: Strategies for an American Renaissance* (Grand Rapids, MI: W. B. Eerdmans, 2001), 77.

10. Deace, "Megan Rapinoe's Antics Spell Out Exactly the Type of Civil War We Are Up Against."

11. Deace, "Megan Rapinoe's Antics Spell Out Exactly the Type of Civil War We Are Up Against."

12. "U.S. and World Population Clock," US Census Bureau, accessed August 22, 2019, https://www.census.gov/popclock/.

13. "U.S. and World Population Clock," US Census Bureau.

14. "Religious Landscape Study," Pew Research Center, accessed August 22, 2019, https://www.pewforum.org/religious-landscape-study/.

15. "Voting and Registration in the Election of November 2018," US Census Bureau, accessed August 22, 2019, https://www.census.gov/data/tables/time-series/demo/voting-and-registration/p20-583.html.

16. "Religious Landscape Study," Pew Research Center.

17. "Exit Polls," CNN, November 23, 2016, https://www.cnn.com/election/2016/results/exit-polls.

18. To join Cindy Jacobs in praying for the president, sign up at generals.org to receive regular prayer alerts.

19. Robert M. Calhoon, "Loyalism and Neutrality," *A Companion to the American Revolution*, Jack P. Greene and J. R. Pole, eds. (Malden, MA: Blackwell Publishers, 2000), chapter 29, https://books.google.com/books?id=xK1NuzpAcH8C&pg; "American Revolution—FAQs," American Battlefield Trust, accessed August 23, 2019, https://www.battlefields.org/learn/articles/american-revolution-faqs.

20. Fox Business, "Trump Will Win in 2020: Pastor Robert Jeffress," YouTube, November 16, 2018, https://www.youtube.com/watch?time_continue=3&v=2BJuMoOFyBQ.

21. Fox 10 Phoenix, "Trump 2020."

CONCLUSION

1. WDBJ7, "I think God calls all of us to fill different roles at different times and I think that he wanted Donald Trump to become president," Sarah Sanders said. "And that's why he's there." Facebook, https://www.facebook.com/watch/?v=1950529201712715.

2. 1 Timothy 2:2.

3. Matthew 6:33.

4. 2 Chronicles 7:14.

5. To find a Nation Builders prayer call near you, visit marycolbert.us and sign up for her newsletter.

6. Matthew 25:14–30.

7. Matthew 25:26, NIV.

8. Matthew 5:44.

9. James 2:26.

10. Matthew 10:16.

EPILOGUE

1. Huckabee, "IMPEACH TRUMP!!! And Other Wacky Things the Left Likes to Do | Huckabee," YouTube, September 28, 2019, https://www.youtube.com/watch?v=QruXhssHLi4.

2. Huckabee, "Judge Jeanine Pirro Tackles the Left's Plot to REMAKE America | Huckabee," YouTube, September 28, 2019, https://www.youtube.com/watch?v=InKYJtCNAZo.

3. Thaddeus Dolbi, "Deep State Operatives Are Attempting Coup d'État of President Trump," YouTube, June 16, 2017, https://www.youtube.com/watch?v=hJrEp6nhXhE.

INDEX

STAY IN TOUCH WITH
STEPHEN E. STRANG

- Follow him on Twitter @sstrang.
- Like him on Facebook @stephenestrang.
- Subscribe to the *Strang Report* twice-weekly newsletter at charismanewsletters.com.
- Download the *Strang Report* podcasts at CharismaPodcastNetwork.com.
- Subscribe to *Charisma* magazine or other Charisma Media publications. Call 1-800-749-6500 during office hours EST, or order online at Shop.CharismaMag.com.
- Watch for his next book from Charisma House!
- Order his other books at stevestrangbooks.com.

If you enjoyed *God, Trump, and the 2020 Election*, tell your friends, including on social media. Also, leave a five-star rating for the book and your personal review at Amazon.com.

FREE Bonus CONTENT!

To further increase your understanding of Donald Trump and how God has used him to make a difference in America, access these additional resources:

- *Why We Are Winning: Hundreds of Ways Trump Has Made America Great Again*

- *Donald Trump and the Jubilean Mysteries: Two Prophetic Stories Told by Jonathan Cahn*

www.GodTrump2020.com/gift

MORE PRAISE FOR
GOD, TRUMP, AND THE 2020 ELECTION

God, Trump, and the 2020 Election is a predictive document. Every page is a wake-up call pointing to what is ahead if we make a "left" turn. Stephen Strang offers a stern warning to God's people, encouraging them not to shirk their responsibility to steer the course of a nation and even the world toward the kingdom plan of heaven. All I can say after reading this book is that there is really no choice in "choose…this day whom you will serve"! Strang fully presents the choice! This book makes you decree, "As for me and my house, we will serve the Lord" (Josh. 24:15, NKJV).

—CHUCK PIERCE
PRESIDENT, GLORY OF ZION INTERNATIONAL MINISTRIES

Stephen Strang uses his gift of storytelling in brilliant fashion. *God, Trump, and the 2020 Election* is a fascinating look at how spiritual warfare is shaping the presidential race.

—JOHN LINDELL
LEAD PASTOR, JAMES RIVER CHURCH, OZARK, MISSOURI

Stephen Strang does it again by putting God first in the upcoming 2020 elections. Let's pray that America follows suit, with a victory for President Donald John Trump. Love never fails. God always wins.

—EVANGELIST ALVEDA C. KING
NIECE OF DR. MARTIN LUTHER KING JR.
EXECUTIVE DIRECTOR, CIVIL RIGHTS FOR THE UNBORN

No one knows the real faith of the real Donald Trump better than Stephen Strang. *God, Trump, and the 2020 Election* reveals what's at stake for every American.

—CHRISTOPHER RUDDY
CEO, NEWSMAX MEDIA

Stephen Strang is a follower of Christ who is willing to wade into the deep and treacherous waters of American political thought and discourse. Yet he avoids all the eddies that could pull him under. How? He writes as one who has the anchor and compass of God's eternal truth. His fundamental concern is not the classic Right versus Left but right versus wrong. Furthermore, he is bold. In a world in which wimps abound, Strang calls it like it is, with Churchillian courage. And oh, one more thing: Strang is right. What he writes we need to read.

—DR. JIM GARLOW
CEO, WELL VERSED

As a longtime citizen of the United States who was born in Caracas, Venezuela, I have personally witnessed the complete destruction, in a short period of time, of a once great and wealthy, freedom-loving nation by socialist and communist forces from within and from abroad. President Donald Trump and his strong base have stood up as a mighty fire wall that protects America from those same destructive and anti-Christian forces. In *God, Trump, and the 2020 Election*, Stephen Strang connects the dots, in his factual and robust style, showing us how socialism (the communist wolf in sheep's clothing, as I call it) has made its way into mainstream American culture and politics. More specifically, he articulates how socialism and the Left will take America down the destructive path of Venezuela—and thus how important the upcoming 2020 election really is.

—MICHAEL SABGA
BUILDER, DEVELOPER, AND ENTREPRENEUR

As President Trump endures and even thrives as he continues this gauntlet-like presidency, it is more and more obvious the hand of God is on him. My dear friend Tom Zimmer spent the last thirty-five years of his life praying every day for humanity and that no soul would ever be lost. Donald Trump was included in those prayers. Tom would say, "It is by being grateful that God allows us to keep what He has given us." The presidency of Donald Trump is clearly a gift from God. I join my prayers together with Stephen Strang's and all his readers' to express gratitude for President Trump and to implore the guidance and protection of our Father; Jesus, His Son; and the Holy Spirit over him, his family, and all his helpers! May God grant the same graces to everyone who reads this book!

—CLAUDE A. CURRAN, MD
PSYCHIATRIST, FALL RIVER, MASSACHUSETTS

President Trump's supporters are enthusiastic about the upcoming election, but in *God, Trump, and the 2020 Election*, Stephen Strang reminds us that the newly engaged (and enraged) Democratic Party, the Washington establishment, and the elitist news media will do anything imaginable to prevent Trump's reelection. In this book not only does Stephen discuss why Trump's victory is vitally important for believers and the future of our nation, but he also outlines eight reasons (read them all!) Trump could lose. This book stirred my heart to pray for the future of our country and for God's plan to be accomplished in the 2020 election. It is a must-read!

—ROB SAUNDERS
WEALTH CODES COACH

In my business I have to understand what Americans are thinking if I'm to be successful. It's impossible to understand what happened in 2016 and what might happen in 2020 without an understanding of evangelical and Pentecostal voters, and Stephen Strang is the one who understands these groups and why they vote the way they do.

—MARK JOSEPH
FILM PRODUCER AND AUTHOR

Stephen Strang has done it again! This new book, *God, Trump, and the 2020 Election*, is a must-read for every conservative in America—especially those in the body of Christ. If Donald Trump does not win this next election, we can all kiss the America we have known goodbye.

—ART ALLY
PRESIDENT AND FOUNDER, TIMOTHY PLAN

God, Trump, and the 2020 Election is a great political and theological book on the 2020 election. Stephen Strang cuts through the highly charged political rhetoric with skill and truth, calling the church and responsible citizens to action.

—JOHN EDWARD JONES
LIEUTENANT COMMANDER, JAG CORPS, US NAVY RESERVE
ATTORNEY AND CERTIFIED MILITARY JUDGE (1970–1991)

God, Trump, and the 2020 Election is a must-read for anyone who cares for and continues to be concerned for the direction in which our nation is going. We, the people, are very fortunate to have an elected president who truly cares as much as he does for this country. Diligently President Trump is working to make the United States strong and independent. Stephen skillfully makes the reader aware of what is at stake if concerned citizens don't get involved in the 2020 presidential election. Many are hoping you won't read this book. Read it so you can be informed.

—EVAN J. TRINKLE
US ARMY COLONEL (RETIRED)

Stephen E. Strang's newest book in the Trump trilogy is informative, providing the reader insight into current events regarding President Trump and his administration. He weaves prophetic insight throughout his book, ending with a "call to action" for Christians who love America, the Bible, and President Trump. Read this book with great urgency to know what God is doing in this season. The 2020 election is fast approaching.

—ALAN YOUNGBLOOD
EDUCATOR
PASTOR, FAITH OUTREACH CENTER, OVIEDO, FLORIDA

The United States is in a very crucial window that God has opened for spiritual renewal, economic stimulus, and necessary legislative reforms that will be part of the great awakening the Lord is bringing to this earth as we enter a new decade. This is why *God, Trump, and the 2020 Election*, written by Stephen Strang, is right on time and right on point to help us know the times and what we must do in this current election year to protect our nation from anti-God agendas, liberal and secular ideologies, and the leftist extremes that are dangerous to our Constitution, our nation, the Lord's church, and future generations. Stephen Strang has brilliantly presented a very informative, insightful, and prophetic viewpoint in his book, making it easy to discern God's agenda for years ahead.

—Hank Kunneman
Pastor, Lord of Hosts Church , Omaha, Nebraska

William Shakespeare mused, "All the world's a stage, / And all the men and women merely players." He was alluding to the plan of a greater providence that was elusive, yet inescapable. The presidential election of 2016 had divine fingerprints all over it. Now it is time to look ahead again—and Stephen Strang is doing just that in his timely new book, *God, Trump, and the 2020 Election*. Stephen's treatise is a practical summary for any God-fearing voter who is seeking wisdom and clarity in this election cycle. He presents a valued position from a biblical perspective that Donald Trump should be reelected to continue the process to "reverse the loss of America's sovereignty, prosperity, and Christian influence." The tough questions that Christians should ponder are dealt with succinctly. I highly recommend that you share this book with your friends and family and within your spheres of influence.

—Frank Amedia
Senior Pastor, Touch Heaven Church, Canfield, Ohio

God, Trump, and the 2020 Election illustrates why for over twenty years I have read, quoted, and steadily grown in my appreciation of the consistently thorough research and proper application of history and theology by publisher and best-selling author Stephen Strang. He has outdone himself again, offering timely, penetrating questions regarding the future of America and the world and why Christian involvement in the political process has never been more desperately needed.

—Thomas Horn
CEO, SkyWatch TV

The late conservative journalist Andrew Breitbart was well known for his tagline "Politics is downstream from culture." He acknowledged that a nation's politics was the fruit of its culture. He could have added that "culture is downstream from religion." As we look at America's fractured culture and its incredibly divided politics, the cause is clear. Millions of American Christians seem to have abandoned any sense of responsibility for the civic well-being of the nation that has given them more freedom and prosperity than any nation has known in world history. Nature loves a vacuum, and as many Christians have deserted the culture and abandoned any sense of civic leadership, the resulting void has been filled by some of the worst among us.

Stephen Strang has done every American citizen a great favor with *God, Trump, and the 2020 Election*. His new book lays out in stark detail the consequences of the 2020 election and the urgent necessity for Christians to vote their values in record numbers. Strang makes it very clear that the 2020 election will be decisive not just for our civic and cultural life, but it will also have a massive impact on the future of Christianity as we know it. A must-read for all who take their faith seriously.

—Trevor Loudon
Author and Political Activist

Stephen Strang is a gifted journalist—a man with a heart for revival and a keen sense of the power of the unseen realm. Strang carefully marshals the facts, studies them through the lens of God's revelation, and adds a volume to his journalistic accomplishments that will drive readers to their knees. For those who want to understand the key players in America's future and be able to pray focused prayers, this is a must-read.

—Dr. Larry Spargimino
Pastor, Southwest Radio Church, Oklahoma City

Stephen Strang's book powerfully analyzes the political and spiritual role of evangelical and Charismatic Christians for the 2020 election. In the 2016 election 81 percent of Evangelicals voted for Donald Trump without knowing what to expect. In 2020 they know full well. And Trump could increase his evangelical support in 2020. Strang recognizes that although God's hand is upon Donald Trump, there is a very real spiritual battle under way to determine our nation's future. These evil forces behind the scenes can be subdued by prevailing, intercessory prayer. Trump's 2016 election cannot be explained in political or cultural terms alone but must be seen as a spiritual event.

—Chaplain E. Ray Moore, ThM
Lieutenant Colonel, US Army Reserve (Retired)
Bronze Star Recipient and Homeschool Leader

Publisher and best-selling author Stephen Strang has a unique anointing on his life to ferret out truth. I absolutely love his new book, *God, Trump, and the 2020 Election*. When I finished reading the manuscript, I was amazed at how refreshed I felt inside. He left no stone unturned and made no excuses. It is clear to me that God has raised up Donald John Trump for this time, and we must back him up and hold him up in prayer—not only for America but for all the freedom-loving people of the entire earth.

—JOHN KILPATRICK
SENIOR PASTOR, CHURCH OF HIS PRESENCE, DAPHNE, ALABAMA

The unprecedented, extraordinary developments in America today necessitate discovering sources of insight and encouragement to understand the times with knowledge of what to do (1 Chron. 12:32). Stephen Strang is a uniquely gifted and experienced journalist whose latest book, *God, Trump, and the 2020 Election*, is an invaluable resource to help us in these turbulent times. It's clear, comprehensive, and cutting-edge. On a scale of one to ten I give it a ten plus double thumbs up!

—LARRY TOMCZAK
AUTHOR AND CULTURAL COMMENTATOR

In this, his third book about the church in the "Trump era," Stephen Strang has produced a work that is equal parts well-documented journalism and impassioned advocacy. *God, Trump, and the 2020 Election* will inspire many and infuriate others, but it will leave no one in doubt about where Strang stands with regard to the next presidential election. This will be a tough read for woke liberals and Never Trump Evangelicals, but read it they should, as should anyone who cares about how their decision in the ballot box may impact the future of the republic.

—DR. MARK RUTLAND
FOUNDER, GLOBAL SERVANTS

God, Trump, and the 2020 Election is written with prophetic clarity and gives Evangelicals a clarion call to action. These pages expose the heart of Donald Trump as well as the long-term political and spiritual implications of the 2020 election. This book by itself has the potential to tip the scales of history in favor of those who love God!

—DR. DOUGLAS WEISS
PSYCHOLOGIST AND AUTHOR

President Trump has been the best friend and president to the Christian believer in well over one hundred years. His executive order overturning the Johnson Amendment was huge. Too many believers still don't understand what that meant. This must-read book will educate and hopefully motivate believers to no longer sit on the sidelines of their involvement in government matters. Faith without works, as the apostle Paul wrote, is worthless. Now is our time to rise up and take a stand to preserve our religious freedoms for future generations. After reading this book, we have no more excuses!

—MARY COLBERT
AUTHOR, MINISTER, AND WIFE OF DR. DON COLBERT

Conventional wisdom advises those in ministry to avoid all political discussion. Of course that was when the lines drawn between political parties were somewhat blurred. Not so today. Lines are clearly drawn but not politically. Rather, they are drawn between righteousness and unrighteousness. One side supports abortion up to the moment of birth and proudly endorses same-sex marriage; however, more recent efforts are even more daunting. In *God, Trump, and the 2020 Election*, Stephen Strang, like a "watchman on the wall," uses his God-given talent to offer a somber warning to Christians who are ambivalent about their voting privilege. This well-researched book is an absolute must-read for all Christians and patriots.

—ARTHELENE RIPPY
HOST, *HOMEKEEPERS*, CHRISTIAN TELEVISION NETWORK

Stephen Strang does an excellent job of defining what the 2020 election is really about. Beyond the conventional dichotomy of Right versus Left, he defines it in Christian terms as a spiritual war. Evangelicals who were skeptical of Trump in 2016 no longer need to doubt the spiritual warfare Trump is in and his willingness to fight for what matters most to Christians. The enemy is trying to keep America from reaching her destiny. For this reason Trump is fighting many battlefronts you will learn about in this book, including social media censorship, judicial activism, collusion among mainstream media, religious bigotry, subversion by the deep state, abortion, unlawful immigration, and endless wars. It is my hope that fair-minded people and evangelical Never Trumpers will read this book and be convinced that at the very least Trump is a disrupter, if not a patriot, and God's agent of justice. Like him or not, his reelection in 2020 matters to all of us.

—STEVE CIOCCOLANTI
PASTOR, DISCOVER CHURCH, MELBOURNE, AUSTRALIA

It's clear that Stephen Strang's long journalistic background has served him well in writing this very informative and timely book. As it relates to Christian broadcasting, he aptly points out that this administration moved swiftly to rewrite antiquated FCC broadcast regulations that were written before videotape was even invented. As Stephen puts it, this didn't just benefit broadcasting, but the entire economy is benefiting from such deregulation.

—MATT CROUCH
PRESIDENT, TRINITY BROADCASTING NETWORK

A fascinating read. The future of America as we know it hangs in the balance.

—DR. TIM CLINTON
PRESIDENT, AMERICAN ASSOCIATION OF CHRISTIAN COUNSELORS
EXECUTIVE DIRECTOR, JAMES DOBSON FAMILY INSTITUTE

Stephen Strang's third installment in his Trump trilogy comes at a critical time for the future of our nation. It's a timely dose of reality and truth that cuts through the noise and confusion surrounding President Trump. Strang brings prophecy and the spiritual realm to the forefront, making a strong case for Trump beyond typical politics and the secular agenda.

—JOSHUA JAMES FORD
CHRISTIAN ENTREPRENEUR, WRITER, AND CONSULTANT

With all the division in our country Christians must ask, "What is God doing today?" In this outstanding book Stephen E. Strang makes clear the passage that God causes kings to rise and fall and uses them to accomplish His purpose. This book helped me understand what's at stake in the 2020 election and was a reminder that we must let our voices be heard. He covers many important issues and provides readers reasons to take this election seriously, because we are in a war for the heart and soul of America.

—GARRY WIGGINS
PASTOR, EVANGEL TEMPLE ASSEMBLY OF GOD, JACKSONVILLE, FLORIDA

In his new book, *God, Trump, and the 2020 Election*, Stephen E. Strang challenges us all to face the reality that the 2020 presidential election is a spiritual battle for the heart and soul of America. Whether you support Donald Trump or not, this book will help you understand why evangelical Christians have continued to support him, what he is really like, what has been accomplished in his first term, what could cost Trump the election, and what that would mean for America.

—JAMES I. BLACK III
ATTORNEY, NEW YORK

Stephen Strang is one of the most gifted journalists I have encountered. He has the ability to see trends and report them through the lens of the Holy Spirit. This is an important book for the future of the United States and needs to be read.

—CINDY JACOBS
COFOUNDER, GENERALS INTERNATIONAL

Make no mistake, if President Trump is not reelected, Christians will face persecution, more babies will be slaughtered using our tax dollars, America will be weakened, Israel will be abandoned, and the land of the free and the home of the brave will be no more. Stephen Strang's book about the consequences of this election is a clarion call to Christians to vote for Donald J. Trump. The choice is easy because the stakes are so high. May God's grace fall on us once again.

—MATHEW D. STAVER, ESQ., BCS
FOUNDER AND CHAIRMAN, LIBERTY COUNSEL

In *God, Trump, and the 2020 Election*, Stephen Strang lays out the blueprint for America's destiny. His opinions are more than political analysis. They are a critical, strategic overview of the forces in conflict that will impact all lives, not only in the United States but also around the world. America was founded on biblical principles. By reference to our times Stephen explains the logical consequences of the spiritual axiom *God is sovereign over man, and man is sovereign over government*. To understand these times and what is at stake for our and our children's future, this book is a must-read for all Americans.

—MARC NUTTLE
INTERNATIONAL LAWYER, AUTHOR, POLITICAL STRATEGIST, AND
PRESIDENTIAL ADVISER

Nobody in our day understands the issues we face as Stephen Strang does. You will be thankful for this book. Give away copies to your friends who are concerned about our future. Stephen has written clearly and in a manner that has shaken me rigid. This book is a wake-up call to every Christian. It should drive us to our knees; those who believe in the power of prayer should intercede before God as they never have before. Never in my lifetime have I witnessed such hatred toward any person in office as I've seen directed toward President Trump. Let's face it, as Stephen Strang says, those who oppose traditional values hate Bible-believing Christians. We must declare our stand before it is too late. This book will convince you of this if you are not persuaded already.

—R. T. KENDALL
SENIOR PASTOR, WESTMINSTER CHAPEL (FOR TWENTY-FIVE YEARS)
AUTHOR OF MORE THAN SIXTY BOOKS

In *God, Trump, and the 2020 Election*, Stephen Strang provides a compelling account of the high stakes in 2020 and why Christians must be engaged and mobilized as never before. Combining a keen understanding of the evangelical community with solid reporting on President Trump, this book is must-reading for any concerned citizen and serious Christian.

—RALPH REED
FOUNDER AND CHAIRMAN, FAITH & FREEDOM COALITION

Question to ponder: Why have *all* the most accurate prophets in America I have personally evaluated for accuracy said, "President Trump is God's choice"? I know God's reason! God needs America strong for end-time evangelism, and He will once more make America great to trump the devil!

—SID ROTH
HOST, *IT'S SUPERNATURAL!*

No one—and I mean *no one*—captures the intricacies regarding America's Christian community and Donald Trump like Stephen Strang. Why do Bible-believing Christians continue to support this president? Not only does this book answer the question, but it similarly equips readers by revealing what's at stake in the 2020 election and preparing them to push back against the unprecedented assault on the president. It's not about a man; it's a war against life, religious liberty, and biblical justice. Every single Christian concerned with life, religious liberty, and doing biblical justice in the name of Jesus must read this book!

—SAMUEL RODRIGUEZ
PRESIDENT, NATIONAL HISPANIC
CHRISTIAN LEADERSHIP CONFERENCE

Electrifying! This carefully, accurately researched book is urgent reading. It's like a fire truck with its sirens screaming as it rushes to a disaster in time to extinguish the flames already roaring out of control. Stephen Strang is the experienced fireman, having chronicled America's struggle to retain its soul and destiny for the last forty years. In this horribly divided nation at the very brink of devolving into violence and cultural and moral suicide, not only does he sound the unmistakable alarm, but he lays out the practical, absolutely essential plan for putting out the fires and saving our country and our precious way of life, which is unequaled in human history but in terrible danger. We can do it—if we act now. Take two days or nights to absorb this vital information—and if you're not moved to positive action, I'll personally refund your purchase price. This is a three-alarm book!

—PAT BOONE
ENTERTAINER, AUTHOR, AND CULTURAL COMMENTATOR